Thinking Critically about Research Methods

Thinking Critically about Research Methods

John G. Benjafield
Brock University

Allyn and Bacon
Boston • London • Toronto • Sydney • Tokyo • Singapore

Vice-President, Publisher: Susan Badger
Executive Editor: Laura Pearson
Editorial Assistant: Marnie S. Greenhut
Editorial-Production Administrator: Annette Joseph
Production Coordinator: Holly Crawford
Editorial-Production Service: Connie Leavitt, Camden Type 'n Graphics
Manufacturing Buyer: Louise Richardson
Cover Administrator: Linda K. Dickinson
Cover Designer: Suzanne Harbison

Copyright © 1994 by Allyn and Bacon
A Division of Paramount Publishing
160 Gould Street
Needham Heights, Massachusetts 02194

Library of Congress Cataloging-in-Publication Data
Benjafield, John G.
   Thinking critically about research methods / John G. Benjafield.
     p.   cm.
   Includes bibliographical references and index.
   ISBN 0-205-13917-5
   1. Psychology—Research—Methodology. 2. Psychology,
Experimental. I. Title.
BF76.5.B46 1994
150'.72—dc20   93-29724
                                                                      CIP

Printed in the United States of America
10 9 8 7 6 5 4 3   98 97 96

Contents

Preface

This book is intended not only for readers who may be thinking about a career in psychology but also for those whose lives will be influenced by psychology, even if they never become psychologists. Since the latter category includes virtually everyone, I have tried to make the book interesting for the general reader as well as for those who may go on to specialize. Although several statistical concepts are presented, such as *power*, they are described in a nontechnical, and mostly nonmathematical, way. While some readers may have had a course in statistics, the book does not require any statistical sophistication whatsoever.

In writing this book, I had two major goals. On the one hand, I wanted to present basic information necessary to the understanding of psychology as a research enterprise. On the other hand, I wanted to make sure that students critically examine the ideas presented. These goals require a different structure from that found in many methods texts. I have *not* tried to write a "cookbook" that fills the student up with standard information about methods. Throughout I have tried to instill critical thinking skills that will enable students to evaluate psychological research and to begin thinking about psychological research they may want to do themselves. I have included not only a critical analysis of basic concepts of research design but also a discussion of the process of scientific creativity and discovery. In general, I have tried to give a thorough, yet concise, description of psychological science as a process.

Recursiveness and *redundancy* are key aspects of the structure of the book. Important ideas are not presented only once and then left behind. Rather, after being presented, they recur at subsequent points in the text. I have structured the book this way partly because repetition is an important pedagogical device (e.g., Bahrick & Hall, 1991). Moreover, I believe that when basic ideas are repeated in different contexts they stand a better chance of becoming interconnected with other important ideas.

In general, I have adopted a historical approach to the presentation of ideas. I have done this in part because, as McCloskey and Kargon (1988) have observed, knowledge of the history of the emergence of ideas and practices helps one to understand why certain ideas and practices have come to occupy the status they currently enjoy. Historical analysis also enables the student to see that numerous intuitively plausible approaches have been tried already and have been found wanting. Thinking critically about the past trains us to think critically about what we may plan to do in the future.

As a cognitive psychologist, I naturally find research from the cognitive area particularly attractive and instructive. I have made a concerted effort, however, to employ illustrations from the full range of psychological research, from comparative psychology to psychotherapy, from the laboratory to the archives, and from the individual to society.

Ken Proctor was the first to suggest that I might want to write this book, and I am very grateful to him for that. Susan Badger, at Allyn and Bacon, has been insightful and supportive, and I am also grateful to her for giving me this opportunity. Lewis Soroka, formerly Dean of Social Sciences at Brock University, was always an enthusiastic advocate of my efforts. Such confidence meant a great deal to me. I am also grateful to the members of my department for many intriguing methodological discussions.

I wish to acknowledge those individuals who reviewed the manuscript for Allyn and Bacon: Sam Church, Fairmont State College; Marie Fox, Metropolitan State College of Denver; Gloria Leventhal, William Paterson College; and Susan Lima, University of Wisconsin–Milwaukee.

Last, I want to thank my wife, Gail, who has understood how important it has been to me to write this book and who has been very generous in accommodating my occasionally eccentric schedule.

1

Thinking Critically about Psychology

Why Do We Need to Think Critically about Psychology?

This book aims to teach you how to think critically about psychology. Psychology is not a simple, straightforward enterprise. As you are probably aware by now, psychologists study a broad range of topics and employ many different methods. A good way to begin would be for you to imagine different topics that you think psychologists should study. Write the list on a piece of paper. Do it now.

Boneau (1990) asked authors of psychological textbooks to rate the importance of a large number of psychological concepts. One result was a list of the "Top 100" concepts: those that every psychology student "should be able to discuss and relate to other terms" (Boneau, 1990, p. 892). This list is given in Table 1-1. How well does it match *your* list? There are probably some things on your list that are not on the "Top 100" list, and vice versa. Keep your list. Perhaps as we go along, you will think of ways of incorporating the items on your list into the existing areas of research of interest to psychologists.

According to a recent count, the American Psychological Association (APA) has a membership of about 68,000 (*Directory of the American Psychological Association*, 1989). This makes psychology a very big discipline indeed, and the growth from only a few psychologists at the beginning of the twentieth century to the many there are today has been one of the great success stories of the modern era. Perhaps psychology has grown so much because it concerns itself with things that are important to every individual. Psychology is a very open discipline and is growing and becoming more differentiated all the time. That is why the topics on your list that are not represented in Table 1-1 may find a place on that list some day. Maybe you will help put them there.

Groups within psychology keep emerging in order to represent the particular interests of psychologists as these evolve. Even the list in Table 1-1 does not fully capture the variety of psychology in the United States. In addition to the APA, a new group of psychologists, the American Psychological *Society* (APS), was formed in 1988. It now has over 13,000 members, some of whom also belong to the APA. The APS was formed in part because of tensions within the APA between psychologists with an "academic/research orientation" and those with a "private practice/health service–provider orientation" (Rodgers, 1990, p. 81); the APS sees itself as more representative of the former group.

You would hardly expect such a large number of people with such a wide range of specialties to agree on everything, would you? There is no point in pretending that psychology is a completely unified discipline, although there are certainly many "common values, goals, and beliefs" that allow psychologists to "identify with a larger psychological 'family' " (Bower, 1992, p. 2). Psychologists do not fit easily into one category but constitute a *pluralistic*

TABLE 1-1 Psychology's "Top 100" Concepts

Absolute threshold	Hypothesis testing
Action potential	Id
Aggression	Independent variable
Anxiety	Infant-mother attachment
Anxiety disorder	Information-processing approach
Artificial intelligence	Instrumental behavior
Associationism	Intelligence
Attachment	Intelligence quotient
Attitude change, factors influencing	Introversion-extraversion
Attitudes and behavior	Just noticeable difference
Attribution theory	Law of effect
Avoidance learning	Long-term memory
Binocular depth cues	Longitudinal research
Central nervous system	Meaning
Cerebellum	Mental illness
Cerebral cortex	Mental imagery
Cerebral hemispheres	Milgram's obedience experiment
Childhood, characteristics of	Nature-nurture controversy
Classical conditioning	Neocortex
Cognitive development	Neurotransmitter
Cognitive dissonance theory	Normal distribution
Conditioned stimulus	Operant conditioning
Conditioned reflex	*Origin of Species*
Conformity	Personality
Consciousness	Phobia
Contrast	Placebo effect
Control group	Positive reinforcement
Correlation coefficient	Prejudice
Correlational method	Prosocial behavior
Dendrite	Psychoanalytic theory
Deoxyribonucleic acid (DNA)	Psychosis
Dependent variable	Psychosomatic disorders
Depression	Psychotherapy
Depth perception	Rehearsal
Determinism	Reinforcement
Developmental stages, theories of	Right hemisphere
Distance cues	Sample
Ego	Semantic memory
Electroencephalograph	Serial position function
Empiricism	Short-term memory
Etiology	Significance level
Evolution and functionalism	Significant difference
Experimental group	Social influence
Extinction	Socialization
Forgetting curve	Socioeconomic status
Free association	Traits
Free recall	Unconscious
Frequency (audition)	Unconscious motivation
Gestalt principles of organization	Visual angle
Gestalt psychology	Visual depth perception

Source: "Psychological Literacy: A First Approximation" by C. A. Boneau, 1990, *American Psychologist, 45,* 894.
Copyright 1990 by the American Psychological Association. Reprinted by permission.

discipline, in the same way that countries such as the United States and Canada can be seen as pluralistic cultures. A pluralistic culture is one in which there are different groups, each with its own unique heritage. While we all share some important things in common, we also value our uniqueness. William James (1890), perhaps the most influential of all American psychologists (Estes, 1990), put it this way:

> One great splitting of the whole universe into two halves is made by each of us; and for each of us almost all of the interest attaches to one of the halves; but we all draw the line of division between them in a different place. When I say that we call the two halves by the same names, and that those names are "me" and "not-me" respectively, it will at once be seen what I mean. The altogether unique kind of interest which each human mind feels in those parts of creation which it can call "me" or "mine" may be a moral riddle, but it is a fundamental psychological fact. (p. 289)

James's point is that it is inevitable that every person will regard some things as closer to him or her than others. The degree to which we feel that something is "mine" will greatly influence the way we think about it (Markus, 1990). This feeling of ownership may be not only a source of pride but also one source of *bias*, which influences the judgments and choices we make. Psychologists may not always be immune to bias. I may judge those parts of psychology in which I specialize, and thus see as mine, differently from the way I judge those parts in which I have less interest.

Given the variety of things that psychologists do, it is not at all surprising that there have always been vigorous discussions within the psychological community concerning how best to practice psychology. Such debates are a sign of the importance of the issues with which psychologists deal. You would not see people getting worked up over things that did not matter. Because psychology *matters*, and because there are so many ways of practicing psychology, we all need to be able to evaluate critically the work that psychologists do. Understanding psychology is a bit like finding your way through a maze like that in Figure 1-1. As you make your way through a maze, you are confronted with points at which you must choose among alternative routes, and you hope that you do not get stuck at a dead end (Newell & Simon, 1962). Similarly, in psychology you may be confronted with a wealth of studies on a topic. The studies may appear to lead in very different directions. Being able to separate the better studies from the inferior ones is an important part of being able to progress as a psychologist. In a maze, the choices you make are relatively blind, because you cannot see far enough ahead to decide rationally on a course of action. In psychology, however, there is no need to behave in quite so blind a manner. As we will see, there are techniques that help us make decisions both about worthwhile procedures in psychology and about

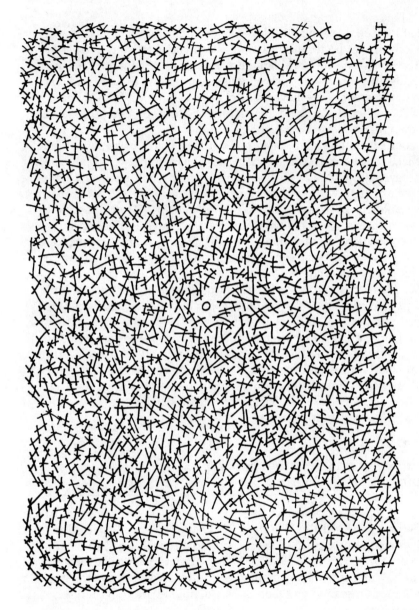

FIGURE 1-1   Go from Zero to Infinity

Source: The Great Maze Book by Greg Bright, 1975. New York: Pantheon, p. 45. Copyright © 1975 by Random House, Inc. Reprinted by permission of Pantheon Books, Inc., a division of Random House, Inc.

practices that may be questionable. Nevertheless, it is important to acknowledge at the outset that no techniques are perfect, and that we can never be certain that we have solved a problem once and for all. As Joseph Priestley, the great eighteenth-century English scientist, is supposed to have said, "In completing one discovery we never fail to get an imperfect knowledge of others of which we could have no idea before, so that we cannot solve one doubt without creating several new ones."

In this book we will be more concerned with the *how* of psychology than with the *what.* This book is about *method:* how psychologists actually do research in psychology. Although the principal focus will be on *academic* research—research that typically goes on in universities—we will not neglect research that takes place in applied or "real life" settings. We will sample a variety of content areas in psychology to illustrate the ways in which different methods have been used. At each point, we will critically examine the choices presented to us by a study or set of studies, and we will try to arrive at reasonable judgments in each case.

Let us begin with an outline of the historical development of research methods in psychology. We will show how some of the basic approaches to research have emerged. As McCloskey and Kargon (1988) argued, the historical development of a discipline often parallels the way a student's thinking evolves. An overview of the history of research methods may make "the student aware of his or her preconceptions" and "may be effective in clearing the ground" in preparation for the acquisition of new skills (McCloskey & Kargon, 1988, p. 66). So, before we consider current research methods, we will have a look at some earlier approaches.

The Development of Scientific Thinking in Psychology: A Brief History

Any account of the development of research methods in psychology must include a discussion of Wilhelm Wundt (1832–1920). Wundt is often credited with establishing the first psychological laboratory, which was in Leipzig, Germany, in the 1870s. The methods used in this laboratory proved to be very controversial. The reaction to these methods played a decisive role in the way that psychological research methods subsequently evolved. What were Wundt's research methods?

Wundt and Introspectionist Experiments

Wundt (1912/1973, p. 151) made a distinction between "simple" and "complex" psychological processes. Laboratory research was appropriate only for relatively simple psychological processes. Complex psychological processes, such as our ability to use language, could not be understood using experimental, laboratory methods. They required instead, observations of the products of language and thought as they occurred naturally (Blumenthal, 1975). In the beginning, therefore, Wundt established the precedent that at least two kinds of methods are necessary in psychology. One was laboratory-based experimentation and was suited to the investigation of simple psychological phenomena. The other involved naturalistic observation and was suited to the exploration of psychological processes as influenced by social and cultural factors (Danziger, 1983). As we will see, a great deal of controversy has developed over this distinction.

Wundt's laboratory procedures involved *introspection*. At the time, it seemed intuitively obvious that introspection would be a useful method. After all, when we want to find out what's "going on" inside ourselves, we naturally "look inside" ourselves, or introspect. Wundt tried to establish introspection as a central research method in psychology. How was introspection supposed to work?

Wundt's method of introspection involved having the subject respond to simple stimuli. This often required the use of apparatus. As we will see, different kinds of apparatus play an important role in the evolution of psychological methods. One apparatus that Wundt (1912/1973, p. 2) discussed at length was the metronome. As you know, if you have ever taken music lessons, a metronome is a device that can be set to emit a sound, or beat, at a regular interval. The beat can be made faster or slower, and the musician can use the beat to guide his or her playing. Nowadays, most metronomes are electronic, but in Wundt's day metronomes looked like Figure 1-2. Essentially,

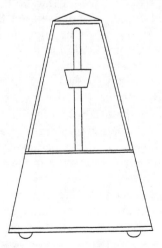

FIGURE 1-2 A Metronome

a metronome was a "clockwork with an upright standing pendulum, on which a sliding weight is attached, so that beats may follow each other at equal intervals in greater or less rapidity. If the weight is fixed at the upper end of the pendulum, the beats follow each other at an interval of two seconds; if at the lower end, the interval is shortened to about a third of a second" (Wundt, 1912/1973, p. 2). How can this apparatus be used in a psychological experiment?

If you have access to a metronome, go get it now. If not, you can simulate a metronome by tapping with a pencil on a tabletop. Suppose you set the metronome at the slow speed that Wundt described: about one beat every two seconds. What do you experience when the metronome (or your pencil) is beating out that particular rhythm? Of course, you can hear the beats, one after the other, but do you experience anything else besides your perception of the beats? Wundt (1912/1973, p. 53) observed that immediately after you hear one beat, you begin to anticipate the occurrence of the next one. You experience increased tension until the next beat occurs. This tension disappears, however, once you hear the next beat, at which point you experience relief. In addition, this slow rhythm tends to make you feel a bit sad, or depressed. By contrast, what do you experience if you speed the metronome up to two or three beats a second? Now the rhythm is no longer depressed; rather, it gives rise to a feeling of excitement.

Wundt claimed that by manipulating the speed of the metronome, one can discover a set of basic feelings. So far we have found two dimensions along which feelings can vary: tension-relief and excitement-depression. Wundt also noted that some rhythms strike us as pleasant and others strike us as unpleasant. These observations led to Wundt's *tridimensional theory of feeling*, illustrated in Figure 1-3. Any feeling can be thought of as located within the three-dimensional space. Wundt believed that this model was completely general: "We find everywhere the same pairs of feelings that we produced by means of the metronome" (Wundt, 1912/1973, p. 59).

There are three things to note about Wundt's metronome experiment:

1. Wundt's experiment is like many experiments in any science. It involves experimental manipulation of something (the speed of the metronome) and observations of the effect of this variation on something else (the feelings you experience). What is manipulated by the experimenter is called the *independent variable*. The experimenter is interested in the effects that the independent variable may have on the *dependent variable*, which is, in Wundt's case, the feelings that are experienced. A dependent variable may change as a result of manipulating the independent variable, just as Wundt claimed feelings change as a result of manipulating the metronome speed. Of course, sometimes manipulation of the independent variable may not lead to any corresponding variation in the dependent variable. Thus Wundt's experiment

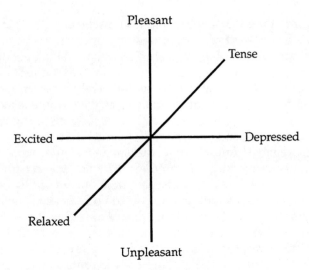

FIGURE 1-3 Wundt's Tridimensional Theory of Feeling

might not have worked in the way that he claimed it did. In principle, the metronome experiment may have failed to show any relationship between the independent and dependent variables. Moreover, as we shall see later, some experiments involve more than one independent variable and/or more than one dependent variable. Wundt's experiment is about as simple as an experiment can be. Although most of Wundt's experiments were simple, he often had to train subjects to make what he believed to be the correct observations.

2. The feelings that subjects observe in response to the metronome are Wundt's *data*. On the basis of these data, Wundt constructs a *theory* (the tridimensional theory of feeling). In science, the distinction between theory and data is very basic. The data consist of observations, which are supposed to be factual. A theory is intended to explain the data.

3. We need to ask some hard questions about Wundt's metronome experiment and the tridimensional theory of feeling. How would you criticize it? Take a moment to think about this question.

Let us begin our critical analysis of Wundt's experiment by looking at the data. The data are observations of feelings. Feelings are subjective experiences. Subjective experiences are private in the sense that I cannot observe your subjective experiences and you cannot observe mine. Wundt has the problem of saying how "immediate experience, [which] is private . . . can be the subject matter of a public science," a science in which all observations are open to scrutiny by anyone (Mischel, 1969, p. 22). One of the characteristics of scientific inquiry is that all observations must be objective. An objective observation is an observation that, at least in principle, can be made by anyone. Wundt's data seem to fail the test of objectivity. Moreover, the fact that subjects were often trained to make observations casts doubt on their objectivity. How can we know that they were not merely experiencing what they were trained to experience, rather than what they would experience without having been biased by their training? Introspectionist subjects often disagreed about the experiences they had. How much faith can one put in data that are not reliable? Important to the success of the experimental method is the ability to produce the same results when the experiment is repeated. Data are reliable if they are consistent from one set of observations to the next. Introspectionist data do not appear to be sufficiently reliable.

Now let us examine the tridimensional theory of feeling. What kind of theory is it? It seems to do little more than summarize the data. It does not appear to explain fully *why* the data are the way they are. (Although, to be fair, as Hilgard [1987, p. 320] points out, Wundt did, in some of his other work, try to provide a more thorough explanation.) What do we want a theory to do for us? This is a question to which we will return often.

In spite of criticisms of Wundt's experimental method, we should not forget the enormous contributions that he made. He succeeded in establishing psychology as an experimental discipline, even while others criticized his methods. In fact, as we indicated earlier, these criticisms were at the heart of the development of a very different set of methods. Let us examine this newer alternative.

Logical Positivism

As psychology became more sophisticated in the 1920s and 1930s, it developed a philosophy that justified it and made its procedures appear to be the same as those followed by other more established sciences. The philosophy it adopted goes under various names. One common name is *logical positivism*, which is associated with a group of physicists, logicians, and mathematicians working in Vienna, Austria, in the 1920s. They were called the Vienna Circle. They tried to formulate general principles or rules for gathering knowledge. These rules were adapted from those of successful knowledge-gathering disciplines such as physics and chemistry.

A good example of the application of logical positivism to psychology is described in a paper by Carnap (1935/1959). Carnap, like other logical positivists, stressed that knowledge is embodied in language. Any science, therefore, is essentially a set of statements referring to observations. The truth of these statements must lie in their correspondence with these factual observations. How can we check to see if the statements we make concur with the facts? There must be a procedure for verifying statements that is open to public scrutiny. The truth or falsehood of statements must be objectively (i.e., publicly) decided. This kind of thinking led to the *verification principle:* the meaning of a statement is its method of verification (Schlick, 1938/1962). "Thus, whenever we ask about a sentence, 'What does it mean?', what we expect is instruction as to the circumstances in which the sentence is to be used; we want a description of the conditions under which the sentence will form a true proposition, and of those which will make it false" (Schlick, 1938/1962, p. 30). From this viewpoint, if we cannot describe a procedure for verifying our statements, then they are of no value; they are meaningless.

According to Carnap (1935/1959), when we do experiments, our observations should be described by *protocol sentences*, which refer to publicly observable events. A meaningful statement is one that can be translated into these protocol sentences. If you are unable to translate a statement into protocol sentences, then it is not a meaningful statement. Once you have translated a statement into protocol sentences, then the protocol sentences *are* the meaning of the statement. There is no *surplus meaning*, in that statements never mean more than the protocol sentences to which they refer.

To understand the procedure that Carnap is recommending, let us reconsider Wundt's experiment. Suppose that, as the experimenter, I play the metronome at a very slow speed (one beat every two seconds). Suppose further that I say, "This metronome speed makes the subject feel sad." How can a statement like that be meaningful, if I cannot observe the subject's emotional experience? If you think about it for a minute, however, you can see what appears to be a way out of this problem. How do you usually find out that someone is sad? You usually observe what the person says and does. If someone says he or she feels sad, and if the facial expression is downcast and posture slumped, you might feel justified in saying, "That person feels sad." Notice that all of your observations (what the person says, the facial expression, and the posture) would have been objective. In Carnap's terms, your observations would be protocol sentences. These descriptions give meaning to your statement "That person is sad." Similarly, in Wundt's experiment, the experimenter can say, "The subject feels sad" and mean that the subject is really saying, "That beat makes me feel sad." What the subject *says* is publicly observable. From Carnap's viewpoint, Wundt was mistaken in believing that the data of psychology consist of private experiences. In fact, the data of psychology consist of publicly observable occurrences in the form of behavior, which includes verbal behavior such as saying, "I feel sad."

Carnap went further and argued that psychology involved what he called *dispositional concepts*. Dispositional concepts are descriptions of lawful relationships between independent and dependent variables. Such statements have the following form: *If X, then Y,* where *X* is an independent and *Y* a dependent variable. Thus the following is a dispositional concept: *If the metronome is played at one beat every two seconds, then the subject will say, "That beat makes me feel sad."*

Dispositional concepts are capable of being falsified (Popper, 1965). *Falsifiability* is an important characteristic of scientific concepts. As long as your observations are consistent with a dispositional concept, the concept can be retained as a law. Should your observations be inconsistent with a dispositional concept, however, it must be replaced with a more likely alternative. This alternative can then be tested against publicly observable data until it is falsified. In this way, our laws more accurately reflect the true structure of behavior.

Operationism

Psychologists have been influenced by another viewpoint that is quite similar to Carnap's suggestion that all psychological concepts ultimately refer to publicly observable occurrences. That viewpoint is *operationism* (Boring, 1945; Bridgman, 1927). Operationism requires the investigator to specify the way in which a concept is to be measured. Such specifications are called *operational definitions*. A researcher should be able to give an operational definition for any psychological concept whatsoever. Thus an operational definition of a concept such as intelligence might be the score a person obtains on an intelligence test (Boring, 1923). Here again, operational definitions provide a way of making sure that psychological concepts refer to publicly observable events.

As useful as operational definitions are, it is not always obvious precisely how psychological concepts should be operationally defined. Thoughtfully working out sensible operational definitions is a major task for the research psychologist. As you consider different examples of psychological research, always ask whether or not the operational definition(s) that a researcher uses are as valid as they could be. A *valid* measure is one that actually measures what it purports to measure. As you consider each research example, try to think of alternative operational definitions for the concepts the researcher has employed.

Hull versus Tolman:
A Case History in Psychological Research

Logical positivism and operationism were extremely influential in psychology during the 1940s and 1950s. A good example of the way research was conducted during this period is the work of Clark Hull (1884–1952). Hull (1952) was the most influential psychologist in this period. While the content of his theory of learning no longer has many adherents, many psychologists still try to emulate the form of the theory. The form of the theory was a logical structure of *postulates* and *theorems* (Logan, 1959). Postulates are intended to describe the basic processes that underlie behavior. They are used to derive theorems that can be tested experimentally. If experimental data are consistent with the theorem, then the postulates are retained unchanged. If a theorem is falsified, however, then the postulates must be changed. New theorems can then be derived and tested. This process goes on and on with the postulates being improved as a result of experimentation. Of course, the postulates must also be consistent with one another. The procedure just described is called the *hypothetico-deductive method*, because the theorems that are *deduced* from the postulates are *hypotheses* that can be tested experimentally. A hypothesis, as defined by the *Oxford English Dictionary*, is "a supposition or conjecture put forth to account for known facts; especially in the sciences, a provisional supposition from which to draw conclusions that shall be in accordance with known facts, and which serves as a starting-point for further investigation by which it may be proved or disproved and the true theory arrived at." In practice, how did Hull's hypothetico-deductive method work?

Hull's postulates contained a set of *intervening variables*. As the name suggests, intervening variables *come between* independent and dependent variables. Intervening variables are intended to explain the relationships between independent and dependent variables. For example, *habit strength* was an intervening variable in Hull's system. Habit strength referred to the connection between a stimulus and a response and was postulated to increase gradually whenever an animal was rewarded for responding to a stimulus. For example, suppose that a food-deprived animal, such as a hungry white rat, is placed in the start box of a maze similar to the one in Figure 1-4. Eventually the animal will reach the end of the maze and be fed. From Hull's perspective, this means that there will be an increase in the strength of the habits that connect the stimuli from the maze to the correct responses that enable the animal to reach the food. Thus, turning left, right, right, left, left, right are the responses that the animal needs to learn. Hull would deduce from his postulate that the time it takes the animal to go from start box to goal box would decline gradually as a function of trials. This hypothesis is deduced from Hull's theory and can be tested experimentally. In fact, experiments in which animals were rewarded on each trial showed the kind of continuous improvement that Hull's theory predicted. Because these data do not falsify the hypothesis deduced from Hull's postulate, they appear to allow that postulate to be retained. The data seem to support the notion that habit strength increases continuously as a function of trials in which the animal is rewarded. These data, however, are not the whole story.

During this period, Edward C. Tolman (1886–1959) was Hull's great competitor in psychology. Although Tolman also made use of intervening variables in his theory (in fact, he invented the term), his view of the nature of learning was radically different from Hull's. Instead of using an interven-

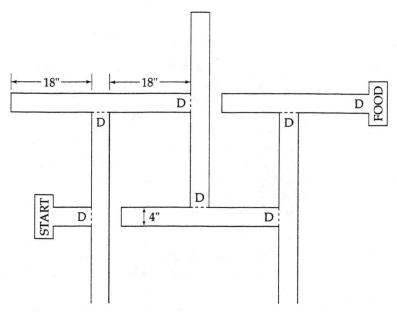

FIGURE 1-4 Six-Unit Alley T-Maze

Source: "The Effect of the Introduction of Reward upon the Maze Performance of Rats" by H. C. Blodgett, 1929, *University of California Publications in Psychology, 4,* 117. Reprinted by permission.

ing variable called habit strength, Tolman used one called *expectancy*. Tolman argued that learning involved the formation of expectations, rather than the formation of habits. According to Tolman, these expectations could be learned in the absence of reward. Simply by exploring the maze in Figure 1-4, an animal could learn what to expect at each point in the maze. The animal might not demonstrate that it had learned anything until it became important for it to do so. What are the consequences of the difference between Tolman and Hull?

Look at Figure 1-5, which contains data from an experiment by Tolman and Honzik (1930). The graph shows data from three groups of rats, each of which was allowed to run once a day through a maze similar to the one shown in Figure 1-4. One group, called HR for "hungry reward," was fed every time it reached the food box. Notice that the group behaves just as Hull would have predicted. They go through the maze faster and faster on successive days until they have apparently learned the maze thoroughly, and there is no further improvement. Another group, called HNR for "hungry no reward," also behaves just as Hull would have predicted. This group receives no reward upon reaching the end of the maze. The rats show no improvement as the days pass, indicating that they may not have learned anything. But wait

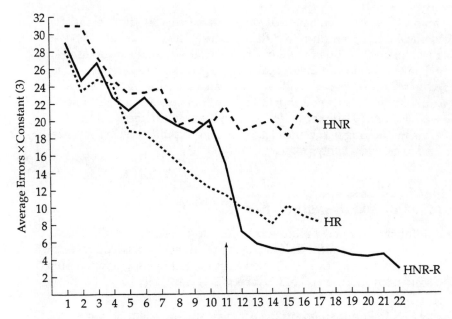

FIGURE 1-5 Data from Tolman and Honzik's "Latent Learning" Experiment

Source: "Cognitive Maps in Rats and Men" by E. C. Tolman, 1948, *Psychological Review, 55,* 195. Copyright 1948 by the American Psychological Association. Reprinted by permission.

a minute. Look at the curve for the group labeled HNR-R, for "hungry no reward-reward." This group is not rewarded for the first ten days. These rats behave just like the no-reward group during this period. According to Hull's theory, they should not have learned anything, because they have not been rewarded. When the rats are rewarded on the eleventh and subsequent days, however, they rapidly begin to perform as well as the rats who have been rewarded all along. Apparently these rats learned the maze without reward but did not display their learning until they were rewarded for doing so. This phenomenon was called *latent learning.* Results such as these led Tolman to make a distinction between *learning,* which could occur without reward, and *performance,* which was influenced by reward. Perhaps you can discover instances of latent learning in your own experience. Can you learn something without anyone else knowing that you have learned it, like the rats in the HNR-R group? Again, like the rats in that group, do you usually show what you have learned only when it is important for you to do so?

You should be able to identify the independent and dependent variables in Tolman and Honzik's experiment. Their study demonstrates how an experiment can provide objective data that allow a researcher to argue in favor of one theoretical interpretation rather than another. The controversy between Hull and Tolman also illustrates how nonhuman subjects can be used to provide data that bear on a theoretical dispute that is quite general and not restricted to only one species. Hull and Tolman's theories were intended to apply to any species whatsoever, not just to rats or people. Although Tolman's theory was challenged on many occasions and eventually replaced by other theories, the underlying assumption that behavior is guided by expectancies has proved to be remarkably popular.

The Context of Discovery versus the Context of Justification

In general, Tolman adopted a much looser and more speculative formulation than did Hull. Tolman's attitude toward the relationship between research and theory in psychology can be gleaned from the following quotation from a paper written toward the end of his career (Tolman, 1959):

> The system may not stand up to any final rules of scientific procedure. But I do not much care. I have liked to think about psychology in ways that have proved congenial to me. Since all the sciences, and especially psychology, are still immersed in such tremendous realms of the uncertain and the unknown, the best that any individual scientist, especially any psychologist, can do seems to be to follow his own gleam and his own bent, however inadequate they may be. In fact, I suppose that actually this is what we all do. In the end, the only sure criterion is to have fun. And I have had fun. (p. 152)

In spite of the apparently whimsical nature of these remarks, Tolman was a very serious investigator whose influence lasted well beyond his lifetime. What is important to note, however, is that Tolman's description of the way in which he *actually did* research contrasts sharply with the way in which philosophers of science, such as the logical positivists, said that we *should* do research. This distinction is often put in terms of a contrast between the *context of discovery* and the *context of justification* (Gigerenzer, 1991; Reichenbach, 1938). The thinking that leads to the discovery of a method for investigating a research problem may be quite different from the thinking that goes into presenting a completed study for consumption by the rest of the scientific community. The latter involves justifying the procedure that was used, rather than explaining how the investigator came up with it in the first place. In this book we will deal with both of these aspects of the research process.

More Recent Developments

Recall that Wundt made a distinction between simple and complex psychological processes. He also thought that there were different research methods that were appropriate for the study of each kind of process. Simple processes could be studied in the laboratory, while complex ones had to be studied as they naturally occurred in the world. This distinction has been echoed often throughout the history of psychology. Nowadays, some psychologists (e.g., Bruce, 1985) take what is called an *ecological approach* to research. They often argue that you cannot understand the complexity of behavior as it occurs in everyday life by means of laboratory-based research alone (Neisser, 1978, 1982). An ecological approach to research involves studying behavior in natural settings (Neisser, 1985). *Ecologically valid* research is a difficult enterprise because it requires the exploration of complex "real-world" situations (Hirst & Levine, 1985). The development of ecologically valid (Neisser, 1976) research methods will be considered in this book, alongside the development of the sort of laboratory-based research methods that have also served psychology well (e.g., Loftus, 1991). In this book we are not interested in taking sides with respect to controversial issues, but only interested in making sure that all sides are given a thorough hearing. You, the reader, are the ultimate judge of the worth of the different research methods we will consider.

Discussions of research methods over the last twenty years have also tended to emphasize the *complexity* of the research process more than earlier discussions did (e.g., Pedhazur, 1982). When we do research, we are often interested in what causes what, but the nature of *causality* is not easy to spell out. The current debate about causality was forcefully anticipated by the German philosopher Immanuel Kant (1781/1929; Mischel, 1967). Kant observed that everyone (not just scientists) tends to organize their experiences in terms of causes and effects. We impose cause-and-effect relationships on the world, though they may not actually exist in the world. Perhaps you have had an experience of the sort that Kant had in mind. For example, "when a gust of wind blows a door shut, and at the same time an electric light happens to go on at the other end of a corridor, the impression of a causal relation is forced upon us" (Michotte, 1963, p. 16). Whenever we experience two events occurring together we tend to interpret one as the cause of the other, even though it may be an illusion to do so. The problem of "illusory" causal relationships is as important for researchers as it is in everyday life. Although researchers often tend to think of independent variables as "causing" dependent variables, it is often very difficult to say anything definite about causal relationships. In fact, we are not always able to specify the relations between independent and dependent variables in an unambiguous manner. The facts may not "speak for themselves" but may need to be understood from within a particular theoretical framework. For example, Pedhazur (1982, p. 575) points out that it is entirely possible for different theories to be consistent with the same data. Being consistent with the data is no guarantee of a theory's validity. An investigator's theory may, at least partially, determine how the data will be interpreted.

Many philosophers have noted that the process of scientific inquiry inevitably contains a subjective aspect, as Tolman suggested. Thomas Kuhn (1970) is among the more influential of these philosophers. T. Kuhn reviewed the historical development of established sciences such as physics. He came to the conclusion that the development of these disciplines had not been smooth. It was *not* the case that they had simply grown and developed by accumulating data that guided the development of an adequate theory. On the contrary, scientific disciplines appeared to develop discontinuously, as there were long periods during which almost all workers in a discipline had the same beliefs about the methods, data, and theory that were appropriate for their discipline. At certain critical junctures, however, there were radical upheavals, and entire scientific communities changed their minds about what were the proper methods, data, and theory in their discipline. The set of fundamental beliefs that guide workers in a scientific discipline is called a *paradigm*. Revolutionary periods occur in which a new paradigm is emerging and an old paradigm is being overthrown. The controversy surrounding the emergence of Darwin's theory of evolution in the nineteenth century would be an example of such a revolution.

T. Kuhn argued that paradigms shape the scientist's view of the world. There can be *paradigm clashes* in which fundamentally different ways of interpreting the data exist. T. Kuhn likened this state of affairs to cases in which we can see different patterns in the same situation. A good example of what T. Kuhn had in mind comes from the work of N. R. Hanson (1969). Consider Figure 1-6A. What is it—a bird or an antelope? If we view Figure 1-6A in the context of Figure 1-6B, we are able to see the similarity between it and a bird. As Hanson (1969, p. 13) points out, it is difficult to see it as an antelope when its similarities to all the other "birds" in Figure 1-6B are so evident. If we view Figure 1-6A in the context of Figure 1-6C, however, then its similarity to an antelope becomes clear. Now it looks different. What was formerly the beak of a bird is now transformed into the horns of an antelope. Hanson's demonstration is intended to make the following point. The two contexts are analogous to two different theories. Each of the "theories" suggests a different interpretation of the same fact, or *datum*. Each theory is equally consistent with the datum. In general, the theoretical context within which we interpret data may literally determine how those data are *seen*. Conflicting interpretations of same data are entirely possible, even inevitable. How to resolve such conflicts will be a recurrent theme in this book.

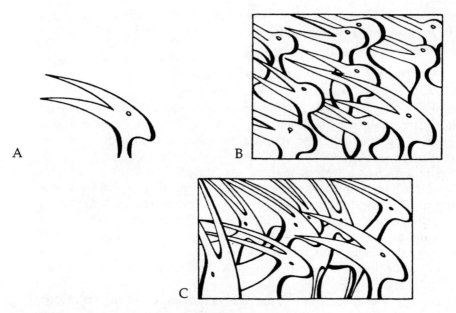

FIGURE 1-6 Is It a Bird or an Antelope?

Source: Patterns of Discovery by N. R. Hanson, 1969, Cambridge: Cambridge University Press, pp. 13–14. Copyright 1969 by the Cambridge University Press. Reprinted by permission.

As Deanna Kuhn (1989) has noted, the way an individual's thinking develops is similar to the historical development of science itself. "Both child and scientist gain understanding of the world through construction and revision of a succession of models, or paradigms, that replace one another" (D. Kuhn, 1989, p. 675). People, including scientists themselves, do not always behave in the way that scientists are supposed to behave. We should revise a theory in the light of new data, but sometimes we get it backwards, and we revise the data to make them fit the theory. In order to properly coordinate theories and evidence, we need to be continuously mindful (Langer, 1989) of the distinction between the two. Being able to bring one's theory progressively into line with reality is not always easy to do. It is a process that "takes place many times over, as the skill mastered or the error avoided in one context remains to be conquered in others" (D. Kuhn, 1989, p. 686). As D. Kuhn (1989) points out, scientific thinking is something that we all do naturally; it is not some weird process fit only for a few select initiates. Everyone can, with some attention and effort, improve their scientific thinking skills. Throughout this book, we will point out the benefits of making such improvements (e.g., Lehman, Lempert, & Nisbett, 1988). A major purpose of the book is to help you become more mindful not only of the more common ways in which we make errors but also of some of the skills needed to do productive research.

A Summary and Some Implications

- Wundt believed that psychological research could take place both in the laboratory and in natural settings. He tried to use introspection as a method for laboratory research, but this method was heavily criticized for being too subjective.
- Operationism is a way of making psychological concepts meaningful by anchoring them to publicly observable events. However, since it is not always obvious precisely how psychological concepts should be operationally defined, you should be careful to use measures that are as valid as possible. Many psychologists now stress the importance of ecological validity—the use of methods that "have something to say about what people do in real, culturally significant situations" (Neisser, 1976, p. 2)
- As the work of T. Kuhn (1970) and others has suggested, the distinction between theory and data is not always as clear as it might be. Keep this distinction in mind as we proceed. In each case, ask yourself questions like the following : What assumptions is this researcher making that are not necessarily justified? If you were doing research in a particular area, what assumptions would *you* make? Are your assumptions justified? Do the data necessarily mean what a particular researcher says they mean? Are there alternative interpretations of the data? How would *you* go about testing an alternative interpretation?

This brief history of the development of research methods in psychology is not complete. There are several recent developments that we will consider later on, particularly in Chapter 7, which is a compendium illustrating a variety of research techniques.

Names and Concepts to Understand and Remember

The following are some of the most influential ideas in the area we have just reviewed. Some concepts are quite general and are not associated with any particular psychologist. In other cases, however, the names of psychologists are paired with the concepts for which they are known. Read through the list. If any of the names or concepts seem unfamiliar to you, then go back and reread the appropriate section of the chapter. The names are in the order in which they are presented in the text, and the concepts are italicized in the text, so they are easy to find. You should be able to define each concept and briefly discuss it. You should also be able to write a brief account of the work done by each person on the list.

Wundt and the nature of introspection and the tridimensional theory of feeling

independent and dependent variables

logical positivism

verification principle

protocol sentences

surplus meaning

dispositional concept

falsifiability

operationism and operational definitions

postulates and theorems

hypothetico-deductive method

hypothesis

intervening variables

Tolman and latent learning

context of discovery versus context of justification

Kant and the concept of causality

T. Kuhn and paradigms and paradigm clashes

ecological approach

validity

Additional Reading

Morawski (1988) contains many interesting observations concerning the development of experimental psychology in the United States. Hulse and Green (1986) provide historical reviews of several important American research traditions. Amundson (1985) gives a thorough look at some of the deeper methodological issues surrounding Tolman's work.

You may have come across some unfamiliar words in this chapter. It is probably a good idea to keep a dictionary close to hand. Reber (1985) is an excellent dictionary of psychological terms.

2

The Psychology of Scientific Thinking

Overview

Is Scientific Thinking Different?
    Confirmation Bias
    Simplicity
    Consistency
    The Psycho-Logic of Disconfirmation
    Concept Formation in Science

Ethical Principles of Research
    Animal Rights?

Names and Concepts to Understand and Remember

Additional Reading

Is Scientific Thinking Different?

One of the more intriguing developments in psychological research has been the growth of the study of the similarities and differences between the way people ordinarily think and the way people think when they are doing science. We will examine this research throughout this book, because it will help us clarify how we should think when we do research ourselves. To get started, and to give you a taste of things to come, let us have a look at the work of one of the pioneers in this area, Peter Wason of the University of London. Wason has been particularly interested in what is called *confirmation bias*. Confirmation bias is the tendency to search for information that will confirm one's hypothesis, rather than to look for information that will disconfirm it. Confirmation bias can lead one to believe that one has found the "right answer," when in fact more critical thinking may be needed.

Confirmation Bias

We will consider a situation in which an experimenter gives an adult subject a reasoning task, and the data consist of what the subject does with that task. Although not unlike what pupils sometimes face in the classroom, the situation is obviously somewhat artificial, as one cannot discover everything about reasoning in everyday life by studying individuals in an experimental context. Still, several interesting things come to light in such studies.

Wason's approach to the study of reasoning (1960, 1966, 1977a, 1977b, 1978; Wason & Johnson-Laird, 1972) is to invent tasks that directly tap intriguing aspects of reasoning. No one, perhaps, has been more clever in the design of psychologically interesting reasoning tasks than Wason, who has invented three tasks we will be considering. At the outset we should note that the results in Wason's experiments tend to be the same across a broad range of subjects. So when we talk about what subjects do in a particular reasoning task, we are talking about "garden-variety" adults, with no special characteristics (although Wason's experiments were usually initially performed with University of London undergraduate students, who probably would not appreciate being described as having no special characteristics).

Wason apparently discovered the *generative problem* in a dream. Although undoubtedly original, Wason's task brings out some of the issues that philosophers such as Wittgenstein (1953) considered when he was wondering what it means to understand a rule. Sternberg (1982, p. 451) has raised similar issues. He has also discussed the ability to discover a rule as an aspect of intelligence. Here is a variant of one of Sternberg's examples. Suppose that on the first day of spring there is 1 daffodil in your garden. On the second day a second daffodil makes its appearance, while on the third day a third daffodil shows up. What would you predict for the fourth day? How many daffodils in total would there be? Most people would say 4, because it seems as if 1 daffodil is being added to the garden every day. Suppose, however, that on the fourth day 2 new daffodils appear, for a total of 5. What would you predict for the fifth day? Is there any rule you can discern governing the growth of daffodils? Suppose that on the fifth day there is a total of 8 daffodils, and on the sixth day a total of 13 daffodils. The growth pattern of daffodils would then be as follows:

Total Number of Days	1	2	3	4	5	6
Total Number of Daffodils	1	2	3	5	8	13

Do you see any pattern here? In fact, the growth of daffodils appears to follow a well-known rule. The rule is this : The total number on any particular day is the sum of the totals on the previous two days. Thus you would predict a total of 21(8 + 13) daffodils on the seventh day. This well-known mathematical rule is called the Fibonacci sequence, named after a thirteenth-century mathematician. The Fibonacci sequence can actually be found in some growth patterns (Stevens, 1974), although not necessarily in daffodils, and it is an example of a rule that can be discovered and then used to predict future occurrences. The discovery of such lawful relationships is an important part of scientific inquiry. Wason's work helps us to understand the processes by which people uncover such rules.

If you were a subject in an experiment using the original version of Wason's generative problem, you would be "told that the numbers 2, 4, 6 conformed to a simple . . . rule which the experimenter had in mind, and that [your] task was to discover the rule by generating sequences of three numbers. . . . [The experimenter] would tell you each time whether the rule held" for the sequence you generated (Wason, 1966, p. 139). At each trial, you would also write down a hypothesis about the rule. When you felt highly confident that you had discovered the rule, then you would be allowed to propose it. You would be told if you announced the wrong rule, and then you would continue with the task until you discovered the rule.

Subjects tend to think that this task is easier than it often turns out to be. They typically assume that the rule is that each number in the series is two more than the one preceding it. They propose sequences of numbers that are consistent with this assumption, such as 8, 10, 12. The rule Wason actually had in mind was *any increasing series of numbers,* and sequences such as 8, 10, 12 are consistent with this rule. Thus when the subject proposes sequences such as 8, 10, 12, he or she will be told that the proposed sequence is consistent with the rule. Because of the positive feedback, subjects become confident that they have discovered the rule, and announce the belief that it is "numbers increase by two." They are then told that their hypothesis is false, and are often very surprised.

The subject may go on for quite a while longer in this fashion. Wason (1966, pp. 140–141) describes cases in which subjects end up proposing quite complex rules, such as "the difference between the two numbers next to each other is the same." On being told that such a rule is still not quite right, subjects, understandably enough, may become annoyed and frustrated. In this respect, at least, their behavior may be quite similar to that of a scientist who keeps trying to come up with an acceptable hypothesis, but, no matter how hard he or she tries, it is never quite good enough.

I have often used a version of Wason's task in my classes. I can report that Brock University students behave remarkably like University of London students, or, for that matter, like people anywhere who have been given this task. This is particularly true if the students start to compete with each other to find the right answer, each trying to be the first to announce the correct rule. This only seems to make matters worse. Competition and clear thinking may not always go hand in hand (Luchins & Luchins 1950/1968, p. 71).

All the sequences that subjects typically propose are consistent with the rule *any increasing series of numbers*, as are 1, 2, 3 or 1, 4, 9 or an infinite number of other possible sequences. If you are a subject in this experiment, it is simply not a very good strategy to propose sequences that are consistent with your hypothesis about the rule. What should you do instead?

What would happen if you suggested a sequence that is *inconsistent* with your hypothesis? For example, suppose you believed that *the rule is that each number is two more than the preceding number*. If you propose a sequence such as 7, 8, 9, which contradicts your hypothesis, then the experimenter will tell you that the sequence you have proposed is, in fact, consistent with the rule that the experimenter has in mind. It follows that your hypothesis is *false*. Notice that the strategy of falsifying your hypothesis, and thus eliminating incorrect beliefs, is the same strategy we discussed earlier. As many philosophers of science have observed, there is no substitute for attempting to falsify hypotheses (e.g., Popper, 1965).

One might be tempted to conclude that subjects in Wason's task are not behaving very much like scientists, since they persist in seeking confirmatory evidence for their hypotheses, rather than actively seeking evidence that would disconfirm them. Wason's experiment, and others like it, show that ordinary reasoning processes do not conform to the usual standards of scientific reasoning. However, there is also evidence suggesting that successful scientists themselves often reason in a way that is typical of the subjects in Wason's experiment, because they also often seek confirming rather than disconfirming evidence (e.g., Gorman 1986, p. 96; 1989). Here is a good example of this tendency, taken from Beveridge (1957, as cited in Gorman, 1986, p. 86), that concerns the blowfly, or fleshfly, which is often the carrier of disease:

When I saw a demonstration of what is known as the Mules operation for the prevention of blowfly attack in sheep, I realized its significance and my imagination was fired by the great potentialities of Mules' discovery. I put up an experiment involving thousands of sheep and, without waiting for the results, persuaded colleagues working on the blowfly problem to carry out experiments elsewhere. When about a year later, the results became available, the sheep in my trial showed no benefit of the operation. The other trials, and all subsequent ones, showed that the operation conferred a very valuable degree of protection and no satisfactory explanation could be found for the failure of my experiment. It was fortunate that I had enough confidence in my judgment to prevail upon my colleagues to put up trials in other parts of the country, for if I had been more cautious and awaited my results they would probably have retarded the adoption of the operation for years. (p. 34)

It is unlikely that one negative experimental result would be allowed to disconfirm a strongly held theory once and for all. If there appear to be good reasons for maintaining the theory in the first place, then that theory may need to be put to the test many times before it is rejected by a majority of members of the scientific community. Beveridge's example shows that such persistence in the face of disconfirmation may sometimes be a positive, rather than a negative, feature of scientific behavior. As you recall, confirmation bias is the name for the tendency to seek confirming, rather than disconfirming, evidence for a hypothesis. It may be as characteristic of the behavior of at least some professional scientists on at least some occasions as it apparently is of the majority of subjects in Wason's experiments. One prominent philosopher of science (Lakatos, 1970) put it like this:

The direction of science is determined primarily by human creative imagination and not by the universe of facts which surround us. Creative imagination is likely to find corroborating novel evidence even for the most "absurd" program, if the search has sufficient drive. This look out for *new confirming evidence* is perfectly permissible. (p. 187)

While we need to be alert to disconfirming evidence, we should not, as the saying goes, be in a hurry to throw out the baby with the bath water. A theory that has repeatedly been confirmed would be worth continued evaluation, even in the face of some negative evidence. Another relevant proverb is "One swallow does not make a summer": neither does one negative result necessarily disconfirm a hypothesis. Perhaps an experiment yielding a negative result was not properly carried out. Perhaps the negative results occurred by chance and are not representative of the experimental results that will be obtained in the long run. One last proverb is appropriate here: "Patience is a virtue."

Conclusions in science are usually regarded as tentative, not as absolute. Many scientists have argued that scientific theories should not be like religious beliefs, to which one commits oneself totally, although, as we will see later, the relationship between science and religion is not straightforward. Sometimes the ideal of "disinterested inquiry" (Russell, 1959, p. 313), in which one explores the implications of one's hypotheses in a dispassionate manner, is advanced as an essential characteristic of scientific inquiry. However, science can also be a demanding, time-consuming pursuit, and some degree of emotional investment in the process may be important. We are reminded (Gorman, 1989) of the prominent physicist Paul Dirac, who is supposed to have said: "It's most important to have a beautiful theory. And if the observations don't support it, don't be too distressed, but wait a bit and see if some error in the observations doesn't show up" (Judson, 1984, p. 43). But what is a beautiful theory? This is not an easy question to answer. The following are some of the qualities that beautiful scientific theories are often said to possess.

Simplicity

A good theory should be as simple as possible. Some of the subjects in Wason's experiments generated hypotheses that became more and more complex as they went along. This may be the wrong way to proceed if you are trying to think scientifically. In the fourteenth century a Franciscan monk named William of Occam advanced the principle that "it is vain to do with more what can be done with less." As a scientific principle, this is often stated as follows: "Do not multiply theoretical entities beyond necessity." Known as *Occam's razor*, this principle admonishes us to keep our explanations as uncomplicated as we possibly can. The unnecessary parts of theories are like whiskers that we should shave off whenever we notice them. In psychology, this principle is identified with one of the first people to study learning in animals, C. Lloyd Morgan (1904), and is called *Lloyd Morgan's canon* (in this context, a canon is a principle or rule). In Lloyd Morgan's words,

> In no case may we interpret an action as the outcome of the exercise of a higher psychological faculty, if it can be interpreted as the outcome of the exercise of one which stands in the psychological scale. (p. 53)

Lloyd Morgan's canon is often called the *principle of parsimony*. A person is said to be parsimonious if he or she is frugal or careful with money, and a theorist is parsimonious if he or she is careful not to create too elaborate a theory. If we follow Lloyd Morgan, we will try to explain behavior in as

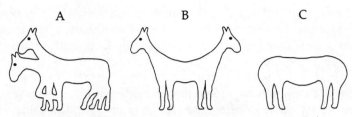

FIGURE 2-1 Simplicity versus Likelihood

Source: "Against the Likelihood Principle in Visual Form Perception" by E. Leeuwenberg and F. Boselie, 1988, *Psychological Review, 95,* 486. Copyright 1988 by the American Psychological Association. Reprinted by permission.

economical a way as possible. If we can explain what people do in terms of what a simpler organism does, then we should do so. Do you agree with this principle? Can you think of any cases in which, in your opinion, it should not be applied?

Whatever the merits of the principle of parsimony, there is evidence that people often prefer to see things as simply as they can. The tendency to see things as simply as possible is called the *simplicity principle* by Leeuwenberg and Boselie (1988). Leeuwenberg and Boselie compared the simplicity principle with the *likelihood principle.* The likelihood principle states that we tend to see the most likely event, whether it is simple or not. Consider Figure 2-1A. It is an example of a reversible figure, which can be seen either as a very unusual creature or as two horses. If our perception followed the likelihood principle, then we would tend to see this figure as two horses. Moreover, if our perception followed the simplicity principle, we might also see two horses, since that would be simpler than seeing one animal with extra heads and legs. Thus figures such as 2-1A do not allow us to decide which of the two principles governs our perception. However, in Figure 2-1B and 2-1C, we tend to see the simplest alternative, which is one animal in both cases, even though it is very unlikely that we have actually seen such creatures before.

On the basis of demonstrations like this, Leeuwenberg and Boselie argue that our perception is determined more by simplicity than it is by likelihood. Thus, of two interpretations of an event, we will tend to prefer the simplest one. However, as we will see at various points in this book, there may be cases in which we must abandon the simplest explanation in favor of a more complex alternative, even if the simplest explanation is more attractive.

Consistency

Theories are supposed to be *internally consistent*—that is, one part of a theory should not contradict another part of the same theory. If a theory is simple, then it should be easy to tell if it is consistent. In practice, however, inconsistency is not always easy to detect. If a theory is complicated, the logical consistency of its parts may not be at all obvious. Special procedures may be necessary to determine consistency. Casting the theory in the form of a computer program is one strategy that is sometimes adopted to determine consistency. Such a program should detect any internal inconsistencies, or "bugs," in the theory. However it is determined, many scientists value consistency very highly, as this quotation from the great Polish logician J. Lukasiewicz (cited in Coope, Geach, Potts, & White, 1970) indicates:

> I should like to sketch a picture connected with the deepest intuitive feelings I always get about logic. This picture throws more light than any discursive exposition would on the real foundations from which this science grows (at least so far as I am concerned). Whenever I am occupied even with the tiniest local problem . . . I have the impression that I am confronted with a mighty construction, of indescribable complexity. . . . This construction has the effect upon me of a concrete tangible object, fashioned from the hardest of materials, a hundred times stronger than concrete or steel. I cannot change anything in it; by intense labor I merely find in it ever new details, and attain unshakable and eternal truths. (p. 7)

Far from being "disinterested inquiry," the process Lukasiewicz is describing is one that involves him totally. Although science is often thought of as being opposed to religion, the feelings Lukasiewicz expresses sound almost religious. Many scientists have been religious people of a variety of persuasions, and others have not been at all religious. Whether or not you are a religious person may color the way you feel about science, but it need not determine whether or not you will do science in a way that is recognized as worthwhile by others.

Simplicity and consistency are values that can combine to make a theory beautiful. Sometimes, however, simplicity must be sacrificed in order to make a theory that does justice to the complexity of the data; and sometimes consistency is not a simple thing to evaluate! As you read this book, try to evaluate the research we review by asking the following questions:

- Is this research derived from a theory that is as simple as possible? Is there a simpler alternative, and, if there is, what hypotheses could be deduced from it?
- Is this research derived from a theory that is logically consistent? Is there a more consistent alternative, and, if there is, what hypotheses could be deduced from it?

Most people are capable of creating what seem to them to be beautiful theories about any number of things. Apparently, we tend to look for evidence that will confirm our beautiful theories, and we tend not to look for evidence that might disconfirm our beautiful theories. We might call these tendencies the *beautiful theory hypothesis*. Of course, the beautiful theory hypothesis might be false. Perhaps you could design an experiment that would provide evidence that the beautiful theory hypothesis is at least misleading, if not completely wrong. What might such an experiment be like?

The Psycho-Logic of Disconfirmation

Let us explore confirmation bias a little further, because we have not yet learned all the lessons that this phenomenon has to teach us about research. Wason's *card selection task* (Wason, 1966, p. 145; Wason & Evans, 1975) has been extensively explored because of its ability to demonstrate confirmation bias. The selection task is illustrated in Figure 2-2. There are four cards, each with a letter on one side and a number on the other. The experimenter gives the subject a rule, and the subject must try to determine if the rule is correct. Here is an example of such a rule: *If a card has a vowel on one side, then it has an even number on the other side.* The subject's task is to say which cards must be turned over in order to find out if the rule is accurate.

The most common response is to turn over the E and the 2, or just the E. Johnson-Laird and Wason (1970) reported that about 79% of subjects given the selection task choose those alternatives. People tend to focus on confirming instances, and thus this task illustrates the operation of confirmation bias. Few people see that you need to turn over the fourth card. If you turn over the 5 and find E on the other side, then that *falsifies* the rule, because there is a card with a vowel on one side and an odd number on the other. While it is necessary to turn over the fourth card, turning over the third card is a waste of time. Suppose you turned over the third card and discovered the letter F. Would that falsify the rule? Think about it.

I hope that you reached the conclusion that discovering a consonant on the other side of the third card does not falsify the rule. The rule does not prohibit the existence of cards with consonants on one side and even numbers on the other. The rule says only that a card with a *vowel* on one side must have

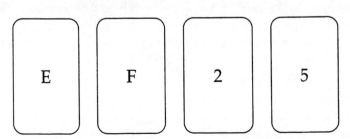

FIGURE 2-2 The Card Selection Task

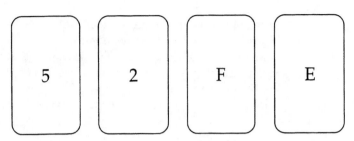

FIGURE 2-3 The Backs of the Cards in Figure 2-2

an even number on the other. That is why the second card is also irrelevant to the rule. Whatever number is on the other side of the *F*, it will not falsify the rule. Thus the only cards you need to turn over are the first and the fourth cards, because they are the only ones that can falsify the rule. You will see that this is the case if you examine Figure 2-3, which represents the backs of the cards in Figure 2-2. In this task we can see particularly clearly the role that falsification can play in the evaluation of a hypothesis.

Wason's selection task illustrates the kind of reasoning necessary when we do research. Recall our previous discussion of dispositional concepts. Dispositional concepts are descriptions of lawful relationships between independent and dependent variables. Such statements have the following form: "If *x* then *y*," where *x* is an independent and *y* a dependent variable. Evidence from Wason's selection task suggests that we tend to look for evidence to confirm such statements, rather than to look systematically for evidence to disconfirm them. Let us examine the logic of *If . . . , then . . .* statements in a little more detail. Such statements are often also called *hypothetical statements*. Hypothetical statements take the form "If *p* then *q*," where *p* stands for an independent variable (or *antecedent*) and *q* stands for a dependent variable (or consequent).

Truth tables were invented by Wittgenstein (1921/1974, p. 32), in order to evaluate the truth or falsehood of statements. A truth table can be used to display the possible combinations of antecedents and consequents. An example of a truth table is given in Figure 2-4, which shows the four possible combinations of antecedent (*p*) and consequent (*q*). The antecedent can be either true (T) or false (F); and the consequent can be either true (T) or false

p	q	If p, then q
T	T	T
T	F	F
F	T	T
F	F	T

FIGURE 2-4 A Truth Table

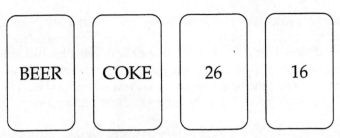

FIGURE 2-5   A Drinking Problem

Source: Adapted from "The Logic of Social Exchange: Has Natural Selection Shaped How Humans Reason?" by L. Cosmides, 1989, *Cognition, 31,* 192. Copyright 1989 by Elsevier Sequoia S.A., Lausanne/Switzerland. Adapted by permission of the publisher and Leda Cosmides.

(F). Let us examine the four possibilities. As a running example, we will use a rule adapted from Griggs and Cox (1982) and Cosmides (1989, p. 192). This example is illustrated in Figure 2-5. Each card has a beverage on one side and an age on the other side. The rule is *If a person is drinking beer, then he or she must be over 21 years old.* The antecedent, *p*, is drinking beer. The consequent, *q*, is being over 21. What card would you turn over in order to detect cheaters? The *BEER* card and the 16 card, right? Let us look at the four possibilities:

1. When both *p* and *q* are true, then obviously the statement "If *p*, then *q*" is also true. The person drinks beer and is over 21.
2. When *p* is true, but *q* is false, then "If *p*, then *q*" is false. This case corresponds to drinking beer, but not to being over 21. This obviously falsifies the rule.
3. If *p* is false, but *q* is true, then "If *p*, then *q*" is still true. The person does not drink beer but is over 21 anyway. People are often surprised that such a case does not falsify the rule. But one must consider the fact that the rule does not *require* a person to drink beer if he or she is over 21. People over 21 can drink beer or not drink beer as far as this particular rule is concerned.
4. Finally, if both *p* and *q* are false, then that does not falsify "If *p*, then *q*." If a person does not drink beer and is under 21, then the rule still stands.

Oakhill and Johnson-Laird (1985) have argued that the active search for information that will disconfirm a rule is one of the characteristics of rational thought:

> Rationality depends on the search for counterexamples. If, say, you hold the prejudice that women are bad drivers, and your curiosity is only provoked by cases of bad driving, then you will never be shaken from

your bias; if a bad driver turns out to be a woman, your prejudice is confirmed; if a bad driver turns out to be a man, your prejudice is not disconfirmed since you don't believe that only women are bad drivers. Unless you somehow are able to grasp the potential relevance of *good* drivers to your belief, then the danger is that you will never be disabused of it, and will never understand the force of counterexamples. (p. 93)

In science, as in everyday life, it is important to be on the lookout for counterexamples. Although, as we have seen, confirming evidence is important as well, there is no substitute for an experimental design that allows us to find disconfirming evidence if it exists. You may already have remarked that the conditional statements we have been examining in this section bear more than a passing similarity to the dispositional concepts we considered in Chapter 1. We observed that dispositional concepts stated hypothetical relationships between an independent and a dependent variable in the form of conditional statements. Notice that p and q in the hypothesis "If p, then q" refer to an independent variable and a dependent variable, respectively. The minimum conditions for the evaluation of a hypothesis are the four alternatives in the truth table in Figure 2-4. These four alternatives can be cast in the form of a 2 × 2 table, such as Figure 2-6, which is adapted from an experiment by Smedslund (1963). The independent variable refers to the presence or absence of a particular disease, while the dependent variable refers to the presence or absence of a particular symptom. Suppose that the disease is *cancer*, and the symptom *weight loss*. At a minimum, if the independent variable is present, then the dependent variable should be also: If someone has cancer, then he or she will be losing weight. What about the other three

Correlation-Relevant Frequency Information on the Relationship between a Hypothetical Symptom and a Hypothetical Disease in 100 Supposed Patients

		Disease		
		Present	Absent	Total
Symptom	*Present*	37	33	70
	Absent	17	13	30
	Total	54	46	

FIGURE 2-6 Relationship between a Symptom and a Disease in a Sample of 100 Cases

Source: "Likeness and Likelihood in Everyday Thought" by R. A. Shweder, 1977, *Current Anthropology, 18,* 639.

cells? If someone does not have cancer but loses weight, does that falsify the hypothesis? No; there may be any number of reasons why someone loses weight. The cell containing people who do not have cancer and do not lose weight also does not falsify the hypothesis. The particularly interesting condition is the cell in which people have cancer but do not lose weight. These cases falsify the hypothesis.

In practice, experiments can be *much* more complicated than the simple case in Figure 2-6. At a minimum, there must be two values of an independent variable (e.g., present or absent, 1 or 0) and two values of a dependent variable. These variables, however, can also be *continuous*. Examples of continuous variables are *height* and *weight*. Such variables can take on any number of values. In subsequent chapters we will explore different procedures for dealing with variables of different kinds.

Concept Formation in Science

Scientific thinking, like any other kind of thinking, involves concepts. Typical psychological concepts include *intelligence, introversion,* and *short-term memory*. Concepts are abstractions. Every time we place someone or something in a category, we are using concepts. As we noted in the section "Operationism" in Chapter 1, scientific concepts are defined in terms of publicly observable events. That does not mean, however, that scientific concepts must have a simple structure. Scientific concepts (or, for that matter, any kind of concept) may be organized in different ways. Table 2-1 lists a number of concepts that have different structures. This list, adapted from Neisser and Weene (1962), is by no means exhaustive; it is intended only to illustrate some of the possibilities.

The simplest kind of concept, labeled Level I in Neisser and Weene's classification scheme, is one in which all the members of a category have one thing in common. Thus all vertebrates have backbones. Some categories, however, are defined by the absence of a characteristic. Animals *without* backbones are invertebrates. To define an animal operationally as either a vertebrate or an invertebrate is easy: either it has a backbone or it does not.

Moving up to Level II, we find *conjunctive* concepts that are defined by the presence of two or more characteristics. *Creativity* is an example of a psychological concept that is often defined at this level. Creativity is typically said to involve "the production of novel, socially valued products" (Mumford & Gustafson, 1988, p. 28). Such a definition acknowledges that creativity cannot sensibly be defined only in terms of the ability to behave in novel, or original, ways. The full meaning of the term also includes some criterion of appropriateness (Vinacke, 1974, p. 354). Behaving in an original way does not qualify as creative unless the product also provides some "solution to a significant social problem" (Mumford & Gustafson, 1988, p. 28). Thus

TABLE 2-1 Concepts Organized by Three Different Levels of Complexity

Name	Description	Example
Level I		
Presence (A)	A must be present	Vertebrate: must have a backbone
Absence (not A)	A must be absent	Invertebrate: must not have a backbone
Level II		
Conjunction (A and B)	Both A and B must be present	Creative: behavior must be both novel and useful
Disjunction (A or B)	Either A or B or both must be present	Allergenic: e.g., a food containing either strawberries or tomatoes
Exclusion (A and not B)	A must be present and B not present	Eligible for driver's license: must have passed test and not committed a felony
Disjunctive absence (not A or not B)	Either A or B, or both, must be absent	Uncreative: behavior that is either not original or not useful
Conjunctive absence (not A and not B)	Both A and B must be absent	Nonallergenic: e.g., a food containing neither tomatoes nor strawberries
Implication (not A or B)	A may be absent; but if A is present, then B must be also	Ineligible for driver's license: must have not passed test or have committed felony
Level III		
Either/or (A and not B)/(not A and B)	Either A or B must be present, but not both together	Half-sister; THOG
Both/neither (A and B)/(not A and not B)	Both A and B must be present, unless neither is	Anti-THOG

Source: Adapted from "Hierarchies in Concept Attainment" by U. Neisser and P. Weene, 1962, *Journal of Experimental Psychology, 64,* 641. Copyright 1962 by the American Psychological Association. Adapted by permission.

researchers who have focused only on the process whereby original behaviors are produced, without considering the criterion of appropriateness, have not necessarily been investigating creativity.

Other concepts at this level are *disjunction, exclusion, disjunctive absence, conjunctive absence,* and *implication.* Examples of each of these are given in Table 2-1 (we have also already considered implication at some length in the previous section). You can see that these concepts require a subtlety of definition, which may not be obvious until you think about it. You must carefully analyze the concepts you use when you do research. In saying this, I am trying to emphasize the point made earlier in this chapter about being thoughtful when you operationally define a concept. While very simple definitions may be attractive, more than one criterion for a concept may be much more appropriate.

Let us move on to the concepts in Level III. The first is called *exclusive disjunction,* and it requires that something have one *or* the other of two properties, *but not both.* For a long time (Bruner, Goodnow, & Austin, 1956) researchers have known that people find it very difficult to think about relationships of exclusive disjunction. Smyth and Clark (1986) invented a problem that illustrates this kind of concept. They used the concept of *half sister* as an example. My half sister has one and only one of my parents as one of her parents. Smyth and Clark constructed a "half-sister problem," which is illustrated in Table 2-2. The names of four women and their parents are listed in the table. My father and Max are two different men, and my mother and Sarah are two different women. If Marilyn is my half sister, which of the others is also my half sister?

The correct answers are that Madge and Mitzi are definitely not my half sisters, and Marlene definitely is my half sister. If you cannot see why this is true after doing some hard thinking, then sit down with someone else and go over the problem again. Smyth and Clark gave American and British university students the half-sister problem and found that 93% solved it correctly. This suggests that people can understand a concrete example of exclusive disjunction fairly easily; but, as we will see, there are other versions of the problem that are much harder.

The half-sister problem is a version of another of Wason's (1977b) inventions, the *THOG problem.* The version of the problem we will use is from

TABLE 2-2 The Half-Sister Problem

Name	Parents
Marilyn	My father and Sarah
Madge	Max and Sarah
Mitzi	My father and my mother
Marlene	Max and my mother

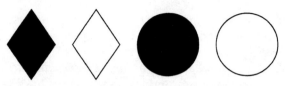

FIGURE 2-7   The THOG Problem

Smyth and Clark (1986, p. 275). Look at the designs in Figure 2-7: a black diamond, a white diamond, a black circle, and a white circle. Suppose that you were a subject in a THOG experiment. The experimenter would tell you that the name of a color (*black* or *white*) and the name of a shape (*diamond* or *circle*) had been written on a piece of paper. Let us call these the *criterial properties* of THOGness. A design is a THOG if it has one, and only one, of these criterial properties. A design is not a THOG if it has *both* or *neither* of these criterial properties. If the black diamond is a THOG, are any of the other designs THOGs?

People have very strong intuitions about this problem (Wason & Brooks, 1979; Griggs & Newstead, 1983) and find it irresistible to conclude not only that the white diamond and the black circle are THOGs but also that the white circle is definitely not a THOG (Wason & Brooks, 1979). The interesting thing about this problem is not that subjects find it so difficult to see the right answer, but that they find it so easy to see the *wrong* answer. Subjects do not react to this problem by saying, "Gee, beats me." Rather they naturally conclude that the white diamond and the black circle are THOGs, and that the white circle cannot be a THOG. In fact, the white circle is definitely a THOG, and the white diamond and the black circle are definitely not THOGs. Wason reports that some of his subjects have simply been unable to solve the THOG problem, no matter how hard they tried. We can conclude that abstract versions of a problem may be much more difficult than concrete, realistic versions of the same problem. Because scientific concepts are often more abstract than the concepts we use in everyday life, more time and effort may be required to understand them.

The THOG problem has the same structure as the half-sister problem (see Table 2-3). The following parts of the problems match: my father = black, Sarah = diamond, Max = white, and my mother = circle. If you cannot see the equivalence of the two, work through the problem with a friend.

The *ANTI-THOG problem* (Wason, 1978) is an example of the last type of concept in Table 2-1. In this case, there is a color and a shape such that something is an ANTI-THOG if it has both or neither. If the black diamond is an ANTI-THOG, then so is the white circle, because it is neither black nor a diamond.

Neisser and Weene (1962) found that Level III concepts were extremely difficult for people to acquire. Griggs and Newstead (1983) proposed an

TABLE 2-3 A Comparison of the THOG and the Half-Sister Problems

Name	Parents	Form
Marilyn	My father and Sarah	Black diamond
Madge	Max and Sarah	White diamond
Mitzi	My father and my mother	Black circle
Marlene	Max and my mother	White circle

explanation for the difficulty of such problems. Errors may be the result of a process called *matching bias*, whereby people see two things as similar to the extent that they share features. Level III concepts, however, require us to group things that are dissimilar. We may overlook many interesting psychological variables because we do not take the time to imagine all the logically possible concepts that may be operating in a situation. For example, being a brother or a sister obviously has important psychological consequences. These days, however, many families contain half brothers and half sisters, and psychologists interested in family dynamics must take such concepts into account. To paraphrase a remark attributed to Einstein, our investigations should involve concepts that are as simple as possible, but no simpler.

We have now considered some basic aspects of thinking in a scientific context. Often we can observe *biases*, such as confirmation bias and matching bias, which may work in many situations, but which also act to keep us from considering rational alternatives. We have also reviewed some basic scientific values, such as simplicity and consistency. These values should be observed whenever possible but we should not adhere to them slavishly. Scientific research is not a rigid, mechanical process, and so it is probably unwise to consider only one position on any issue to the exclusion of all others. The great Cambridge biologist D'Arcy Thomson (1929) noted that the ancient value of the Golden Mean probably applies to scientific behavior, as it does to most things. The Golden Mean can be summarized in a few words: Neither too much nor too little, neither excess nor defect. In what follows, we will try to take a balanced approach to scientific inquiry, considering both how scientists actually think and how they *should* think, not favoring one to the exclusion of the other. Our aim is to allow you to appreciate both the process of science and its goals, and to enable you to become a sensible researcher and a well-informed critic of psychology.

Ethical Principles of Research

Becoming a researcher in psychology involves acquiring the skills to evaluate hypotheses competently. Research is both a cognitive and a *moral* enterprise (e.g., *Ethical principles in the conduct of research with human participants*, 1982;

Ethical principles of psychologists and code of conduct, 1992). Researchers need to follow ethical guidelines. Psychologists have spent a great deal of time debating the ethical issues surrounding their activities. After many years of discussion, the principles listed in Table 2-4 were adopted by the American Psychological Association. Read these principles over carefully.

Research is undertaken only after a serious consideration of alternative courses of action. The researcher must take into consideration not only the scientific merits of the research but also its general worth. It is necessary to ask what benefits will come in the long run, from the line of research being pursued. The benefits may be small, but they should be articulated nonetheless. It is also important to obtain advice from colleagues on the ethical consequences of proposed research. If your research meets standards for an ethical project, and if you decide to go ahead with it, then you must behave in a way that is not only consistent with the laws and regulations that apply in your case, but that is also sensitive to the feelings of the participants in your study.

There may very well be a committee on research with human subjects at your institution. Such a committee reviews research projects to determine whether they meet ethical standards. Depending on the nature of your project, you may be required to submit a research proposal to the committee for approval. The risks to participants must be assessed. Such risks can include physical pain and embarrassment. If you are doing a collaborative study, then you and your fellow investigators are jointly responsible for its ethical status. Ethics cannot be delegated to someone else; ultimately, they are your responsibility.

Researchers should make a full disclosure to participants concerning those aspects of the research that they may wish to know in order to make a decision about whether or not to participate. You should think about what sorts of things participants need to know in order to make a decision. Obvious information includes how long they will be needed, what kind of behavior will be required, and how you will dispose of data collected from them. Normally, participants should be given enough information to enable them to give their informed consent to participating in the research. There may be exceptions to this principle, but only under special circumstances, and only after careful consideration has been given to alternatives. Typically, participants may withdraw at any time in the research process. This is a particularly tricky rule when participants are members of a subject pool in a university or college. It may be a course requirement that they act as subjects in an experiment. Under such circumstances, potential participants should be given as many options for participation as possible so that they are not coerced into participating in any one study.

It is the investigator's responsibility to notify participants of any adverse consequences of participation, *even if these come to light only after the study is*

TABLE 2-4 Ethical Guidelines for Conducting Research

Planning Research

a. Psychologists design, conduct, and report research in accordance with recognized standards of scientific competence and ethical research.

b. Psychologists plan their research so as to minimize the possibility that results will be misleading.

c. In planning research, psychologists consider its ethical acceptability under the Ethics Code. If an ethical issue is unclear, psychologists seek to resolve the issue through consultation with institutional review boards, animal care and use committees, peer consultations, or other proper mechanisms.

d. Psychologists take reasonable steps to implement appropriate protections for the rights and welfare of human participants, other persons affected by the research, and the welfare of animal subjects.

Responsibility

a. Psychologists conduct research competently and with due concern for the dignity and welfare of the participants.

b. Psychologists are responsible for the ethical conduct of research conducted by them or by others under their supervision or control.

c. Researchers and assistants are permitted to perform only those tasks for which they are appropriately trained and prepared.

d. As part of the process of development and implementation of research projects, psychologists consult those with expertise concerning any special population under investigation or most likely to be affected.

Compliance with Laws and Standards

Psychologists plan and conduct research in a manner consistent with federal and state law and regulations, as well as professional standards governing the conduct of research, and particularly those standards governing research with human participants and animal subjects.

Institutional Approval

Psychologists obtain from host institutions or organizations appropriate approval prior to conducting research, and they provide accurate information about their research proposals. They conduct the research in accordance with the approved research protocol.

Research Responsibilities

Prior to conducting research (except research involving only anonymous surveys, naturalistic observations, or similar research), psychologists enter into an agreement with participants that clarifies the nature of the research and the responsibilities of each party.

Informed Consent to Research

a. Psychologists use language that is reasonably understandable to research participants in obtaining their appropriate informed consent (except as provided in Standard 6.12, Dispensing With Informed Consent). Such informed consent is appropriately documented.

b. Using language that is reasonably understandable to participants, psychologists inform participants of the nature of the research; they inform participants that they are free to participate or to decline to participate or to withdraw from the research; they explain the foreseeable consequences of declining or withdrawing; they inform participants of significant factors that may be expected to influence their willingness to participate (such as risks, discomfort, adverse effects, or limitations on confidentiality, except as provided in Standard 6.15, Deception in Research); and they explain other aspects about which the prospective participants inquire.

c. When psychologists conduct research with individuals such as students or subordinates, psychologists take special care to protect the prospective participants from adverse consequences of declining or withdrawing from participation.

d. When research participation is a course requirement or opportunity for extra credit, the prospective participant is given the choice of equitable alternative activities.

e. For persons who are legally incapable of giving informed consent, psychologists nevertheless (1) provide an appropriate explanation, (2) obtain the participant's assent, and (3) obtain appropriate permission from a legally authorized person, if such substitute consent is permitted by law.

Dispensing with Informed Consent

Before determining that planned research (such as research involving only anonymous questionnaires, naturalistic observations, or certain kinds of archival research) does not require the informed consent of research participants, psychologists consider applicable

Continued

TABLE 2-4 *Continued*

regulations and institutional review board requirements, and they consult with colleagues as appropriate.

Informed Consent in Research Filming or Recording

Psychologists obtain informed consent from research participants prior to filming or recording them in any form, unless the research involves simply naturalistic observations in public places and it is not anticipated that the recording will be used in a manner that could cause personal identification or harm.

Offering Inducements for Research Participants

a. In offering professional services as an inducement to obtain research participants, psychologists make clear the nature of the services, as well as the risks, obligations, and limitations. (See also Standard 1.18, Barter [With Patients or Clients].)

b. Psychologists do not offer excessive or inappropriate financial or other inducements to obtain research participants, particularly when it might tend to coerce participation.

Deception in Research

Psychologists do not conduct a study involving deception unless they have determined that the use of deceptive techniques is justified by the study's prospective scientific, educational, or applied value and that equally effective alternative procedures that do not use deception are not feasible.

b. Psychologists never deceive research participants about significant aspects that would affect their willingness to participate, such as physical risks, discomfort, or unpleasant emotional experiences.

c. Any other deception that is an integral feature of the design and conduct of an experiment must be explained to participants as early as is feasible, preferably at the conclusion of their participation, but no later than at the conclusion of the research. (See also Standard 6.18, Providing Participants With Information About the Study.)

Sharing and Utilizing Data

Psychologists inform research participants of their anticipated sharing or further use of personally identifiable research data and of the possibility of unanticipated future uses.

Minimizing Invasiveness

In conducting research, psychologists interfere with the participants or milieu from which data are collected only in a manner that is warranted by an appropriate research design and that is consistent with psychologists' roles as scientific investigators.

Providing Participants with Information about the Study

a. Psychologists provide a prompt opportunity for participants to obtain appropriate information about the nature, results, and conclusions of the research, and psychologists attempt to correct any misconceptions that participants may have.

b. If scientific or humane values justify delaying or withholding this information, psychologists take reasonable measures to reduce the risk of harm.

Honoring Commitments

Psychologists take reasonable measures to honor all commitments they have made to research participants.

Care and Use of Animals in Research

a. Psychologists who conduct research involving animals threat them humanely.

b. Psychologists acquire, care for, use, and dispose of animals in compliance with current federal, state, and local laws and regulations, and with professional standards.

c. Psychologists trained in research methods and experienced in the care of laboratory animals supervise all procedures involving animals and are responsible for ensuring appropriate consideration of their comfort, health, and humane treatment.

d. Psychologists ensure that all individuals using animals under their supervision have received instruction in research methods and in the care, maintenance, and handling of the species being used, to the extent appropriate to their role.

e. Responsibilities and activities of individuals assisting in a research project are consistent with their respective competencies.

f. Psychologists make reasonable efforts to minimize the discomfort, infection, illness, and pain of animal subjects.

g. A procedure subjecting animals to pain, stress, or privation is used only when an alternative procedure is unavailable and the goal is justified by its prospective scientific, educational, or applied value.

Continued

TABLE 2-4 *Continued*

h. Surgical procedures are performed under appropriate anesthesia; techniques to avoid infection and minimize pain are followed during and after surgery.

i. When it is appropriate that the animal's life be terminated, it is done rapidly, with an effort to minimize pain, and in accordance with accepted procedures.

Reporting of Results

a. Psychologists do not fabricate data or falsify results in their publications.

b. If psychologists discover significant errors in their published data, they take reasonable steps to correct such errors in a correction, retraction, erratum, or other appropriate publication means.

Plagiarism

Psychologists do not present substantial portions or elements of another's work or data as their own, even if the other work or data source is cited occasionally.

Publication Credit

a. Psychologists take responsibility and credit, including authorship credit, only for work they have actually performed or to which they have contributed.

b. Principal authorship and other publication credits accurately reflect the relative scientific or professional contributions of the individuals involved, regardless of their relative status. Mere possession of an institutional position, such as Department

Chair, does not justify authorship credit. Minor contributions to the research or to the writing for publications are appropriately acknowledged, such as in footnotes or in an introductory statement.

c. A student is usually listed as principal author on any multiple-authored article that is substantially based on the student's dissertation or thesis.

Duplicate Publication of Data

Psychologists do not publish, as original data, data that have been previously published. This does not preclude republishing data when they are accompanied by proper acknowledgment.

Sharing Data

After research results are published, psychologists do not withhold the data on which their conclusions are based from other competent professionals who seek to verify the substantive claims through reanalysis and who intend to use such data only for that purpose, provided that the confidentiality of the participants can be protected and unless legal rights concerning proprietary data preclude their release.

Professional Reviewers

Psychologists who review material submitted for publication, grant, or other research proposal review respect the confidentiality of and the proprietary rights in such information of those who submitted it.

Source: "Ethical Principles of Psychologists and Code of Conduct," 1992, *American Psychologist, 47*, 1608–1610. Copyright 1992 by the American Psychological Association. Reprinted by permission.

completed. The researcher's responsibility does not end when the data have been collected. Researchers should fully debrief the participants and ameliorate any consequences of contributing to the study. Participants should also be fully aware of the ways in which their data may be shared with people other than the investigator.

The preceding is only a cursory overview of complex ethical questions. Other ethical principles, such as honest reporting of research results, are also important (e.g., Johnson, 1990a). The American Psychological Association principles we have discussed are not to be seen as final, universal ethical rules. For example, you may need to pay attention to considerations that arise in the particular place in which you work. Moreover, ethical principles are not written in stone but are open to continuous reevaluation. We will consider ethical questions further as we review examples of research throughout this book.

Animal Rights?

Thus far we have been concerned with ethical principles that apply to research with humans. However, a persistent issue in psychological research is the proper treatment of animals. The American Psychological Association has also published guidelines for the proper treatment of animals used in research, a summary of which is given in Table 2-4. (You might also wish to examine *Guidelines for ethical conduct in the care and use of animals*, 1985.) You may be surprised to learn that experimentation on animals has a long history. In the seventeenth century, the great French philosopher Descartes took an attitude toward animals that many people would find offensive today. "Animals were . . . not conscious, not really living—machines without will or purpose or any feeling whatever. [Descartes] dissected them alive (anesthetics were far off in the nineteenth century), amused at their cries and yelps since these were nothing but the hydraulic hisses and vibrations of machines" (Jaynes, 1973, p. 170).

Figure 2-8 is from a newspaper article written in 1913. "Experimental work on live animals" has often been seen by the general public as an opportunity for researchers to use techniques that would be unacceptable if performed on humans. Figure 2-8 speaks to the long-standing fear, on the part of some people, that what is done to research animals today will be done to people tomorrow, particularly to people who are not in a position to object to maltreatment. Lederer (1985) provides an excellent review of the early period of the controversy concerning experimentation on animals.

Recently, the controversy over animal experimentation has entered a new phase. The nature of the current debate is well illustrated by the reaction to a recent article by Johnson (1990b). Johnson argued that there are currently two contrasting views of what constitutes ethical treatment of research animals. The first he calls *animal welfare*, and the second *animal rights*.

1. Animal welfare is consistent with the Judeo-Christian tradition, which has always maintained that while people are of greater value than animals, people have a responsibility to promote the welfare of animals. From this viewpoint, however, the use of animals in research that will benefit people is ethical. Without animal subjects, we will be forced to abandon research "that would have saved lives or eased the pain" of people who may be suffering from one disorder or another (Johnson, 1990b, p. 214). Of course, the use of animals in research should be as humane as possible with no unnecessary suffering.

2. The animal rights activists adopt a different value system. People are not necessarily superior to other life-forms. Both people and animals are capable of experiencing pain. Pain is a great leveler. To inflict pain on any animal, human or otherwise, is immoral. This principle eliminates research with animals that would not be ethical if done with humans.

Only a Step

FIGURE 2-8 Only a Step

Source: Reprinted from the *New York Herald* in the *Open Door* for July 1913. Reprinted by permission of the Rockefeller University Press.

In his article, Johnson came out strongly in favor of the animal welfare position. The animal rights position, however, is certainly not without its advocates among psychologists. Estes (1991), the editor of the journal in which Johnson's article originally appeared, observed that it had elicited "a rather massive response." There are intense feelings on both sides, and "the optimization problem of allowing maximum benefits from animal research while minimizing the concern of people who sympathize strongly with the animals has not yet been solved" (Estes, 1991, p. 202). It is useful to keep the following points in mind:

- Animal rights activists constitute a very large group of people, numbering in the hundreds of thousands. While there is a wide range of views within this group, most would ban animal research outright (Plous, 1991). Its large numbers and strongly held views make the animal rights movement a potent political force.

- It is important for animal researchers to make a persuasive case that animal models are necessary in order to investigate and ultimately alleviate the causes of human suffering. Some critics have even suggested that animal research has not produced the kind of understanding that its proponents have claimed for it (e.g., Ulrich, 1991), and the arguments of these critics must be addressed. As stated in Table 2-4, "subjecting animals to pain, stress, or privation is used only when an alternative procedure is unavailable and the goal is justified by its prospective scientific, educational, or applied value."

Devenport and Devenport (1990) have proposed a way of doing animal research that may meet at least some of the conditions of both sides in this dispute. The solution they propose is the use of pets as subjects! At first, this may sound like an outrageous suggestion, and there are obviously very serious limits on what pets owners will allow you to do with their pets. Nevertheless, Devenport and Devenport point out that there are over 50 million dogs and 50 million cats in the United States. Data on these animals are available from veterinarians. Many interesting experiments can be done with pets in their own homes with the permission of their owners. Devenport and Devenport report that pet owners are very positive about such research. They list the following benefits of research on pets:

- Since animals are in their usual, familiar surroundings, they are calmer and easier to work with. One can argue that this setting is more "natural" than the laboratory.
- Pets are not destroyed at the end of the experiment.
- The researcher does not have to pay the cost of maintaining the animal; the pet owner does!

We have not yet mentioned what is perhaps the best reason for studying animals: an intrinsic interest in animal behavior. If you have such an interest, perhaps you should consider the "pet alternative." As Devenport and Devenport point out, there are many pets besides dogs and cats that could be studied, providing a plethora of information about different species and broadening the database of animal research.

Names and Concepts to Understand and Remember

The following are some of the most influential ideas in the area we have just reviewed. Some concepts are quite general and are not associated with any particular psychologist. In other cases, however, the names of psychologists are paired with the concepts, for which they are known. Read through the list.

If any of the names or concepts seem unfamiliar to you, then go back and reread the appropriate section of the chapter. The names are in the order in which they are presented in the text, and the concepts are italicized in the text, so they are easy to find. You should be able to define each concept and briefly discuss it. You should also be able to write a brief account of the work done by each person on the list.

confirmation bias

Wason's generative problem

Occam's razor, Lloyd Morgan's canon, and the principle of parsimony

simplicity principle versus likelihood principle

internal consistency

beautiful theory hypothesis

Wason's card selection task

conditional reasoning

antecedent and consequent

truth table

types of concept: conjunction, disjunction, exclusion, disjunctive absence, conjunctive absence, implication, exclusive disjunction

Wason's THOG and ANTI-THOG problems

intuitive errors

matching bias

ethical principles in the conduct of research with human participants

animal welfare

animal rights

Additional Reading

The literature on cognitive biases is enormous. A good place to start is Arkes and Hammond (1986). A classic introduction to the study of concept formation in science is Brunswik (1952), a work that has recently begun to receive renewed attention. Somewhat more complex approaches are collected in Lycan (1990). Additional guidelines for the use of animals in research can be found in *Animal Behaviour*, 1981, *29*, 1–2.

3

Designing Experiments

We have already seen that the procedure for testing a hypothesis is at least as important as the hypothesis itself. It is no good having a hypothesis if you do not know how to go about evaluating it. In this chapter we will review some of the more influential proposals concerning proper methods for hypothesis testing. As in the previous chapter, we will take a historical approach, outlining major developments in roughly the order in which they occurred. If you have already taken a statistics course, then some of the concepts discussed may be familiar to you. Nevertheless, the chapter will provide a useful review, and you may see some well-known ideas presented in a different way.

You will come across the concept of cause fairly often in this chapter. As we noted in Chapter 1, the nature of causality is difficult to spell out (e.g., White, 1990). We cannot, however, avoid the concept altogether, and for now we will adopt the *Oxford English Dictionary*'s definition of the verb *cause:* "to bring about, produce, or make." Thus an independent variable can be seen as a cause to the extent that it is responsible for bringing about, producing, or making possible a dependent variable. While this is not a rigorous definition, it will do for the time being.

Mill's Methods

John Stuart Mill wrote the most famous guide to experimental method. In *A System of Logic, Ratiocinative and Inductive* (1846/1973), he outlined four methods of experimental inquiry. The four methods are described below. In his discussion, Mill made use of the terms *antecedent* and *consequent,* and we will use the terms *independent variable* and *dependent variable* interchangeably with these terms. You should remember these concepts from our earlier discussion. If you are a bit hazy about them, then you should review the previous chapter now.

The Method of Agreement

Following Mill, we will denote independent variables by capital letters (e.g., A, B, C), and dependent variables by lowercase letters (e.g., a, b, c). Suppose we are curious about the possible effects of A. Mill (1846/1973, p. 388) noted that it is important to examine carefully cases in which the phenomenon of interest occurs. We can examine the consequences of A in combination with other independent variables, such as B or C. We find that whenever A occurs, then a does also. It does not matter whether A is paired with B or with C. In either case, the presence of A leads to the occurrence of a. As an example, consider the possible connection between the occurrence of frost (A) and the sudden death of plants in gardens (a). (Cohen & Nagel [1934, p. 251] used a similar example.) Gardens vary a great deal in size and in other ways, but such factors do not invariably precede the sudden death of plants. When frost occurs it is not the case that the plants in small gardens (B) suddenly die, but the plants in large gardens (C) do not. Frost is the only common factor in situations when the plants suddenly die. Therefore, we tend to attribute a sudden increase in plant mortality to the frost and not to the size of gardens. Thus the *method of agreement* involves identifying recurrent regularity: those conditions (such as frost) that are *always* present when the phenomenon of interest (such as sudden plant death) occurs.

- The method of agreement is not foolproof. There are some very real problems associated with its use. What might some of these problems be? Try to think of situations in which this method would not necessarily allow you to identify the cause of a phenomenon.

Mill himself realized that unless we can experimentally produce the dependent variable by manipulating the independent variable, then we must remain in considerable doubt as to its cause. Experimental control over a phenomenon is a very desirable source of evidence. Otherwise, we can never be sure that the independent variable does not precede the dependent variable as "day precedes night or night day" (Mill, 1846/1973, p. 390). Another way in which this point is often made is to say that we should not believe that events that always occur together bear a causal relationship to one another. Remember our earlier discussion of confirmation bias. Just because night always precedes day, we should not believe that night *causes* day.

In the summer of 1992, a well-publicized controversy surrounding Acquired Immune Deficiency Syndrome (AIDS) developed that illustrates Mill's point. According to those on one side of the controversy, the virus called HIV is the cause of AIDS. People on the other side, however, point to cases in which people carry the HIV virus but do not develop AIDS. They argue that there must be factors in addition to, or other than, HIV that are responsible for the emergence of AIDS. According to the first argument, HIV precedes AIDS as night precedes day. The fact that HIV and AIDS always occur together may not mean that HIV causes AIDS. In this case, as in many others, there may be conditions of which we are unaware that are responsible for the phenomenon of interest.

At this point, it is useful to distinguish between *necessary* and *sufficient* causes. A necessary cause must be present in order for the effect to occur. A necessary cause may not be sufficient, however, to produce the effect. In the preceding example, HIV may be a necessary cause of AIDS, as AIDS may never occur unless HIV is present. However, HIV may not be a sufficient cause, since something else in addition to HIV may need to be present for AIDS to appear.

The Method of Difference

This method involves observing whether or not the phenomenon of interest occurs in the absence of a particular independent variable. If there is only one *difference* between situations in which an event occurs and situations in which it does not occur, then that difference is the cause of the event. Mill (1846/1973, p. 391) uses the example of someone perfectly healthy who dies when shot through the heart. We infer that it was the condition of being shot that caused death, because we routinely observe that, all other things being equal, perfectly healthy people do not just die. If the independent variable (being shot through the heart) does not occur, then neither does the dependent variable (dying).

Mill (1846/1973, p. 392) notes that both the method of agreement and the method of difference are *methods of elimination*. The experimenter tries to eliminate all possible causes but the right one. For example, one might suspect that any of *A, B,* or *C* might cause an event *a.* What would you have to do to determine whether or not *A* was the cause of *a?* Using the method of difference, one would have to observe the effect of *A* in combination with *B* and *C*, and then the effect of *B* and *C* in the absence of *A.* If *a* occurs in the former case, but not in the latter, then one would conclude that *A* was causally related to *a.*

- Are there any limitations on the method of difference? How practical is it? Can you think of any cases in which it either could or should not be used?

Mill was well aware that nature does not arrange itself for the benefit of experimenters. Events do not come nicely packaged in the combinations that the method of difference requires. If we are interested in the effect of *A* and *A* typically occurs in the presence of *B* and *C,.* it may be impossible to find a naturally occurring case in which only *B* and *C* occur. It may be possible for the experimenter to artificially produce such a situation, by withholding *A* from the subject, for example. However, suppose that the absence of *A* may harm the subject in the experiment. Does that not raise ethical questions about the study? Here are two examples illustrating these problems.

1. Defining intelligence is a complex matter. However, no matter how one defines it, one cannot deny that, over the years, a raging debate in psychology has been whether or not intelligence is inherited or acquired. The person who started the debate was Francis Galton, who wrote a book called *Hereditary Genius* in 1869. Galton, who was a cousin of Charles Darwin and born into a wealthy family, believed that intelligence tended to run in families. However, even if Galton was correct in this belief, it does not necessarily mean that

intelligence is innate. After all, a wealthy family provides a different environment than a poor family, and it is possible that this environmental disparity is at least partially responsible for any observed differences in intelligence (e.g., Anastasi, 1965, p. 106). It has not been easy to separate the effects of innate and environmental factors because of the difficulty of finding cases in which one factor is present and the other absent. Environmental and innate factors are present together. It is likely that the causes of intelligence are much more subtle than Galton thought that they were (e.g., Lerner, 1986, chap. 5). We must be very careful when we interpret data bearing on this question (e.g., Loehlin, 1987, p. 17; 1989).

2. There has been a tradition in psychology of investigating the effects of visual deprivation on perception in nonhuman animals. Much of the early work is reviewed by Hinde (1970, p. 471). The goal of these experiments was to determine whether an animal's ability to perceive its surroundings accurately was innately determined, or whether it was the result of perceptual experience. The research strategy in these studies was simple. By rearing animals in the dark, for example, one could eliminate early perceptual experience, and then later determine whether the absence of perceptual experience caused a change in the behavior of the animal relative to the behavior of animals who had not been deprived. This strategy illustrates the method of difference well. Nowadays, however, many animal rights activists would have misgivings about deprivation experiments of any kind. Moreover, it is unthinkable that such deprivation experiments would be conducted on human infants. Thus some research questions cannot be answered simply by using the method of difference. More complicated approaches are needed. We will consider them later on.

The Method of Residues

A *residue* is a remainder, or something left over. Consider an experimental situation in which there are three independent variables (A, B, C) and three dependent variables (a, b, c). Suppose further that we already know from other experiments that B causes b, and C causes c. We can then infer that A causes a. Mill (1846/1973, p. 398) notes that this inference must remain speculative unless we can isolate A experimentally and observe its influence on a. However, the value of the method of residues, according to Mill, is that by analyzing known cause-effect relationships, we may discover new causes that we previously overlooked. If the known causes do not exhaustively explain a phenomenon, then we must seek additional factors that might be responsible.

• Rosch (1988, p. 17) provides an example that illustrates what Mill meant by the method of residues. As Rosch observes, we are often tempted to try to explain a phenomenon in terms of only one cause, and yet there may be many causal factors at work in a situation. To illustrate this point, Rosch asks us to imagine a study of reading ability in third-grade children (leaving aside for the moment precisely how one would measure reading ability). Rosch (1988) notes that a variety of factors are known to account for reading ability, including "number of books in the home, father's income, number of siblings, mother's age at marriage, length of time at present school" (p. 17). Of course, some of these factors may be more important than others in accounting for reading ability. Nevertheless, even when we take all these factors into account, they do not fully account for reading ability. There is a residue of reading ability that is left unexplained, and we may try to discover the factors that account for that residue.

The Method of Concomitant Variation

Concomitant means "simultaneously," or "at the same time." Mill (1846/1973) realized that in many cases it is possible to observe variation in both the independent variable and the dependent variable. If variation of an independent variable *A* is accompanied by variation in the dependent variable *a*, then it seems reasonable to claim that *A* and *a* bear a causal relationship to one another. Mill remarked that this type of variation tends to be *quantitative*. For example, variables such as *height* are measured using a quantitative scale (such as feet or meters) and can be related to variables such as *weight*, which can also be measured using a quantitative scale. We will consider the nature of different scales of measurement later; for now it is enough to realize that when we are interested in concomitant variation, we are typically interested in variables that can be quantified.

- Suppose that we examine people who vary in height, and discover that there is a corresponding variation in weight, such that the taller a person is, the more he or she weighs. This relationship will not be perfect, as some tall people may weigh less than some short people. Still, can we conclude from the concomitant variation in height and weight that height and weight bear a causal relationship to one another?

In fact, we cannot be sure that height bears a causal relationship to weight. Perhaps there is some other factor, such as diet or genetics, that is responsible for both height and weight and thus explains the observed concomitant variation between height and weight. The existence of concomitant variation between two variables does not necessarily mean that they are causally connected.

The method of concomitant variation is closely related to the *concept of correlation*. In fact, this relationship is so intimate that we will immediately turn to a discussion of correlation. Two variables are correlated to the extent that "where one is the other is, and where one is not the other is not" (Jevons, as cited in Stigler, 1986, p. 298).

Galton and the Concept of Correlation

We have already mentioned Galton in connection with his views on the inheritance of intelligence. Galton contributed to many areas of psychology and scientific method. Accounts of Galton's discovery of our contemporary *concept of correlation* are given by Fancher (1979; 1985). Galton initially considered a phenomenon called *regression to the mean*. A *mean* is the average of a series of values. Thus, the mean height of 10 people would be calculated by adding all 10 heights and dividing by 10.

Regression toward the Mean

According to the *Oxford English Dictionary*, *regression* means "the action of returning to a place or point of departure." The dictionary notes that the word has the following technical sense in genetics: regression occurs when children "slip back toward the average of the population from which the parents were chosen." To understand what this means, take a look at Figure 3-1. The line labeled *M* represents the average, or *mean*, height of parents of a set of parents sampled from the British population in the nineteenth century. The left vertical axis represents the parents' height. You can read the graph by first noting the parents' height. Thus, at the point labeled *A* the parents' height is less than 65 in. Observe that the children's height at the corresponding point *C* is closer to the mean value, *M*. Now look at the opposite end of the distribution, at point *B*, where the parents' height is close to 72 in. Note that the children's height (point *D*) is closer to the mean. You should be able to verify for yourself that for all values of parents' height, the children's height is closer to the mean. In general, the children tend to *regress toward the mean*.

Variables are usually not *perfectly* correlated. In fact, most of the correlations we deal with in psychology are far from perfect. Correlation is usually expressed using a scale that varies from −1 through 0 to +1, where −1 means perfect negative correlation, 0 means no correlation, and +1 means perfect positive correlation. A negative correlation occurs when large values on one variable go with small values on the other variable, and vice versa. Such a correlation might exist, for example, between "number of children attending college" and "surplus income." One might expect that, in general, a family

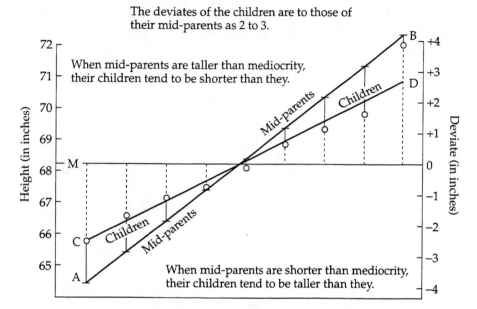

Rate of Regression in Hereditary Stature

The deviates of the children are to those of their mid-parents as 2 to 3.

The circles give the average heights for groups of children whose mid-parental heights can be read from the line AB. The difference between the line CD (drawn by eye to approximate the circles) and AB represents regression toward mediocrity.

FIGURE 3-1 Regression Lines for Parents' and Children's Heights

Source: "Regression toward Mediocrity in Hereditary Stature" by F. Galton, 1886, *Journal of the Anthropological Institute, 15,* 253. Copyright 1886 by the Royal Anthropological Institute. Reprinted by permission.

would have a smaller surplus income the greater the number of children it has in college. A positive correlation occurs when the values on both variables increase (or decrease) together. The data in Figure 3-1 represent a positive correlation.

Regression toward the mean occurs as a mathematical necessity whenever two variables are not perfectly correlated (Cohen & Cohen, 1983, p. 45). Galton (1889, as cited in Senders, 1958) described it as follows:

The law of Regression tells heavily against the full hereditary transmission of any gift. Only a few out of many children would be likely to differ as widely as the more exceptional of the two parents. The more bountifully the Parent is gifted by nature, the more rare will be his good fortune if he begets a son who is endowed yet more largely. But the law is even-handed: it levies an equal succession-tax on the transmission of badness as of goodness. If it discourages the extravagant hopes of a gifted parent that his children will inherit all his powers; it no less discountenances extravagant fears that they will inherit all his weakness and disease. (p. 106)

- Regression to the mean is a very common occurrence. Cohen and Cohen (1983), p. 46) and Tversky and Kahneman (1974) give several examples. Suppose that you do badly on one intelligence test, even though your average performance on intelligence tests is quite high. The logic of regression toward the mean suggests that your next intelligence test would yield results that are closer to your average level of performance. Such a result would require no other explanation than regression to the mean, even though we might be tempted to give a causal explanation, such as that the second test was easier, or that we were less tired. "Thus, on the average over time, overweight people lose weight, low IQ children become brighter, and rich people become poorer" (Cohen & Cohen, 1983, p. 45). Researchers who are unaware of the existence of regression to the mean may make unwarranted causal interpretations of such phenomena.

Here are two important things to keep in mind as we proceed:

1. When we make measurements, such as height and weight, we do not measure everyone in the *population*. That is, we do not measure everyone whom, at least in principle, we could measure. Rather we measure a *sample* drawn from the population. We will deal with the way in which we take this sample in detail below.
2. On any measure, individuals will vary. For example, not everyone is the same height or weight. In order to describe the sample as a whole, we need statistics that characterize the sample as a whole, such as the average, or mean.

How sure can we be that our sample is representative of the population from which it is drawn? When we calculate statistics like the mean for a sample, how close is that value likely to be to the mean of the population? It is very important to answer such questions.

The Law of Large Numbers

The *law of large numbers* was discovered by Jacob Bernoulli in the seventeenth century (Newman, 1956, pp. 1450–1451). Bernoulli observed that games of chance are usually arranged so that everyone knows the odds of any one alternative occurring. In coin tossing, for example, we assume that the probability of getting a head is the same as getting a tail: both have a 50% chance of occurring. However, in many other real-world situations we do not know in advance what the probabilities of the various alternatives are. Bernoulli (as cited in Newman, 1956) put it this way:

> But what mortal, I ask, could ascertain the number of diseases, counting all possible cases, that afflict the human body in every one of its many parts and at every age, and say how much more likely one disease is to be fatal than another. . . . Or again, who can pretend to have penetrated so deeply into the nature of the human mind or the wonderful structure of the human body that in games which depend wholly or partly on the mental acuteness or the physical agility of the players he would venture to predict when this or that player would win or lose? (p. 1452)

Bernoulli goes on to point out that even though there are many situations in which we cannot know in advance the chances of one event or another occurring, we may still make reasonable predictions based on the assumption that the future will resemble the past. However, in order to make such predictions we need a sample of past events. This sample will have to be reasonably large. For example, we obviously cannot make a decision about the likelihood of dying from a particular disease if we have information only about one or two cases. If we know of two cases of people who had a disease, and one of them died, then we would not have a very good sample on which to base a conclusion concerning the likelihood of dying from the disease. As Bernoulli said, "The larger the number of pertinent observations available, the smaller the risk of falling into error" (Newman, 1956, p. 1452). A small sample may not reflect the population from which it is drawn. The larger the sample, the more likely it is to match the population as a whole.

Suppose that I toss a coin twice, and it comes up heads both times. I should not reject the idea that the coin is unbiased, because two coin tosses is a very small sample. I would still expect the coin to come up heads 50% of the time in the long run, consistent with the law of large numbers. You should not, however, confuse the law of large numbers with the so-called *law of averages*. The law of averages is a widely held belief that if one of a number of alternatives has failed to occur for some time, then the likelihood of its occurrence has increased. For example, suppose we toss a coin three times, and it comes up heads every time. If we believe in the law of averages, then we may be willing to bet that the coin will come up tails on the next toss, in order to begin to equalize the previous number of heads. The intuitive appeal of the law of averages is very great, since some sort of balancing process would seem to be required in order to compensate for the string of heads.

However, consider the following example from Schuh (1968, pp. 211–212). Suppose that a coin comes up heads three times in a row, and then comes up head 500 heads and 500 tails over the next 1,000 tosses. Thus, over the last 1,000 tosses there is no balancing process whatsoever, since both alternatives occur with equal frequency. This would give 503 heads and 500 tails, and 503/(502+500) is very close to 50%. This is all that the law of large numbers requires: the larger the sample, the better will it tend to represent the population from which it is drawn.

The law of large numbers says nothing about any particular event. Thus the results of any one coin toss are independent of the results of any other coin toss. It is wrong, therefore, to believe that the likelihood of tossing a tail is greater following a series of heads than following a series of tails. To believe otherwise is an example of what is called *the gambler's fallacy*.

The law of large numbers implies that the larger the sample, the more confident we can be that a sample statistic is a good approximation of the population value. For example, if we calculate the mean of a small sample, then that value may be quite different from the population value. Similarly, the observed correlation between two variables based on a few cases only may be quite different from the actual correlation between the two variables as it exists in the population. In general, a particular sample of events may not reflect the values that are in the entire population. Yet people often act as if they believe that small samples really are representative of the population.

The "Law of Small Numbers"

Even though the law of large numbers has been well understood for a long time, most people still appear to behave in accordance with a false belief that Tversky and Kahneman (1971) have called *the law of small numbers*. The law of small numbers leads us to believe that a small sample will have the same characteristics as the population from which it is drawn. As Tversky and Kahneman (1971, p. 106) observe, a scientist who believes in the law of small numbers "will have exaggerated confidence in the validity of conclusions based on small samples. To illustrate, suppose he is engaged in studying which of two toys infants will prefer to play with. Of the first five infants studied, four have shown a preference for the same toy. Many a psychologist will feel some confidence at this point" that infants have a real preference. In fact, you can draw no inferences about population preferences from these results. As Kahneman and Tversky (1971, 1972) observe, attempting to draw conclusions from small samples is too risky to be worthwhile.

Most of us have another regrettable tendency noted by Tversky and Kahneman (1971). We tend to be overly influenced by the *patterns* found in small samples. For example, a sequence of coin tosses such as H H H H T T T T does not appear to most people to be particularly representative of a random sequence, even though it is perfectly plausible that it was generated by a random process. At this point it is useful to distinguish between a *random process* and a *random product* (Lopes, 1982). Even though both H H H T T T and H T H T T H could be generated by a random process, the second sequence seems to most of us to be a better representative of a random product. Because the sample is so small, we need to resist the tendency to give a causal explanation of the pattern we detect in the first sequence.

- When we are doing research, we must be careful not to base our decisions on the law of small numbers. We must also be careful not to confuse a random process with a random product. If we sample events randomly from a population, that does not necessarily mean that those events will appear to be random.

The Normal Distribution

We need to understand another idea at this point. It too is an idea that Galton helped to popularize. It is known as the *normal distribution*. To get a sense of what a normal distribution is, take a look at Figure 3-2, which is a drawing of a device similar to one used by Galton (Stigler, 1986, p. 276). You can make such a device easily, and I urge you to do so. You use this contraption as follows. Drop a metal ball in the opening at the top. Below this opening are several rows of pins. The ball will hit a pin in each row, being deflected to the left or right each time it hits a pin. Eventually, the ball will end up in some position at the bottom of the apparatus. Suppose we drop several balls in this manner. The balls will tend to pile up at the bottom in the way shown in Figure 3-2. Most of the balls end up more or less in the middle of the device, fewer fall a bit farther away, and fewer still fall at the extreme ends of the instrument. There is an exact mathematical description of this kind of distribution, but for our purposes we need only observe that this normal distribution is easily generated and characterizes the way in which events are often distributed in the real world. Notice that this distribution is *symmetrical*, with equal numbers of events on the left and the right. Measurements, such as height and weight, may be distributed in this fashion. Galton himself made many measurements of such things as *keenness of eyesight, breath capacity, strength of hand squeeze, height, arm span,* and *weight* (Johnson, MacClearn, Yuen, Nagoshi, Ahern, & Cole, 1985). He was a great believer in the notion that most measurements are normally distributed.

When measurements are normally distributed, then the mean value is at the center of the distribution. This is illustrated in Figure 3-3. The mean is a measure of the *central tendency* of the distribution. Notice that it is also the case that the most frequently occurring cases are at the mean. The most

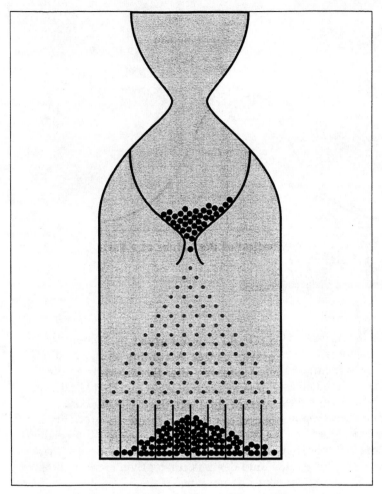

**FIGURE 3-2 Galton's Device for Demonstrating the Normal
Distribution**

Source: Reprinted by permission of the publishers from *The History of Statistics: The Measurement
of Uncertainty before 1900* by Stephen M. Stigler, Cambridge, Mass.: The Belknap Press of Harvard
University Press. Copyright © 1986 by the President and Fellows of Harvard College.

frequently occurring value is called the *mode*. Notice further that the mean is
also the point that divides the distribution in half. The *median* is the name for
that value for which 50% of the cases are higher and 50% lower. In a normal
distribution, the mean, median, and mode are the same.

Not all measurements are normally distributed, however. S. J. Gould
(1991) gives an important example of a distribution that is *skewed* (i.e., not

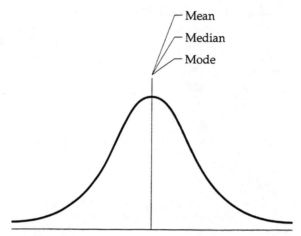

**FIGURE 3-3 Normal Distribution of the Values of a Variable
(e.g., height)**

Note: The mean, median, and mode coincide.

symmetrical). As it happened, Gould was informed in 1982 that he had
abdominal mesothelioma, a form of cancer. According to the best medical
advice, this disease is incurable. Moreover, after the disease has been diagnosed, patients have a median time to death of eight months. That is, 50% of
all people with the disease die within eight months of diagnosis.

Gould, writing in 1985, pointed out that the distribution of mortality is
skewed, as shown in Figure 3-4. This means that the mode is less than eight
months, and the mean is more than eight months. Most people die in less than
eight months, but the average time until death is greater than eight months.
The three measures of central tendency do not agree.

In thinking about his own case, Gould reasoned that there were several
factors that would put him in the right-hand side of the distribution. For
example, he lived in Boston, which has some of the best medical facilities in
the world. Thus his life might be prolonged well past the usual expectations.
Notice that Gould, like anyone in his position, is interested in determining
where *his* case lies in the distribution. Distributions are made up of *individual
cases*, and as researchers we can be interested in the individual case, as well
as the entire distribution of cases. Research methods used to study the individual case differ from those used to study distributions of cases. We will
examine methods used for studying individual cases throughout the book.
Now, however, we will explore experimental methods that involve gathering
data on a sample of cases, rather than focusing on only one case.

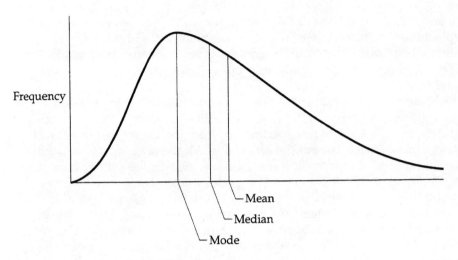

FIGURE 3-4 A Skewed Distribution

Note: The mean, median, and mode do not coincide.

Doing Experiments

As Gigerenzer and Murray (1987, p. 18) point out, experiments done in Wundt's day consisted largely of exhaustive descriptions of individual cases, with no explicit rules for making generalizations. Such experiments proved not to be very convincing to most twentieth-century academic psychologists, partly because, as we saw earlier, Wundt's experiments involved subjective interpretation that seemed to be unscientific. Many psychologists found a better way of thinking about experiments in the work of R. A. Fisher (1925/1991), who is generally acknowledged to be one of the most important methodologists of all time (Rao, 1992).

Fisher's Approach to Designing Experiments

Fisher was an English gentleman who made his major contributions in the 1920s, and so the research that amused him might not appeal to everyone today. For example, one experiment he considered involved evaluating a claim made by "a lady [who] declares that by tasting a cup of tea she can discriminate whether the milk or the tea . . . was first added to the cup" (Fisher, 1925/1991, p. 11). She must have been a person of some refinement and gentility—I certainly could not tell whether the milk or the tea had been added first! Assertions like this are similar to claims I have heard some people make that they can discriminate wines made in California from those made in New York. Once again, I would not make such a claim, but it is interesting to consider how one would put such declarations to the experimental test.

In designing an experiment to test tea-tasting ability, Fisher proposed to give the subject eight cups of tea: four with milk added to tea, and four with tea added to milk. In Fisher's experiment, the subject knows that there will be four cups of each kind, but the order in which the cups are given to the subject is random. A random order is not "determined arbitrarily by human choice" (Fisher, 1925/1991, p. 11) but is determined by a purely chance procedure such as rolling dice. Why does Fisher insist on a random order? One reason is that a random order of presentation makes it possible to determine how likely the subject is to make the correct choices by chance alone. It turns out that there are 70 different orders in which the cups can be presented, and so the subject has 1 chance in 70 of making the correct choices. The odds are heavily against the subject accomplishing this task by chance alone. Thus should the subject make the correct choices, then we would feel fairly secure in believing that the subject did not make the correct choices by chance.

Fisher notes that we could make the task even more difficult to accomplish by chance alone by increasing the number of cups. Alternatively, we could make the task easier to accomplish by chance alone by decreasing the number of cups. What degree of chance are we willing to accept? By convention, researchers adopt a criterion of 1 chance in 20, or 5%. To comprehend what this means, consider a tea-tasting experiment in which there are six cups. As Fisher points out, there are 20 different ways in which the six cups can be presented. Therefore, if a subject gets the order right, there is only a 1 in 20, or 5%, likelihood that the subject did it just by luck. However, if we use fewer cups, then we will lose confidence in the results. If we present the subject with four cups, then there are only 6 ways in which the cups can be presented. These orders are given in Table 3-1. In this situation the subject has a 1 in 6, or 17%, chance of guessing the correct order. So should the subject make the correct choices, then most researchers would be unwilling to reject the possibility that the subject has just been lucky, and that this had come about by chance alone.

Suppose we do the experiment with eight cups, and the subject indeed makes all the right choices. Should we conclude that the subject has made good her claim to be able to "discriminate whether the milk or the tea . . . was first added to the cup"? Fisher observes that doing the experiment only once is not as persuasive as being able to *replicate the results*. This is a very important idea. Of course, virtually any result could have come about by chance, including getting all the answers right. Therefore, one has more

TABLE 3-1 The Six Different Ways of Presenting Four Cups of Tea

	Order		
1	2	3	4
Milk	Milk	Tea	Tea
Milk	Tea	Milk	Tea
Milk	Tea	Tea	Milk
Tea	Milk	Milk	Tea
Tea	Milk	Tea	Milk
Tea	Tea	Milk	Milk

Note: Two have milk poured first (Milk), and two have tea poured first (Tea).

confidence in an experimental result to the extent that it has been found over and over again.

There are three general points that emerge from this discussion of tea tasting:

1. Randomization allows the experimenter to make appropriate inferences from the data.
2. The sample of data must be large enough to enable the experimenter to make the appropriate inferences.
3. As the saying goes, "One swallow does not make a summer." There is no substitute for replicating an experimental result.

The Null Hypothesis

You may be familiar with the concept of a *null hypothesis*. According to Fisher (1925/1991, p. 16), when we do an experiment we typically assume that any differences between the experimental conditions are due only to chance; that is, we establish a null hypothesis. In this case, *null* means "no difference." In the tea-tasting experiment, the null hypothesis is that the order in which milk and tea are mixed makes no difference. Should the subject guess the sequence of cups correctly, then we may reject the null hypothesis, which "is never proved or established, but is possibly disproved, in the course of experimentation. Every experiment may be said to exist only in order to give the facts a chance of disproving the null hypothesis" (Fisher, 1925/1991, p. 16).

A classic example of the use of a null hypothesis is an experiment designed to explore the possible existence of extrasensory perception (e.g., Guilford, 1942, p. 156). Consider a deck of cards consisting of four different suits (clubs, hearts, diamonds, and spades). Suppose one person sits in one room with the deck of cards, and another person sits in another room. The deck is shuffled, and the first person looks at the top card, attempting to "transmit" its suit to the person in the other room. The second person attempts to "receive" whatever signal the first person may be sending, and writes down what he or she thinks the suit might be. This procedure is continued until all 52 cards in the deck have been "transmitted." Suppose we repeat this experiment with a large number of "senders" and "receivers." The null hypothesis here is that the "receivers" will guess the correct suit at no more than a chance level. Since there are four different suits, we would expect the "receivers" to guess the correct suit by chance 1 time out of 4, or 25% of the time. If the "receivers" manage to guess the correct suit at a level much higher than mere chance would lead us to expect, then we would *reject the null hypothesis* and look for some explanation of the results other than chance. We would now believe that something other than chance was at work in this situation, although we would not know what it was. We would, of course, have to investigate several possibilities, such as that the subjects were cheating. Rejection of the null hypothesis does not tell you which alternative hypothesis is correct.

To summarize:

- Researchers are often interested in testing the null hypothesis. This is a hypothesis of no difference.
- Typically, one assumes the null hypothesis and does an experiment to see if the null hypothesis can be rejected.

There is much controversy surrounding the concept of the null hypothesis (Gigerenzer & Murray, 1987). Over the years, however, many psychologists have tended to accept the notion that one can only reject the null hypothesis. One can only falsify the null hypothesis. By so doing, one does not confirm an alternative, *research hypothesis*. A famous methodologist, Jacob Cohen (1990), has given the following example of null hypothesis testing, from the early stage of his career:

> I found that if, for example, I wanted to see whether poor kids estimated the size of coins to be bigger than rich kids, after I gathered the data, I couldn't test this *research hypothesis*, but rather the null hypothesis that poor kids perceived coins to be the same size as did rich kids. (p. 1307)

This point is worth reemphasizing. If your data allow you to reject the null hypothesis, that does not mean that any particular alternative hypothesis is correct. It only means that the null hypothesis is apparently false. We will see later on that the research situation may be more complicated than this, and the formulation of an alternative to the null hypothesis (a research hypothesis) can be part of the design of an experiment. For now, however, we will concern ourselves only with procedures for testing the null hypothesis.

Blocks and Plots

Fisher was extremely interested in agricultural experiments. In agriculture it is important to determine which of several different kinds of seed will yield the best crop. Fisher (1925/1991, pp. 50–51) considered a case in which the experimenter wished to evaluate five different types of seed. How would you go about doing this? Take a moment to think about it.

One approach would be to plant samples of the five different types of seed in five different *plots*. Of course, the assignment of seed types to plots would have to be random. Fisher also proposed using eight *blocks* of land, each block being divided into five plots. Within each block, seed types were to be assigned randomly to plots. Fisher (1925/1991, p. 51) is careful to point out that random assignment does not mean "any order that occurs" to the experimenter, but order determined by a truly random process, such as rolling dice. The design of the experiment is given in Table 3-2 and was called a *randomized block design* by Fisher. In Table 3-2, I have assigned each variety to a plot by using a table of random numbers. Such a table consists of a list of numbers 0 to 9, each one of which is equally likely to occur at any point in the list. Notice that by using a method of random assignment (a random process) we may not have generated a design that strikes you as truly random (a random product). Whether or not the assignment of varieties to plots *seems* to be a random product is irrelevant; we are concerned only that the process of assignment be random. Although there are other assignment procedures that result in more "balanced" arrangements, randomization is the simplest and most widely used technique.

Suppose we grow five different varieties of a crop in each block. At the end of the growing season, we measure the yield from each plot. Such a measure could be the weight of the crop produced on each plot. Once we

TABLE 3-2 Fisher's Randomized Block Design

		Plots				
		A	B	C	D	E
Block	1	V3	V1	V5	V2	V4
	2	V1	V4	V5	V2	V3
	3	V5	V3	V1	V4	V2
	4	V4	V2	V5	V1	V3
	5	V2	V1	V5	V3	V4
	6	V4	V1	V3	V2	V5
	7	V1	V2	V5	V3	V4
	8	V1	V3	V4	V5	V2

In this case, there are five plots and eight blocks. Five varieties (V1 through V5) are assigned randomly to the plots in each block.

know the yield for each plot, we can find the yield for each variety of crop. Within a particular block, we cannot tell whether differences among varieties is due to differences in productivity between varieties or to differences between the plots. For example, it could be that one variety outperforms all others by a very wide margin. Is this because that variety is more productive, or is it because the plot on which it was grown is more fertile? Nevertheless, because we have eight blocks, we can calculate a mean yield for each variety across all eight blocks. Remember that each variety has been *assigned randomly* to one of the plots in each block, and so any overall differences among the varieties is unlikely to be due simply to the plots on which they were grown. By using this design, we can test the null hypothesis that there is no difference in yield among the five varieties. A major reason for using blocks in this particular experiment is to provide *replications*. Each block is a repetition of the experiment (Winer, 1971, p. 240).

- Enough about agriculture! Variations of the type of design we have been considering are widely used in psychology. Can you think of any applications of such a design? Take a few minutes to think about it. What might be analogous to blocks in psychological research? How about plots (not the conspiratorial kind)?

In general, a design like the one in Table 3-2 is used in psychology when different blocks represent different kinds of subjects, while different plots represent different experimental treatments. In a true randomized blocks experiment, the subjects within each block are matched on the basis of some characteristic. The characteristic used to match subjects should be one that is believed to be related to the dependent variable. An example often used to illustrate this kind of design is one in which students are grouped ("blocked") using a variable such as academic ability. For example, one could have a design in which one block consists of high school seniors who have been classified as academically successful by their teachers, and the other block consists of high school seniors who have been classified as academically unsuccessful. The treatments (plots) might be different kinds of course projects, such as essays versus classroom presentations. Such a design is given in Table 3-3. Within each block, students would be randomly assigned to one of the projects. The dependent variable could be the final examination results in the course.

Since this is a hypothetical experiment, it is hard to say how it might turn out. The null hypothesis would be that the type of project would make no difference to the final examination grades. Data gathered using a randomized block design are typically analyzed by means of the *analysis of variance*, examples of which may be found in virtually any statistics textbook.

Here is another example of an experiment in which the blocks correspond to different subjects. This time, the experiment we will consider is a real one.

TABLE 3-3 Another Example of Blocks and Plots

	Plots (Type of project)	
Blocks (Type of student)	Essays	Presentations
Academically successful		
Academically unsuccessful		

It is related to Paivio's (1971) theory of the relation between *concreteness* and *imagery*. *Concreteness* is defined as the degree to which a word refers to "concrete objects, persons, places, or things that can be heard, felt, smelled or tasted" Toglia & Battig, 1978). A *concrete* word is one like *cat* that refers to something easily experienced by our senses, while an *abstract* word is one like *unseeable* that refers to something that cannot be experienced directly by our senses. *Imagery* refers to the ease with which a word will arouse mental images. A *high imagery* word is one like *boxer* that arouses a mental image easily and quickly, while a *low imagery* word is one like *permission* that probably arouses a mental image only with difficulty. To measure concreteness and imagery, subjects rate words on seven-point scales anchored by *high concreteness* vs. *low concreteness* or by *high imagery* vs. *low imagery*. Examples of such scales are given in Figure 3-5. Imagery and concreteness are usually found to be very highly correlated (e.g., Paivio, Yuille, & Madigan, 1968). Paivio has argued that concrete words will be easier to learn and remember than will

Low :___:___:___:___:___:___:___: High

Imagery

Low :___:___:___:___:___:___:___: High

Concreteness

FIGURE 3-5 Imagery and Concreteness Scales

abstract words. This is because concrete words elicit mental images more easily than abstract words, and imagery is a process that facilitates memory.

One of Paivio's earliest studies (1965) examined the role of imagery in learning. The study employed a *paired-associate learning task*, which is a traditional method for studying learning. In such a task, subjects learn a list consisting of pairs of items. In the Paivio study, there were four groups of 25–34 subjects each. Each group learned a different list of 16 pairs of words. Each list of 16 words contained 4 sets of stimulus-response pairs. In each of the 4 lists, 4 of the 16 items were pairs in which both words were concrete (e.g., coffee-pencil), 4 were items in which the first member of each pair was concrete and the second abstract (e.g., string-idea), 4 were items in which the first member was abstract and the second concrete (e.g., virtue-chair); and 4 were items in which both words were abstract (e.g., event-theory). Thus, in this experiment, the 4 groups of subjects provide replications of the basic experiment in which subjects learn 16 paired associate items. Within each group, each subject is given all 4 possible combinations of stimulus and response abstractness-concreteness. Each list is presented in a different random order to the subject on each trial. The first learning trial occurred when subjects heard the entire list of words, following which they were given the first word of each pair and were asked to write down the second word. The data consist of the number of correct responses made after four such trials.

The 4 groups of subjects in this experiment are analogous to the blocks in Fisher's experiment. The four different types of paired associate items are like the plots in Fisher's experiment. The subject receives these items in a random order. Yet there is a major difference between Fisher's design and Paivio's. The difference is that in Fisher's experiment each variety of seed was sown on only one plot in each block, whereas in Paivio's experiment each subject hears all items. Experiments in which each subject receives all of the treatment conditions are called *repeated measures* designs. We will consider them in more detail below. Another difference between Paivio's and Fisher's experiments is that the four item types can themselves be classified as shown in Table 3-4. Such an arrangement is called a *two-way classification*.

When Paivio examined the data from his experiment, it turned out that there were no differences between the groups of subjects, and so the data were pooled across groups. The pooled data are presented graphically in Figure 3-6. Consistent with Paivio's theory, concreteness facilitated recall of the words. The most words are recalled when both pairs are concrete, and recall is worst when both pairs are abstract. An important additional result is that concrete stimuli lead to much better recall of the response than do abstract stimuli, due perhaps to the image-arousing potential of these concrete stimuli. Other investigators have also found results similar to these (e.g., Marschark, Richman, Yuille, & Hunt, 1987; Paivio, 1983).

TABLE 3-4 Paivio's Experimental Design (1965)

Group 1		Response	
		Abstract	Concrete
Stimulus	Abstract		
	Concrete		

Group 2		Response	
		Abstract	Concrete
Stimulus	Abstract		
	Concrete		

Group 3		Response	
		Abstract	Concrete
Stimulus	Abstract		
	Concrete		

Group 4		Response	
		Abstract	Concrete
Stimulus	Abstract		
	Concrete		

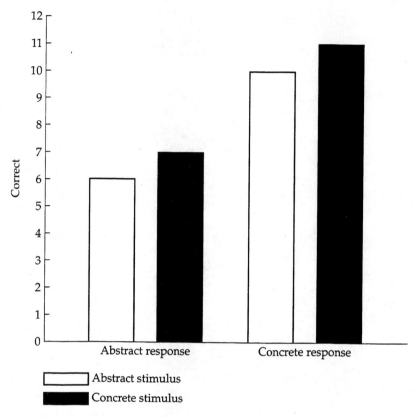

FIGURE 3-6 Paivio Data

There is another simple experiment that illustrates (albeit imperfectly) another design variation. Holmes and Buchanan (1984) were interested in evaluating the widespread assumption that a person's color preference is linked to his or her personality characteristics (e.g., Luscher & Scott, 1969). In order for such a color preference/personality relationship to exist, people must have stable color preferences. Holmes and Buchanan believed that the color that a person preferred would not be stable but would depend on which object was being considered. A person might prefer one color for a couch, but another for a car. Their experiment involved 58 women and 31 men, all of whom were undergraduate psychology students. Each subject filled out a form in class containing the list of objects in Table 3-5. As you can see, the list was slightly different for men and women, but within each sex each list was presented in the same order to all subjects. Subjects wrote the name of the color that they preferred for each object, as well as giving the color that was their overall favorite.

TABLE 3-5 Number of Times Subjects Chose a Color for Eight Different Objects

					Women's Choices				
Color	Overall Favorite	Auto-mobile	Blouse	Skirt	Dress	Carpet	Sofa	Chair	Walls
Red	1	13	10	3	5	0	1	0	0
Blue	27	15	9	19	18	4	5	3	10
Green	2	0	2	1	0	2	0	3	0
Yellow	2	0	3	0	2	1	1	0	4
Brown	0	2	1	8	3	19	29	35	14
Purple	6	0	3	2	5	0	0	0	0
Pink	4	0	6	0	4	2	2	1	0
Orange	2	0	0	0	1	2	2	1	1
Black	0	9	1	7	4	0	1	0	0
White	1	2	6	1	3	1	2	3	22
Gray	0	3	0	9	1	1	0	0	0
Other	7	7	11	1	4	4	5	4	1

					Men's Choices				
Color	Overall Favorite	Auto-mobile	Shirt	Slacks	Suit	Carpet	Sofa	Chair	Walls
Red	3	8	1	0	0	2	2	2	0
Blue	23	8	14	15	10	4	2	0	5
Green	1	2	1	0	1	1	0	0	0
Yellow	1	1	4	0	0	0	1	2	1
Brown	0	1	2	2	7	6	5	1	2
Purple	0	0	0	0	0	0	0	0	0
Pink	0	0	0	0	0	0	0	0	0
Orange	0	0	0	0	0	0	0	1	0
Black	1	3	1	3	1	0	2	1	0
White	1	0	4	2	0	1	3	1	14
Gray	1	3	0	4	7	0	0	0	0
Other	0	3	1	0	1	0	1	1	0

Source: Adapted from "Color Preferences as a Function of the Object Described" by C. B. Holmes and J. A. Buchanan, 1984, *Bulletin of the Psychonomic Society, 22,* 424–425. Adapted by permission of Psychonomic Society, Inc.

Now look at the color preferences given in Table 3-5. Those data are a simplification of the data reported by Holmes and Buchanan. Is there any reason to reject the null hypothesis that people prefer colors equally regardless of the object described? Clearly there is. Different objects appear to have characteristic color preferences. Moreover, although blue is the most preferred overall color, brown is chosen very frequently for specific objects, without ever being named as the overall favorite. In light of these data, it would be hard to maintain that color preference is not a function of the object described. Holmes and Buchanan also note that color preferences do not appear to be the same for both sexes. That is, the null hypothesis that there are no differences between the sexes in color preferences would seem to be questionable. Notice that pink and purple are used by women but not at all by men.

- Now spend a few minutes thinking about this experiment. How might you criticize it? What changes would you make if you were to redo this experiment? Remember, *no psychologist has ever done a perfect experiment.* While some psychologists have done very clever experiments, all experiments are only partial sources of knowledge. There are always things to be learned by criticizing the experiments you come across. Such criticism can lead you not only to do an improved version of an experiment but also to discover a new line of inquiry.

The experiment by Holmes and Buchanan is not a famous experiment; it is simply a typical experiment, which has a number of positive and negative aspects. On the positive side, it is an experiment that explores a topic of interest to a large number of people. Moreover, there is a substantial literature on color preferences that relates to this experiment. For example, there is some good evidence that most people in Europe and North America say that their favorite color is blue (e.g., McManus, 1981), just as the subjects did in this experiment. Thus the Holmes and Buchanan study did not take place in a vacuum but is part of a large body of research into a topic of importance.

On the negative side, there are the following three criticisms. You may be able to think of more.

1. Recall that Fisher was adamant about random assignment. In this experiment all subjects got the list of objects *in the same order*. Is it not possible that a different order of presentation might not have elicited different preferences? You might not think so, but how are we to know? If you were to repeat this experiment, it might be a good idea to give each subject a different random order of presentation of objects.

2. Subjects were allowed to name whatever color they wanted. This led some subjects to name colors such as "rust," which are difficult to classify reliably. This problem could have been avoided by forcing subjects to choose from a set of standard color names. What would you prefer—letting subjects say whatever they want, or forcing them to choose? If you do the former, then your data may be difficult to classify and analyze. If you do the latter, then your data will be "cleaner," but you may miss some interesting quirks that the idiosyncrasies of individual subjects can contribute. There is no easy answer to this problem. Perhaps the best strategy is to attempt to balance the sensitivity of one's measure with as standard a set of measures as possible.

3. All the subjects were undergraduate students. The undergraduate student is the most feverishly studied individual in history. Because they are so accessible to experimenters, undergraduates are much easier to do research with than other individuals. But are results based on this group generalizable to the larger population? What would happen if we redid this experiment with different kinds of subjects? Does age make a difference, for example? Such *subject variables* can be very important, but it is not always easy to gain access to different kinds of subjects.

In the Holmes and Buchanan experiment, all subjects were asked to give their favorite color for all objects. In this respect, the Holmes and Buchanan experiment differs from Fisher's randomized block experiment. In Fisher's experiment, each variety of seed was sown on only one plot in each block. Similarly, in the Holmes and Buchanan experiment, each subject could have been asked to name a favorite color for only one object. Then we would have needed a separate group of subjects for each object. Thus we could ask one group to say what their favorite color was for automobiles, another group their favorite color for carpets, and so on. Of course, we would assign each subject to a different group on a random basis. Notice that we would need many more subjects if we did the experiment this way. Since there are eight objects, we would have needed eight times as many subjects if we were to obtain as many preferences as did Holmes and Buchanan. There is an important lesson here. By getting subjects to respond repeatedly in the same experiment, we can drastically cut the number of subjects needed.

Because repeated measures designs are so efficient, you should use them whenever it makes sense to do so. Unfortunately, it does not always make sense to use repeated measures designs. If exposure to one of the conditions will influence the subjects' response to one or more of the other conditions in ways that make interpretation of the data difficult, then it may be a better idea to use *independent groups* of subjects. There is no hard and fast rule here, but thinking about this issue before you do your experiment is crucial.

Correlational Designs

We have been considering experiments in which the independent variables can be classified discontinuously. For example, in the Paivio study, the variable abstract versus concrete was *dichotomized*, or broken into two, using only very abstract words or very concrete words. Yet one could regard the abstract-concrete dimension as continuously varying from concrete to abstract. Many variables in psychology can be treated as either continuous or discontinuous. When a variable is treated as continuous, it facilitates the use of *correlational designs*. Although strictly speaking these designs have the same underlying principles as designs that involve the use of discontinuous variables (Cohen, 1968), they are a sufficiently different tradition to merit separate treatment (e.g., Cronbach, 1957; Hilgard, 1987, chap. 20).

In a typical correlational design, the experimenter obtains a number of different measures on a set of subjects. For example, in the study referred to briefly earlier in this chapter, Galton obtained measures of several hundred English subjects in the late nineteenth century (Johnson, MacClearn, Yuen, Nagoshi, Ahern, & Cole, 1985, p. 887). His measures included, among other things, social class and physical measures, such as height. For Galton's data, social class can be measured by different occupations, ranging from professional (e.g., physicians) to unskilled workers. There was a very close relationship between social class and the physical measures, with upper-class subjects being larger. The existence of such a correlation allows us to reject the null hypothesis that there are no social-class differences in physical characteristics. One may then speculate about the possible causes of such differences (e.g., better diet for upper-class subjects).

Notice that in Galton's study, the correlation between social class and physical measures was not arrived at by experimental manipulation; it was obtained through measuring existing characteristics in the population. Very often, however, correlational data are obtained by using a *mental test* constructed to measure a psychological variable of interest. Moreover, correlational data can also be useful in an experimental context. Carl Rogers (1952) performed an experiment on the effectiveness of client-centered therapy that illustrates both of these points. In a nutshell, this form of therapy involves seeing "the client as the client sees himself, [looking] at problems through his eyes" in an "atmosphere of complete psychological security," the idea being that the client will "reorganize the structure of self in accordance with reality and his own needs" (Rogers, 1952, p. 67). The null hypothesis is that clients do not change as a result of therapy. Rogers's study is an attempt to test this null hypothesis.

A central notion in Rogers's theory of therapy was the "self-concept." A discrepancy between the person's self-concept and the way the person wished to be (the ideal self) was one source of discomfort. In order to measure the self- and ideal self concepts, Rogers and his coworkers employed a card-sorting technique that uses 100 self-descriptive statements, such as "I am a submissive person," "I don't trust my emotions," and "I have an attractive personality" (Rogers, 1961, p. 232). Before therapy (the pretest) clients sorted the cards to represent themselves and then sorted the cards to represent the person they would like to be (ideal self). They repeated this procedure immediately after therapy (first posttest) and again some time later at a follow-up session (second posttest).

The null hypothesis for this experiment is that the correlation between the self and the ideal self will not be different on any of the three test occasions. In fact, Rogers presented data that allowed him to reject this null hypothesis. The correlation between the self- and ideal-self card sorts was typically lower before therapy than it was for either of the posttests. Rogers (1961, p. 235) took this to mean that the self became "more positively valued, i.e., . . . more congruent with the ideal, or valued, self" as a result of therapy.

- Do these results mean what Rogers thought they meant? Are there any other explanations possible of the increased correlations?

One difficulty in interpreting these data is that we do not know whether or not the outcome is due merely to repeated testing. Perhaps simply retaking the test results in a higher correlation. The increased correlation may not be due to therapy at all. Rogers himself was acutely aware of this problem. The difficulty is devising a procedure that will allow the investigator to make appropriate inferences from these kinds of data. Appropriate procedures would rule out, or make less likely, the kind of alternative explanation we have just considered. In the next chapter we will examine some of the procedures that are needed.

Names and Concepts to Understand and Remember

The following are some of the most influential ideas in the area we have just reviewed. Some concepts are quite general and are not associated with any particular psychologist. In other cases, however, the names of psychologists are paired with the concepts for which they are known. Read through the list. If any of the names or concepts seem unfamiliar to you, go back and reread the appropriate section of the chapter. The names are in the order in which they are presented in the text, and the concepts are italicized in the text, so they are easy to find. You should be able to define each concept and briefly discuss it. You should also be able to write a brief account of the work done by each person on the list.

Mill and the methods of agreement, difference, residues, and concomitant variation

Galton and the concepts of correlation and regression to the mean

population

sample

law of large numbers

"law of small numbers"

random process versus random product

law of averages

gambler's fallacy

normal distribution

measures of central tendency: mean, median, mode

skewness

replication

Fisher and the null hypothesis, blocks and plots, randomized block design, analysis of variance

research hypothesis

paired-associate learning

repeated measures

two-way classification

subject variables

random assignment

independent groups

dichotomized

correlational designs

mental test

Additional Reading

Bakan (1967) is the classic consideration of many of the underlying themes of this chapter, and Cowles (1989) supplies a useful history of many of those themes. A very thoughtful exposition of the history of psychological research is found in Danziger (1990).

Meehl (1978) provides a provocative criticism of Fisher's approach to research.

4

Control and Power

You might think from the title of this chapter that this book has suddenly changed into a consideration of international politics. Nothing could be farther from the truth. *Control* and *power* are not only political terms but, as we shall see, central concepts regulating the design of experiments.

The Problem of Control

Fisher (1925/1991, p. 24) had noted that, even in a simple situation such as the tea-tasting experiment, there are many potential obstacles to conducting an experiment that is a fair test of the null hypothesis. For example, suppose that different kinds of tea were used, so that the subject was not given the same kind of tea across all trials. The subject might discriminate between the teas, which might confuse the subject and make it harder to come to the correct decision. Since the type of tea is not a variable of interest in the experiment, it can only distract from the sensitivity of the experiment. There are many potential variables in any psychological experiment, and it is in the experimenter's interest to be able to *control* as many of them as possible.

When the experimenter does not have control over relevant variables, then the inferences drawn from an experiment may not be warranted or may even be completely wrong. Suls and Rosnow (1988) have reviewed a number of reasons why an experiment might go astray because of lack of control. We will consider some of the cases they describe.

Clever Hans

The story of *Clever Hans* is one of the most famous in the history of psychology and has offered a significant challenge to psychologists' methodological practices. Hans was a horse who could answer questions by tapping his hoof. For example, if asked the sum of three plus two, the horse would tap five times. Hans could also answer questions of much greater complexity and was a truly mysterious phenomenon in his day. Through careful observation and experimental procedure, a psychologist named Oscar Pfungst (1911) showed how Hans was able to do this. Among other things, Pfungst discovered that the kind of spectators made a difference. If the spectators knew the right answer to the question Hans was asked, then Hans would also get the right answer. If, however, the spectators did not know the right answer, then Hans did not know either. It turned out that Hans was picking up information from the spectators' behavior. They would make subtle head movements when Hans reached the right answer. Hans was apparently being influenced by the spectators' behavior, not arriving at answers on his own.

Rosenthal and Experimenter Bias

The "Clever Hans phenomenon" (Rosenthal, 1967, p. 363) may also be important in research. Perhaps subjects play the role of Clever Hans, picking up
subtle cues from the experimenter that tell them what the experimenter
expects them to do (Rosenthal, 1966). The experimenter may unwittingly *bias*
the outcome of the experiment. There may be subtle interactions between
experimenter and subject, influencing the other's behavior in ways that may
escape notice.

Rosenfeld and Baer (1969) provided an interesting example of experimenter-subject interactions. Although their experiment involved deception
and featured only two subjects, it still gives us insight into a potentially
important aspect of psychological research and may be used as the basis for
some generalizations about experimenter-subject interactions. One of the
subjects was an "experimenter" who thought that he was trying to control the
behavior of a "subject," but the "subject" was actually the real experimenter.
This is not as confusing as it sounds. To begin with, a male graduate student
in psychology was told by his professors that his job in the experiment was
to increase the frequency with which a subject emitted a particular behavior.
The behavior selected was chin rubbing. The graduate student was to have a
series of interviews with the subject during which he would nod and say
"Yeah" every time the subject rubbed his chin. We will call this graduate
student *the interviewer*. The interviewer believed that the hypothesis of the
study was that nodding is a social reinforcer that acts to increase the rate at
which the subject rubs his chin, without the subject becoming aware of this
relationship. Meanwhile the person that the graduate student thought was
the subject, who was also male, had actually been told by the same professors
that *his* job was to rub his chin every time the person who thought he was the
experimenter said "Yeah." This second person, whom we will call *the interviewee*, knew all about what the interviewer thought was going on. Thus the
interviewer thought that he was the experimenter but was actually the subject, while the interviewee pretended to be the subject but was actually the
experimenter. The relationship between the interviewer's behavior and the
interviewee's behavior is diagrammed in Figure 4-1.

The data suggested that the interviewee succeeded in getting the interviewer to emit more "Yeah"s by rubbing his chin. The resulting increase in
chin rubbing on the interviewee's part meant that the interviewer was able to
think that he was controlling the other person's chin rubbing by nodding his
head. Careful questioning of the interviewer during pauses in the experiment
revealed that he did not realize what was going on. Thus the experiment
offers an example of the way in which our behavior can be controlled by
others without our being aware of it. Rosenfeld and Baer point out that many
social interactions may have this quality. In conversation, for instance, we

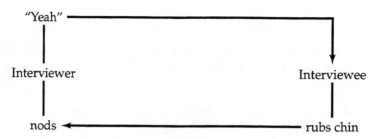

FIGURE 4-1 **Relationship between Interviewer's Behavior and Interviewee's Behavior in the Rosenfeld and Baer (1969) Experiment**

often take turns controlling the behavior of others and letting others control our behavior. To observe this aspect of interaction in your own experience, try to carry on a conversation with someone *without* nodding at them or saying "Yeah" or "Mm-hmm" occasionally. Such social reinforcers are the "glue" that holds our interactions together. Thus researchers must remember that such subtle controls may be present in the experimental situation and may bias the results. The research situation may afford an opportunity for uncontrolled communication between subject and experimenter. Such a potential source of bias should be avoided.

Orne and Demand Characteristics

Subjects may have beliefs about how they should behave in an experiment as a result of assumptions they make about the phenomenon being studied. Their behavior, then, may be determined by these expectations, rather than being under the control of experimental manipulations. Orne (1965) argued that even if subjects are ignorant of the experimenter's hypothesis, their behavior may nonetheless be influenced by what they believe to be the nature of the experiment. Such beliefs may arise from many different sources. When they are recruited, for example, subjects usually are informed at least partially concerning the nature of the study. Subjects may also be given instructions in the course of the study that influence their assumptions about the purpose of the investigation. Orne (1965, p. 96) called sources of information about the experiment other than those explicitly manipulated by the experimenter *"demand characteristics* of the experimental situation" (italics added). According to Orne, subjects need not even be aware of the implicit beliefs about the experiment that are influencing their behavior.

If experimental results are the outcome of variables such as experimenter bias and demand characteristics, rather than the outcome of variables of explicit interest to the experimenter, then the results are said to be artifactual. An *artifact* is any uncontrolled variable in the research situation that could potentially account for some or all of the observed results. The elimination of artifacts is a very important aspect of the research process, involving thoughtful evaluation of potential artifacts and the invention of procedures designed to control for them. The best way to get some idea of how to incorporate sensible experimental controls is to examine an experiment that makes use of some sophisticated techniques to investigate an elusive phenomenon.

A Well-Controlled Experiment

Greenwald, Spangenberg, Pratkanis, and Eskanazi (1991) did an experiment to determine whether or not so-called subliminal self-help audiotapes have any effect. No doubt you have come across such tapes, which are advertised as being able to help you lose weight, quit smoking, increase self-esteem, and so on. Often the tapes contain nothing but music, although it is claimed that they include "subliminal" messages that will affect you. The idea is that the messages have the power to influence you without your being aware of them. What is the proper method for evaluating such claims? Greenwald et al. (1991) list four required procedures. These requirements work well in the Greenwald et al. experiment and are also very useful techniques to apply in a wide variety of experimental situations.

1. A *double-blind* method is necessary. A double-blind method ensures that neither the experimenter nor the subject knows the experimental condition into which the subject is placed. Both experimenter and subject are "blind" with respect to the experimental treatment. Such a procedure attempts to control for the possible effects that demand characteristics and experimenter bias may have in the experimental situation. A double-blind method often involves the use of a *placebo*. A placebo is a treatment that appears to be the experimental treatment but is not. For example, one group of subjects might receive a tape that appears to be "subliminal" but is not, while another group receives a "subliminal" tape. Neither the subjects nor the experimenter would know which tape they had received.

2. The experiment should take place under conditions that are as close to "real world" conditions as possible. That is, the experiment should be as ecologically valid as possible. (You should recall our previous discussion of *ecological validity*. If you do not, reread that section now.) The ecological validity of the present experiment would be reduced if subjects listened to the tapes in a laboratory. The experiment can be made more ecologically valid by having subjects use the tapes under conditions similar to those under

which they would ordinarily be used. That is, subjects should be allowed to take the tapes home and use them as they would typically be used.

3. It is important to use the right kind of subjects. Attention to relevant subject variables can be very important. What kind of subjects are appropriate for the Greenwald et al. (1991) experiment? People who buy the tapes wish to change in the ways advertised by particular tapes. People who do not want to lose weight are unlikely to purchase a "subliminal" weight-reduction tape. Subjects should be people who are interested in using "subliminal" tapes.

4. There should be both *pretest* and *posttest* measures of the behavior that is supposed to be changed by the experimental treatment. Unless there is some *baseline* measure of the behavior the subject is trying to change, it is difficult to evaluate the effect of the treatment on the behavior.

How were these principles applied in this particular experiment?

Greenwald et al. (1991) advertised for subjects who were interested in "participating in a study of memory and self-esteem subliminal audiotapes," and acquired commercially available audiotapes that claimed to be "subliminal" self-help tapes designed to aid either memory or self-esteem. After completing standard pretests of self-esteem and memory, subjects received an audiotape labeled either "memory" or "self-esteem." In fact, the labels were randomly assigned to the tapes, so that some tapes labeled "self-esteem" were actually tapes that purported to improve memory, and some tapes labeled "memory" were actually tapes that purported to improve self-esteem. Subjects were told to take the tapes home and listen to them daily for one month. Subjects then returned to the laboratory and received posttests of memory and self-esteem.

Thus the experimental design is quite simple. (Remember our earlier admonition to "keep it simple"!) One independent variable is *tape label*, and it has two levels: *memory* and *self-esteem*. The other independent variable is *"subliminal" content*, and it also has two levels: *memory* and *self-esteem*. This design, given in Table 4-1, consists of four independent groups of subjects. The procedure of randomly labeling tapes ensures that the assignment of subjects to groups is random. Each subject is given a pretest and a posttest of memory and self-esteem, so that there are two dependent variables, relating to gains in memory and self-esteem. In the Greenwald et al. (1991) experiment, there were between 49 and 73 subjects in each group.

The null hypothesis is that listening to the tapes made no difference in memory and self-esteem. The data, however, allow the null hypothesis to be rejected, in a particularly interesting way. In general, Greenwald et al.'s results showed that memory and self-esteem scores improved in all of the four conditions. That is, no matter which of the four tapes subjects received, their memory and self-esteem scores improved. This is a *placebo effect,* because it apparently occurs simply as a result of participating in this kind of study and

TABLE 4-1   Experimental Design for the Greenwald et al. (1991) Experiment

		"Subliminal" Content	
		Memory	Self-Esteem
Tape Label	Memory		
	Self-Esteem		

cannot be attributed to any improvement-inducing property of the independent variables. (We will have more to say about this effect below.)

Subjects were also asked if they thought that the tape had its desired effect. Now look at Figure 4-2. It shows that if subjects received the tape labeled "self-esteem," they were more likely to believe that their self-esteem had in fact improved than if they received the tape labeled "memory," *regardless of whether or not they had actually received the "subliminal" self-esteem tape.* If, however, subjects received the tape labeled "memory," they were more likely to believe that their memory had improved than that their self-esteem had improved, again *regardless of whether or not they had actually received the "subliminal" memory tape.* Thus the tape label, rather than the actual content of the tape, determines whether or not the subject thinks that he or she has improved. Greenwald et al. call this result an *illusory placebo effect.* The subjects have the illusion that they have improved in one dimension more than in another, even though on average they have done equally well in both.

You may be wondering whether or not there actually were "subliminal" messages on any of the tapes. Greenwald et al. (1991) did not report any attempts to determine whether or not such messages were present. They did say that all that were audible on the tapes was music or nature sounds. One of the strengths of the Greenwald et al. study is that the claims of those who market "subliminal" audiotapes were evaluated without determining whether "subliminal" messages were present. The study also shows the impact and significance of placebo effects.

The Greenwald et al. study is one example from a very large class of psychological investigations. Psychologists are often concerned with evaluating the potential of a treatment to change behavior over time. Examples abound in education and psychotherapy, to mention only two areas of great interest to psychologists. Let us now examine experimental designs that allow such treatments to be evaluated.

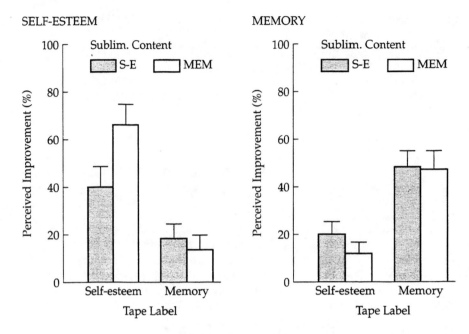

FIGURE 4-2 Percentage of Subjects Perceiving Improvement in Self-Esteem and Memory as a Function of Audiotape Subliminal Content and Tape Label

Source: "Double-Blind Tests of Subliminal Self-Help Audiotapes" by A. G. Greenwald, E. R. Spangenberg, A. R. Pratkanis, and J. Eskanazi, 1991, *Psychological Science, 2,* 121. Copyright 1991 by Cambridge University Press. Adapted by permission.

The Solomon Four-Group Design

In a series of extremely influential papers, Solomon (1949; Solomon & Lessac, 1968) recommended appropriate controls for experiments involving behavioral change over time. Although Solomon's recommendations have not been universally employed over the years, they have recently been reconsidered and reapproved (Braver & Braver, 1988).

Solomon (1949) pointed out that the concept of a *control group* is a relatively recent invention. Simply put, a control group is a group of subjects that does *not* receive the experimental treatment. The *experimental group does* receive the experimental treatment. Thus a very simple experiment has one control group and one experimental group, corresponding to Mill's method of difference. Such experiments are often quite limited, however, in terms of the conclusions that can be drawn from them. For example, Solomon noted that a typical psychological experiment had the following two-group design:

Experimental group
Pretest ⇨ Experimental treatment ⇨ Posttest

Control Group
Pretest ⇨ *No* treatment ⇨ Posttest

The hope is that by using this design one can evaluate the effect of the treatment. Subjects may be randomly assigned to one of the groups or may be matched on the basis of some relevant characteristic. Notice that such a design could have been used by Rogers in the study described earlier to evaluate the effect of psychotherapy. In fact, in some studies, Rogers did use a design like this. Solomon describes a variety of experiments in which this design has been employed, including studies of learning and of attitude change.

Solomon argued that the two-group design did not allow the experimenter to evaluate properly the effect of taking the pretest. For example, it is possible that the pretest sensitizes subjects to the nature of the experiment; and so, in addition to providing a baseline measure, the pretest may also have an unintended effect on the subjects' behavior. This may very well have happened in the Greenwald et al. (1991) experiment we have just reviewed. In fact, Greenwald et al. noted that the placebo effect that they found may have been due to subjects becoming familiar with memory and self-esteem items on the pretest. Their improvement on the posttest would then be seen as a kind of practice effect, which takes place independently of any intervening treatment. To take the possibility of such pretest effects into account, Solomon recommended the addition of a second control group, so that the design looked like this:

Experimental Group
Pretest ⇨ Experimental treatment ⇨ Posttest

Control Group 1
Pretest ⇨ *No* treatment ⇨ Posttest

Control Group 2
No pretest ⇨ Treatment ⇨ Posttest

This way one can compare the behavior of subjects receiving the pretest and training with the behavior of subjects receiving only the training. There is, however, still one logical possibility left: a group receiving only the post-test. The third control group would be as follows:

Control Group 3
No pretest ⇨ *No* treatment ⇨ Posttest

The resulting four-group design has the structure shown in Table 4-2.

Solomon (1949, p. 146) noted that Control Group 3 is particularly valuable if some uncontrolled event or events intervene between the experimental treatment and the posttest. The possibility of uncontrolled events is particularly problematic in studies done over relatively long periods of time. An example similar to one given by Solomon is as follows. Suppose that in 1990 we were interested in the effect of information about Russian history on North American high school students' attitudes toward ethnic Russians. Suppose further that we gathered pretest data on the Experimental Group and Control Group 1 and gave the relevant information to the Experimental Group and Control Group 2 just before the dramatic events in the Soviet Union leading to its breakup. Now the posttest data can be influenced by the events in the Soviet Union. The events in the Soviet Union might interact with the pretest and/or the experimental treatment in unpredictable ways. Control Group 3 is a relatively pure comparison group, which can be used to evaluate the possible effects of uncontrolled events occurring during the course of the experiment. If we had used only a two-group, or even a three-group, design, we would not have been able to properly evaluate the data.

- Design a Solomon four-group experiment to evaluate the possibility that the placebo effect in the Greenwald et al. (1991) study was due to the effect of the pretest.

If you use the Solomon four-group design in your own research, you should be aware that the analysis of the resulting data can be quite complex.

TABLE 4-2 The Solomon Four-Group Design

		Pretest	
		Present	Absent
Experimental Treatment	Present	Experimental group	Control group 2
	Absent	Control group 1	Control group 3

Braver and Braver (1988) have provided a useful guide to the analysis of data obtained using this design.

External versus Internal Validity

We are now in a position to appreciate the distinction between *internal validity* and *external validity* (Campbell & Stanley, 1963, p. 5). An experiment is internally valid to the extent that it allows the experimenter to conclude that there either was or was not a relationship between the independent and dependent variables. For example, a well-designed experiment minimizes the likelihood that the experimenter will be making a mistake when the null hypothesis is either accepted or rejected. We will discuss internal validity further below. External validity refers to the extent to which an experiment can be generalized to settings other than the one in which it was performed. The Solomon four-group design is one way to increase the external validity of an experiment. By adding control groups, one is able to separate the possible effect of an independent variable (treatment) from the confounding effects of other variables, such as the pretest.

External validity is similar to ecological validity. Experiments performed in laboratories may not be easily generalized to nonlaboratory situations. Moreover, the world outside the laboratory provides many opportunities for research (e.g., Gigerenzer, 1981).

Experiments done in naturally occurring contexts are often called *field studies*. Such research often employs what are known as *quasi-experimental designs*.

Quasi-Experimental Designs

When working in the field, it is often not possible to use the same experimental procedures that one would employ in the laboratory. It may not be possible to assign subjects randomly to experimental and control groups. For example, suppose that one is interested in how well individuals remember what they learned in school. In one such study, Bahrick and Hall (1991) wanted to evaluate the effects of such variables as number of algebra courses taken and number of years since the last algebra course taken on long-term retention of algebra. Obviously, one would not do such a study by randomly assigning subjects to conditions in which they take algebra courses, and then waiting until several years after the subjects have left school to measure retention of algebra knowledge. Such a procedure is too time consuming (the experimenters may die before the data is collected!). Moreover, who is going to tell students that some have randomly been chosen to take algebra, and others not to take algebra? The only alternative is to accept the existing natural division of students into those who have taken algebra and those who have not. Experiments that use such preexisting distinctions are termed *quasi-experiments* (Campbell, & Stanley, 1963, p. 2).

A Quasi-Experimental Example

Schachter, Christenfeld, Ravina, and Bilous (1991) did an instructive quasi-experiment on hesitation pauses. Hesitation pauses in normal conversation have been extensively studied over the years, but Schachter and his coworkers at Columbia University studied hesitation pauses by university lecturers in different disciplines. They were particularly interested in *filled pauses*, or cases in which the speech of lecturers contains "ums," "ers," "uhs," and "ahs." (You may have noticed your lecturers emitting such *speech disfluencies*.)

Observers were trained to attend lectures and count the number of filled pauses. Measurements were obtained on the frequency of filled pauses in the speech of 47 lecturers in 10 departments at Columbia. These departments were distributed across three faculties: Natural Science (e.g., Chemistry), Social Science (e.g., Political Science), and Humanities (e.g., English). The administrative structure of Columbia is similar to that at most universities, except that at Columbia, Psychology is in the Faculty of Natural Science, rather than in the Faculty of Social Science. The resulting data, grouped by faculty, are shown in Figure 4-3.

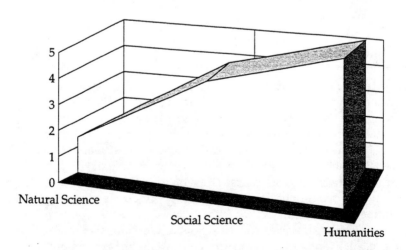

FIGURE 4-3 **Mean Number of Filled Pauses in the Schachter et al. (1991) Study**

The different faculties appear on the x (vertical) axis; the frequency of filled pauses per minute on the y (horizontal) axis. These data allowed Schachter et al. (1991) to reject the null hypothesis that there are no differences between the faculties in hesitation pauses during lectures. Natural science lecturers generate filled pauses much less frequently than do either social science or humanities lecturers.

- Schachter and his colleagues noted that there are a variety of possible interpretations of the observed differences between faculties. What explanations can you think of?

The interpretation that Schachter et al. (1991) found most plausible involves the distinction between disciplines that are concerned with teaching *facts*, and disciplines that are relatively more concerned with teaching *interpretations*. Science lecturers may be more concerned with teaching facts, while lecturers in the other disciplines are concerned more with interpretations. Schachter et al. used the following example. Suppose that I was a physics lecturer who began the mathematical sentence "$E = MC \ldots$" For most (and hopefully all) physics lecturers, there is no ambiguity concerning what comes nest: "squared" completes the sentence. If I say, "$E = MC \ldots$ uh ... cubed," then it is simply the case that I do not know what I am talking about. Suppose, however, that I was an English professor who said, "The explanations of Hamlet's indecisiveness include the following possibilities ... uh. ..." The cause of my pausing at that point may not be that I do not know what the possibilities are, but only that I am searching through the alternatives in order to select the one I want to talk about next.

What kind of data might support Schachter et al.'s (1991) interpretation? Schachter et al. report data from an undergraduate honors thesis by Wanner (1990), who examined the frequency of filled pauses per minute for 19 lecturers in both undergraduate and graduate courses. For 15 of the 19 lecturers, the number of filled pauses was greater when they were lecturing to graduate students than when they were lecturing to undergraduates. On Schachter et al.'s account, this is because there is more uncertainty at the graduate level, and thus more choosing between alternatives as one speaks. Humanities and social science lecturers seem to pause equally often, regardless of the level, which suggests that interpretations are their stock-in-trade.

Notice that in the Schachter et al. (1991) study, none of the independent variables is under the control of the experimenter. Type of faculty (natural science, social science, or humanities) and type of lecture (undergraduate or graduate) are distinctions that are given to the experimenter. In spite of the lack of direct control, Schachter and his colleagues were able to gather data that provide information about an important aspect of teaching. Their interpretation of the data is open to question; you may have other interpretations that you find more plausible. Perhaps you can think of a quasi-experiment that would follow from your interpretations. Quasi-experiments are typically more "open-ended" than laboratory experiments in that they lend themselves to diverse interpretations.

Studies may vary in the extent of their "quasiness" (Campbell & Stanley, 1963, p. 64). As we have just seen, some studies have no independent variables under the direct control of the experimenter. Other studies are mixtures of experimenter-manipulated variables and variables that are given in the field. We will examine several such studies throughout the book.

Logical Spaces and the Partial Nature of Experiments

You will have noticed by now that experiments are always partial. That is, no matter how well designed an experiment is, it always leaves us wanting to know more. There are good reasons why experimental inquiry is never finished. Sometimes science is portrayed as an activity that will eventually lead us to understand everything that can be known. This view is misleading, however. It is likely that we will never be able to understand all possible events in the world and their interrelationships, or "know it all." To see why this is so, we need first to consider what it was like when we knew even less than we do now. That was the state of our knowledge when we were children.

Piaget and the Development of a "Logical Space"

The study of the development of the ability to think logically owes more to Jean Piaget than to anyone else. When we are children, says Piaget, we easily confuse class concepts. Piaget (1957, p. 4) described an experiment in which children who were between five and eight years of age were shown a set of twenty wooden beads. The beads were either brown or white, with the majority being brown. Although you might think that anyone, regardless of age, would say that there are more wooden beads than brown beads, these children were inclined to say, "There are more brown beads than wooden beads, because there are only two or three white ones" (Piaget, 1957, p. 5). Children at this age cannot think in terms of one class (brown beads) being a member of a larger class (wooden beads). Rather, children believe that if we take the brown beads away from the wooden beads, then the only wooden beads left are the white beads, and there are more brown beads than white beads.

Eventually, however, children come to understand that something can be the member of one class (brown beads) and the member of another class (wooden beads) at the same time. To put it more formally, children realize that something can belong to both a *subordinate class* (e.g., brown beads, white beads) and a *superordinate class* (e.g., wooden beads). An important next step is the *multiplication of classes*. Multiplication of classes becomes a possibility when children realize that something can belong to more than one superordinate class. For example, in experimental psychology we often classify people in more than one way simultaneously. An example is shown in Figure 4-4. Subjects in our experiments can be classified by such variables as *intelligence* and *income* as well as by any number of additional variables. Suppose we let *A* be one superordinate class (such as intelligence) and *B* be another superordinate class (such as income). We can further classify people as *above* average in intelligence (*A*1) or *below average* in intelligence (*A*2) and as *rich* (*B*1) or *poor* (*B*2), resulting in the four classes in Figure 4-4: above average and rich, below average and rich, above average and poor, below average and poor. Figure 4-4 looks like an experimental design, and indeed it is. The multiplication of classes makes it possible for us to think experimentally. We can imagine different possible independent variables, such as *height* and *income*, and formulate hypotheses concerning their possible effects on behaviors of various sorts. We can then test these hypotheses against data.

The two-by-two classification in Figure 4-4 is, of course, only one possibility. One could think of any number of alternative classes that could be multiplied, such as *age* (old versus young), *gender* (men versus women), and so on. Depending on the experiment, different classifications would be relevant. Moreover, there is no reason to limit ourselves to multiplying only two dimensions. Psychologists often do experiments that classify subjects using three or more variables (e.g., *gender* by *age* by *intelligence*). Could one do an experiment that involved multiplying all possible classes? That would

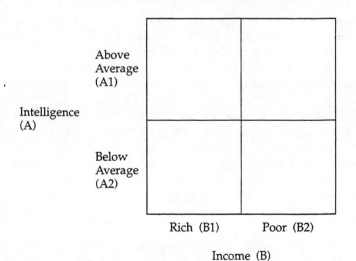

FIGURE 4-4 Multiplication of Classes

result in a "logical space" that contained all possible events. Wittgenstein (1921/1974) put it like this:

> Logic deals with every possibility, and all possibilities are its facts. . . . If I know an object, I also know all its possible occurrences in states of affairs. . . . Each thing is, as it were, in a space of possible states of affairs. This space I can imagine empty, but I cannot imagine the thing without the space. (p. 71)

Even though I can imagine *some* of the possibilities, I cannot do an experiment that takes *all* possible states of affairs into account. In any possible experiment, I can include only a part of the logical space. Any possible experiment can explore only some of the independent variables that may be important, and I cannot know in advance what the result of considering other variables might be.

Given that any experiment can only sample some of the possible variables, it is obviously very important to select your variables carefully. Before you go to the time and trouble of conducting an experiment, you should do as much work "up front" as possible to make sure that the variables you select are likely to be important ones. A good question to ask is, Will the independent variables I have selected actually have a strong effect on the dependent variable(s) in which I am interested? This is a complicated question, but there are some guidelines to help you answer it.

Power

Researchers often have two hypotheses in mind when they do an experiment. On the one hand, an experiment is designed to test the null hypothesis, which we will symbolize as H_0. On the other hand, the experimenter may also be interested in an alternative hypothesis, the research hypothesis, which we will symbolize as H_1. We considered research hypotheses briefly when we cited Cohen's (1990, p. 1307) example of the research hypothesis that "poor kids estimated the size of coins to be bigger than rich kids" versus "the null hypothesis that poor kids perceived coins to be the same size as did rich kids."

Fisher, as we have seen, was the inventor of null-hypothesis testing. Neyman and Pearson (1928a, 1928b) explored the relation between null hypotheses (H_0) and research hypotheses (H_1). Their work was never accepted by Fisher but has had an important impact nonetheless (Cohen, 1990; Gigerenzer & Murray, 1987). Let us explore some of the concepts that they introduced.

We will begin by considering a concrete example. Suppose you were to redo the Schachter et al. (1991) experiment at your university or college. The null hypothesis (H_0) would be that you would find no differences between the faculties in filled pauses. The research hypothesis (H_1) would be that science lecturers emit more filled pauses than social science or humanities lecturers. Suppose that you did your experiment and failed to find any differences between the faculties in filled pauses. You would then have failed to replicate the Schachter et al. study. You would not reject the null hypothesis (H_0), but you would reject the research hypothesis (H_1). By deciding not to reject H_0 but to reject H_1, you may be making a mistake. Perhaps H_1 is actually true, and your experiment has simply failed to detect it. For example, if you had included only one lecturer from each faculty in your study, you should not be terribly surprised if H_0 is not rejected. Remember the law of large numbers: the larger the sample, the more confident we can be that results obtained from it are reasonably representative of the underlying population. The values obtained of a small sample (especially a very small sample, such as one per group) may be quite different from the underlying population values. In order to test a hypothesis adequately, we must have a sufficiently large sample.

Let us consider another possibility. It may be that your attempted replication of Schachter et al.'s experiment (1991) succeeds. That is, your results may turn out to have the same pattern as did Schachter et al.'s results. Under those circumstances you would reject the null hypothesis (H_0) and accept the research hypothesis (H_1). Of course, rejecting H_0 does not automatically mean that H_1 is true. It just means that H_1 is the alternative hypothesis that you have decided to accept provisionally. As your research progresses, you may modify H_1 or eventually abandon it altogether.

Let us generalize a bit on the basis of these examples. When you make inferences from experimental data, there are two errors that can occur. Rejecting the null hypothesis (H_0) when H_0 is true is called a *Type 1 error*. Rejecting the research hypothesis (H_1) when H_1 is actually true is called a *Type 2 error*. Thus if your attempted replication of Schachter et al.'s experiment (1991) led you to *reject* H_0 when it was in fact true, then you would have made a Type 1 error. Alternatively, if your attempted replication of Schachter et al.'s experiment led you to *accept* H_0, and thus reject the research hypothesis (H_1) when H_1 was in fact true, then you would have made a Type 2 error.

Obviously we would like to avoid making errors of any sort. Since there is no way to be certain that we are not making an error, we must accept a certain level of risk. The problem is to set the risk at an acceptable level. As we observed earlier, psychologists typically accept a 1 in 20, or 5%, chance of rejecting the null hypothesis (H_0) when H_0 is true. This means that psychologists generally accept a 1 in 20, or 5%, chance of making a Type 1 error. But what about Type 2 errors? How should we avoid making Type 2 errors?

Several years ago, Cohen (1962) reviewed 70 articles in the area of abnormal-social psychology. He observed that many of the studies were not designed in a way that would make it very likely that they would reject the null hypothesis (H_0). Another way of putting Cohen's findings is to say that, in general, the experimenters conducting the studies typically ran a high risk of making a Type 2 error (i.e., rejecting H_1 when H_1 is true). The studies Cohen reviewed were generally of low *power*. In this context, power refers to the likelihood that the null hypothesis will be rejected (Cohen, 1988, p. 4). A recent review by Sedlmeier and Gigerenzer (1989) suggested that current studies are no more powerful than those considered by Cohen in his original review (1962). Thus while many psychologists acknowledge the importance of doing studies with adequate power, as yet they have tended not to use procedures for making sure that their studies are powerful enough. Recent developments, however, suggest that the concept of power will become increasingly influential in psychological research.

Power depends on three things:

1. Power increases as the probability of making a Type 1 error increases. Usually we accept a 1 in 20, or 5%, risk of making a Type 1 error. If we were to decide to accept a 1 in 10, or 10%, risk of making a Type 1 error, then our experiment would have more power. Conversely, if we were to accept a more stringent criterion for rejecting H_0, such as a 1 in 100, or 1%, risk of making a Type 1 error, then our experiment would have less power. There is a trade-off between Type 1 and Type 2 errors. The more we guard against making one type of error, the greater the risk of making the other type of error.

2. Power increases as the magnitude of the hypothesized effect increases. Suppose that you expect that your independent variable(s) will produce a big difference between your experimental conditions. Ideally, you should be able to say just how big an effect you expect to find. This will require you to be very specific in the formulation of your research hypothesis (H_1). In any case, the larger the *effect size*, the greater the power of the experiment. It might be helpful to think of effect size in terms of the correlation between variables. You should recall that correlations vary from 0 to + or − 1. The closer the correlation is to 1, the larger the effect size. For example, if two variables have a correlation of .9, then they are very closely related. Such a relationship represents a large effect size, because any large variation in one of the variables also yields a large variation in the other variable. By contrast, a low correlation, such as .2, represents a small effect size. In that case, a large variation in one of the variables yields only a small variation in the other. An illustration of effect size in terms of correlation will be given below.

3. Power increases as the size of the sample increases. We have noted several times that to reject the null hypothesis one must use an appropriately large sample. The larger the effect, however, the smaller the sample size needed to reject the null hypothesis. If the effect you are studying is small, then you may need a very large sample to find the effect reliably. Using small samples to search for small effects is not a wise procedure.

Cohen (1988) outlined a procedure for calculating power in a variety of situations. If you wish to calculate power precisely, you should consult his book. For our purposes, it is necessary for you only to understand that power is determined by all three of these characteristics of experiments: Type 1 error rate, effect size, and sample size. If the value of any one of these characteristics changes, then so does power. Increasing power is important, because it is a shame to invest time, effort, and perhaps money in a study that is so underpowered that it cannot detect a real effect. Sample size is an obvious feature of an experiment that will increase power and is relatively easy to change. Cohen (1962) recommended paying close attention to the size of the sample you use. Alternatively, before you do an experiment, you can try to be as sure as possible that the effect you are investigating is strong. Paying close attention to previous research done in your area of interest is an important way of becoming familiar with the strong effects in that area. In a subsequent chapter, we will review areas of research that have shown strong effects.

• Cohen (1990) provided an example that illustrates why paying attention to such things as effect size is important. He cited a 1986 account of a newspaper article reporting a correlation between *height* and *IQ scores*. Apparently, even after one controls for other variables, such as age, sex, and socioeconomic status, there is a relationship such that tall people have higher IQ scores than short people! When such a relationship is stated baldly like that, it sounds like bad news for short people. Perhaps society will become prejudiced against short people, believing that they are just not as smart as tall people. Should short people be depressed over this study?

It turns out that in this case the effect size is extremely small. The correlation between height and IQ scores is about .1. The following example shows that we should not take a small effect size such as this very seriously. According to Cohen (1990, p. 1309), "for a 30-point increase in IQ it would take only enough growth hormone to produce a 3.5 ft increase in height, or with the causality reversed, a 4 in. increase in height would require an increase of only 233 IQ points." That is, enormous changes in one variable produce only small changes in the other. How did these investigators discover such a small effect? Remember that sample size is a determinant of power, with large samples needed to detect small effects. The sample for this study was 14,000 children between 6 and 17 years of age. With such a large sample, one can detect even very small effects. The moral of the story is this. We are constantly being bombarded in the media with stories about findings such as those concerning the height/IQ relationship. Some of us take these stories seriously, as we believe that such relationships must be important. It is impossible, however, to evaluate the significance of a relationship without knowing the kind of information we are discussing. The proper evaluation of a study requires that it be placed in proper

TABLE 4-3 **Aspirin's Effect on Heart Attack**

Condition	MI Absent	MI Present
Presence or Absence of MI in Aspirin and Placebo Conditions		
Aspirin	10,933	104
Placebo	10,845	189

Fatal and Nonfatal MIs in Aspirin and Placebo Conditions		
	Nonfatal MI	Fatal MI
Aspirin	99	5
Placebo	171	18

Source: "Statistical Procedures and the Justification of Knowledge in Psychological Science" by R. L. Rosnow and R. Rosenthal, 1989, *American Psychologist, 44,* 1279. Copyright 1989 by the American Psychological Association. Reprinted by permission.
Note: MI = Myocardial Infarction.

context, and knowledge of such things as the effect size and sample size is a crucial aspect of that context.

Rosnow and Rosenthal (1989) have also discussed some of the reasons why we need to pay attention to power. One of their most impressive examples comes from a recent study of the role of aspirin in reducing the risk of heart attack, or myocardial infarction (Steering Committee of the Physicians' Health Study Research Group, 1988). Some results of that study are shown in Table 4-3. Notice the extremely large sample size: a total of nearly 22,000 subjects, divided into two groups of roughly 11,000 each. One group takes aspirin every other day, and the other group takes no aspirin. During the period of the study, 104, or 1.7%, of the subjects in the aspirin group had heart attacks, and 189, or .9%, of the subjects in the no aspirin group had heart attacks. In media accounts of this study, these data were interpreted to mean that the subjects taking aspirin were only about half as likely as the no aspirin subjects to have a heart attack. That interpretation is sort of correct, since the aspirin heart-attack rate (.9%) divided by the no aspirin heart-attack rate (1.7%) gives a value of .53. Notice, however, that the effect size is very small. The relative magnitude of the groups is shown in Figure 4-5. We are talking about only 85 more people having heart attacks in the no aspirin group out of a sample of over 11,000. This translates into a correlation of about .03 (Rosnow & Rosenthal, 1989, p. 1279) between taking aspirin versus no aspirin and presence versus absence of a heart attack. Thus we have here another example of a small effect being detected by a very large sample. Obviously, aspirin has an effect. You would be unwise, however, to rely on aspirin alone

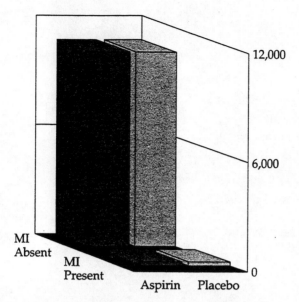

FIGURE 4-5 Graphical Display of the Data in Table 4-3

to prevent heart attacks. As you can see from these examples, issues relating to the power of a study are important not only when you are designing a study but also when you are interpreting its outcome.

Names and Concepts to Understand and Remember

The following are some of the most influential ideas in the area we have just reviewed. Some concepts are quite general and are not associated with any particular psychologist. In other cases, however, the names of psychologists are paired with the concepts for which they are known. Read through the list. If any of the names or concepts seem unfamiliar to you, then go back and reread the appropriate section of the chapter. The names are in the order in which they are presented in the text, and the concepts are italicized in the text, so they are easy to find. You should be able to define each concept and briefly discuss it. You should also be able to write a brief account of the work done by each person on the list.

control
Clever Hans
experimenter bias
demand characteristics

artifact
double-blind
placebo
pretest
posttest
placebo effect
illusory placebo effect
Solomon four-group design
external validity
internal validity
field studies
quasi-experimental designs
logical space
Neyman and Pearson and Type 1 and Type 2 errors
power
effect size

Additional Reading

A classic introduction to measures that are useful for quasi-experiments is Webb, Campbell, Schwartz, and Sechrest (1966). Cohen (1992) offers a very straightforward introduction to the concept of power.

Sources of Data

On Being "Objective"

At several points we have noted the existence of biases that influence the interpretation of events. We have also observed that it is crucial to eliminate these biases as far as possible so that the observations that constitute the data gathered in an experiment are as objective as possible. This is not always as easy to do as it might seem. Sometimes we believe that we are being objective when we are not. This is particularly true when we look upon *objectivity* as a personal characteristic, rather than as a property of the data. Though we may believe that we are objective observers, and have been trained to make objective observations, our description of a situation will not necessarily be accurate. We may sincerely believe that we are describing a situation objectively, when we are actually giving a biased account. Earlier we considered the way in which one's theory influences one's interpretation of the data. Now it is important to make the additional point that objectivity is not something that a person *is*, but is the result of employing proper *methods*. Objectivity is the result of what one does, not the result of what one *is*. The following examples help make this point.

Do Chemists Make Better Scientists?

Psychologists often look to the established sciences, such as physics and chemistry, for models of scientific behavior. The crucial question is, Does expertise in one area of science translate into expertise in another area? If a person becomes a noted chemist, for example, does that mean that he or she has acquired skills that will allow him or her to be a successful scientist in another discipline, such as psychology or sociology? Sometimes social-science disciplines are criticized because they appear to some to lack the rigor of the physical sciences. Perhaps someone trained in physical science would do a better job in psychology than someone trained in psychology!

In this context, it is instructive to consider the research of Gordon R. Freeman (1990), a prominent chemistry professor. Freeman reported that there had been an increase in cheating on his introductory chemistry examination in recent years, compared with when he began teaching the course in 1958. He wished to determine the cause of this change. As he correctly states, "In social science wisdom is necessary in the gathering and interpretation of pertinent data" (Freeman, 1990, p. 795). Freeman goes on to say, however, that "information gained by 'surveys and experiments with controls' is likely to be distorted by the artificiality of the gathering situation, so I do not use that method. My controls are my experiences with about 2500 students during the period 1958–1983" (p. 796). Freeman's data come from interviews and discussions with individuals and groups of students.

On the basis of these "data," Freeman (1990) concludes that "the tendency to cheat correlates strongly with the absence of a full-time mother in the home when the child was growing up, until the young adult left home. . . . About half the children of two-career families suffer serious psychological damage. It accumulates during their first 14 years or so and causes anti-social behavior during their puberty and later years" (p. 796). You may or may not agree with Freeman's belief that mothers who work outside the home contribute to an increase in "drug abuse, compulsive eating, cheating on exams, not telling the truth in controversial situations, and other behavior society finds destabilizing" (p. 797). Your own personal beliefs are just that—*yours*, while Freeman's personal beliefs are also just that—*his*. It is a free country, and people can believe whatever they want. Our concern, as methodologists, is not whether or not Freeman can believe whatever he wants. We are concerned about whether or not the evidence he presents in support of those beliefs meets the criteria for evidence gathered in a methodologically sound way.

- Think about the various possible sources of bias that may have entered into Freeman's data-gathering procedure.

My own belief is that Freeman's study is unlikely to have been published in a *peer-reviewed* psychology journal. (Although in a later chapter we will see that psychology journals are not entirely free of bias either.) Peer review is a process whereby papers intended for publication are sent out to experts in the field for review. Only if expert opinion supports the value of the work, will the paper be accepted for publication. Peer review is a means of quality control. In general, journals that have high standards of peer review are more respected and more influential than journals that do not have such standards. Freeman's study was published in a journal that had a peer review system, but it was a physics journal. You will have spotted some of the the methodological flaws in his study, such as the potential for experimenter bias. Yet, in spite of these flaws, Freeman's paper was accepted for publication and published. (In a later chapter, we will examine research that evaluates the peer review process itself.)

The Freeman incident shows that scientists who have very high standards in their own fields may be unaware of appropriate standards in other fields. Training in the methods of one discipline does not automatically make you an expert in the methods of another field. Lehman, Lempert, and Nisbett (1988) reviewed the training procedures in several different disciplines. They noted that "chemistry provides no improvement in statistical or methodological reasoning. . . . There is little need to differentiate among the various types of causal relations because chemistry deals primarily with necessary-and-sufficient causes. . . . The luxury of not being confronted with messy problems that contain a substantial uncertainty and a tangled web of causes means that chemistry does not teach some rules that are relevant to everyday life" (p. 441). Quasi-experimental designs are not necessary in chemistry!

- Remember that as a student of psychology you are acquiring a set of skills that allow you to gather data in a meaningful way and to interpret those data appropriately. The skills that you are acquiring are *not* the same as the skills acquired by students in other disciplines, although there is obviously some overlap. Do not be intimidated by scientists in other fields, particularly in the older, more established sciences. They do not necessarily have more *relevant* expertise than you do!

Does Experience Always Make You an Expert Observer?

You might agree that a person must have *domain-specific training* (Nisbett, Krantz, Jepson, & Kunda, 1983) in order to be an expert methodologist in a particular area. You might still believe, however, that people who have a lot of experience observing events of a particular kind will be more accurate observers than those who lack such experience. There may be some truth to this, but consider the following study, which appears to cast doubt on the ability of even highly practiced observers to see what is actually going on.

Gilovich, Vallone, and Tversky (1985) investigated the common belief in the so-called *hot hand*. There is a surprisingly widespread intuition that players of virtually any sport can have runs when they are playing especially well. In basketball, spectators often say a player has a hot hand if the player has a run during which all or most of his or her shots go in the basket. Players themselves may comment on feeling particularly "hot" during such a sequence.

Let us consider what it actually means to say that a player has a hot hand. A player would have a hot hand if he or she was more likely to shoot a basket after shooting a series of baskets than after missing a series of baskets. In their study of the Philadelphia 76ers in the 1980–1981 season, Gilovich et al. (1985) could not find any evidence for such "streak shooting." Players were not more likely to shoot a basket after a run of baskets than they were after some other sequence. In fact, sequences of baskets occurred about as often as you would expect by chance. Gilovich et al. concluded that hot hands were an illusion. The fact that spectators and players alike misperceive the existence of hot hands may be due to some of the errors we considered earlier.

- Recall our discussion of the *law of small numbers*. People erroneously tend to believe that a small sample of behavior should resemble the population from which it is drawn. Consider a basketball player who typically makes

50% of his or her shots. That does not mean that every small sample of that player's shooting behavior will show a shooting percentage of 50%. It is quite consistent with the *law of large numbers* to observe a player's shooting percentage varying quite a bit in the short run. The law of large numbers applies only in the long run. The observed short-run variations require no explanation other than chance. It is entirely possible that a small sample of, say, ten shots may contain a much higher (or lower) percentage of baskets. Yet, on the basis of such small samples, spectators may conclude that a player has a hot (or cold) hand.

- Recall our discussion of *random processes* and *random products*. People tend to believe that a sequence of events that is generated by a random process should contain frequent alternations between "hits" and "misses." A sequence of "hits" does not look "random," and so spectators believe that it must be generated by a nonrandom process. A short run of baskets does not look like a random product and seems to require an explanation other than chance. The hot hand is an attempt to explain the observed sequence of baskets, even though such an explanation is not actually required.

- Gilovich et al. (1985) noted that the players themselves may have strong feelings about the existence of the hot hand phenomenon. This may very well be true not just in basketball but in any sport or endeavor. People may feel strongly that they are either having a run in which they are doing exceptionally well ("I'm hot") or having a run in which they are doing exceptionally badly ("I'm cold"). However, the strength of one's feeling that something is the case may not correspond to the reality of one's behavior.

The behavior of the fans and players is surprising because it contradicts one easy assumption. That assumption is that repetitive perception of behavior will make those perceptions more objective. Spectators and players alike believe that they actually *perceive* streak shooting when it occurs, that there is a phenomenon called streak shooting that one can perceive. It turns out that streak shooting may not be perceived at all. Rather, it may be something that spectators and players simply *infer* rather than perceive.

- If streak shooting does not actually exist, then it would make little sense to do experiments to determine what causes it. Let us generalize on the basis of this important example. Before you conduct an investigation into the causes of a phenomenon, try to make sure that the phenomenon actually exists. You must do a lot of work to find a reasonable way of measuring the phenomenon you believe may exist. Rigorous observational methods, rather than casual perception, are necessary in order to make a such determination.

Theory-Driven Observations

We have noted several times that what scientists perceive can be determined in part by the theory they hold. This is true for "ordinary people" as well. They possess the kinds of *cognitive illusions* that McCloskey (1983a, 1983b; McCloskey & Kargon, 1988; McCloskey & Kohl, 1983) has been studying. A cognitive illusion is a false way of thinking about something that colors our perception of it. For example, even though most of us are not very well acquainted with physics, we all are nevertheless familiar with the way that objects move about in the world. In spite of this familiarity, many of us apparently believe that objects move in radically different ways than they actually do.

McCloskey and his coworkers at Johns Hopkins University have investigated the kind of motion that is illustrated in Figure 5-1. The subjects' instructions for one of these studies were as follows (McCloskey & Kargon, 1988):

> Imagine that someone has a metal ball attached to a string and is twirling it at high speed in a circle above his head. In the diagram you are looking down on the ball. The circle shows the path followed by the ball, and the arrows show the direction in which it is moving. The line from the center of the circle to the ball is the string. Assume that when the ball is at the point shown in the diagram, the string breaks where it is attached to the

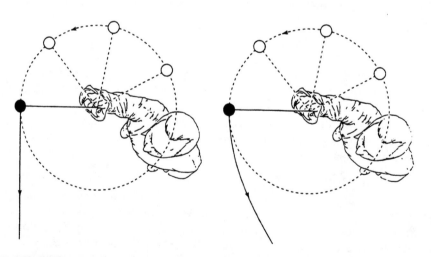

FIGURE 5-1 Illustration of the Curvilinear Impetus Principle

Source: "Intuitive Physics" by M. McCloskey, 1983, *Scientific American, 284,* 128. Copyright © 1983 by Scientific American, Inc. All rights reserved.

ball. Draw the path the ball will follow after the string breaks. Ignore air resistance. (p. 146)

Many subjects believe that the alternative shown on the right of Figure 5-1 is correct. They apparently believe that a body that was moving along a curved path will continue to move along a curved path even after the string breaks. McCloskey calls this the *curvilinear impetus principle,* a way of thinking about motion that was common in the Middle Ages but that is incorrect. Many of us appear to have an old-fashioned theory of motion according to which circular motion can be transferred to the object. The object then continues to move in a circular fashion after receiving an initial circular *impetus*. This "impetus theory" turns out to be wrong. As a matter of fact, the ball moves in a straight line when the string breaks, and so the alternative given on the left in Figure 5-1 is correct.

This is an interesting example because it shows that naive observers do not merely *lack* knowledge. Rather, naive observers often have fairly well-developed belief systems that may color their perception of events. As McCloskey and Kargon (1988, p. 66) remark, to enable the observer to become aware of alternative possibilities, it may be necessary to undo an incorrect or questionable belief. Naive observers must not only acquire new knowledge but must be made aware of the false or questionable beliefs that they possess. To enable this awareness we must know what these questionable beliefs are.

- Before you design your experiment and begin gathering data, try to be as self-critical as possible concerning any possible "hidden" assumptions you may be making about the phenomenon you are studying. These assumptions may color the alternative possibilities your experiment may be able to clarify.

Scales of Measurement

In previous chapters, we concentrated on the process of creating well-designed experiments. The identification of independent variables and their relationships to one another is central to this process. Dependent variables are equally central to the process of experimentation. After all, it is dependent variables that represent the phenomena in which the experimenter is interested. Let us examine some of the more important characteristics of dependent variables.

Every dependent variable involves *measuring* something. This is true in every experiment we have considered so far. For example, the Schachter, Christenfeld, Ravina, and Bilous (1991) experiment had as its dependent variable a measure of the frequency of filled pauses. A filled pause was operationally defined as the occurrence of any one of the following: *um, er, uh,* and *ah*. A tally of the number of times such sounds were emitted gave the dependent variable in this study. Measuring dependent variables is sometimes as straightforward as it was in the Schachter et al. study, but it can often be quite tricky. Moreover, there are several *kinds* of measurements that can be made, and you should know what they are. In what follows we will focus on measurement of dependent variables, but you should also keep in mind that independent variables also involve measurement, so that what we say about dependent measures applies also to independent measures.

Stevens (1951, 1968) proposed a system for classifying measurements. Although Stevens's classification has occasionally given rise to controversy (e.g., Gaito, 1980), it has also had numerous defenders (e.g., Maxwell & Delaney, 1985). In any case, Stevens's measurement system is one with which you should be familiar.

Nominal Scales

Look at Table 5-1. It lists four *levels of measurement*. The most primitive type of measurement uses a *nominal scale*. *Nominal* means "named" or "labeled." On a nominal scale events are simply put into one class or another according to whether or not they are the same or different on the basis of some criterion. For example, in the aspirin study described in Chapter 4, subjects were classified as either receiving aspirin or not receiving aspirin. The classification of people into two groups on the basis of whether or not they had a heart attack is also an example of nominal scaling, because subjects are labeled as being in one group or another. When a nominal scale is used, there can be many or few classes, and as few as one member of each class. Thus the numbers that team members wear on their uniforms constitute a nominal scale. If there are 24 members on a team, each with a different number, then there are 24 classes, each with one member. By contrast, in the aspirin study, there were four classes in all: (1) aspirin/no heart attack; (2) aspirin/heart

TABLE 5-1 Levels of Measurement

Type of Scale	Relationship	Example
Nominal	Same; different	Presence/absence of heart attack
Ordinal	Greater than; less than	Color preferences
Interval	Equal intervals	Imagery; concreteness
Ratio	Equal intervals and a true zero	Height; weight

attack; (3) no aspirin/no heart attack, and (4) no aspirin/heart attack. When a nominal scale is used, it is usually of interest to count the number of cases in each class. The most frequently occurring class is the mode. The mode is the only measure of central tendency available when a nominal scale is used.

Ordinal Scales

An *ordinal scale* has all the properties of a nominal scale but in addition permits comparisons between individual measurements. For an ordinal scale, one measurement is *greater than* (>) or *less than* (<) any other measurement. Suppose that you were asked to rank order your color preference for a shirt among blue, green, yellow, black, and red. You might say, for example, that blue was your first choice, red your second choice, yellow your third choice, green your fourth choice, and black your fifth choice. This *rank order* is an example of an ordinal scale: rank 1 is greater than rank 2, which in turn is greater than rank 3, and so on. The difference between the ranks may not be equal, however. You may prefer blue just a little bit more than red but prefer both of them much more than green. Another example is the variable of *social class*, which we considered previously in relation to Galton's work. Social class can be measured by different occupations, ranging from professional (e.g., physicians) to unskilled workers. A third example of an ordinal scale is *academic rank*. While professors rank higher than associate professors, who in turn rank higher than assistant professors, it would be difficult to argue that there are equal intervals between the ranks.

When an ordinal scale is used, then one can calculate not only the mode but also the median of the resulting distribution of scores. Since scores are arranged from low to high, one can calculate the percentage of scores above or below any scale value, and the median is, of course, that value above and below which half of the scores lie.

Interval Scales

At the next level, *interval scale*, the differences between adjacent values of the scale are equal. These equal differences constitute the *unit* of the scale. *Temperature* is often used as an example of this kind of scale (e.g., Stevens, 1968). For example, the Fahrenheit temperature scale has a unit called a *degree* (°). The difference between 68° and 69° is the same as the difference between 69° and 70°. When an interval scale is used, one can calculate the mean (average) of a set of scores, as well as the median and mode.

A great deal of data in psychology is treated as interval-scale data. For example, earlier we considered Paivio's rating scales for imagery and concreteness. Rating-scale data are generally regarded as interval-scale data. That is, intervals between adjacent values of the rating scale are assumed to be equal. Any time you find a study in which a mean has been computed, then the investigator is assuming that the scale underlying the data has at least the properties of an interval scale.

Ratio Scales

Ratio scales have all the properties of interval scales, plus a true zero. Variables such as *height* and *weight* are measured using ratio scales. Such scales have units, such as *meters* and *kilograms*, and these scales begin at 0. In psychology, ratio scales are often used to measure physical properties such as height and weight. *Time* is also measured using a ratio scale, since time is measured in units such as hours, minutes, and seconds and can be calculated from a true zero. Time is a very frequent measure in psychology. The time taken to perform a task, for example, is a staple dependent variable in many psychological experiments. Of course, on a broader level, developmental studies also typically involve time. Measurement of the time at which events occur during a person's life span is a common variable in psychology. We will examine some experiments involving time throughout the book.

Standard Research Materials

Psychological investigators often use standard research materials to gather data. Such materials include many psychological tests, such as intelligence and personality tests. Your department may maintain a test bank that includes tests that are available for you to use in your research projects. You should check with your instructor concerning the test policy in force at your institution. Some tests require supervision when they are used, and others may be used only by researchers who have met certain professional criteria. There are a number of research materials, however, that are in the public domain and are used widely in many types of research. These materials are so numerous as to preclude a thorough review, but we will examine a few representative examples.

- Wherever possible, you should use established research materials and procedures. Through their use you will become familiar not only with existing practices in psychology but also with both the strengths and weaknesses of research in a particular area.

Linguistic Norms

One way or another, a great deal of psychological research involves the use of *words*. Because language is such an important part of people's lives, it inevitably finds its way into many kinds of psychological research. Linguistic units, such as words (e.g., Benjafield & Muckenheim, 1989), proverbs (e.g., Benjafield, Frommhold, Keenan, Muckenheim, & Mueller, 1993; Higbee & Millard, 1983), and metaphors (Katz, Paivio, & Marschark, 1985) are often used as stimulus materials in psychological experiments. Psychologists have spent a great deal of time and effort uncovering some of the more important psychological characteristics of these linguistic units. Once these characteristics are known, they can be used to control for a variety of factors in psychological experiments. There are several sources that provide useful normative data on words.

Word-Frequency Norms

One of the classic works on words, a *word frequency* book, was produced by Thorndike and Lorge (1944). It provides estimates of the relative frequency of occurrence of words in the English language. Thorndike and Lorge arrived at their estimates by counting the frequency of occurrence of words in magazines. The frequency with which a word occurs in a language is an independent variable that can have substantial effects in many experimental situations. For that reason, experiments often need to control for word frequency. More recently, Kucera and Francis (1967) have compiled a word frequency book that is probably the most frequently used work of its kind. If you have a need for word-frequency norms, the Kucera and Francis source should probably be your first choice, because it is so widely used and well known. The norms provided by Carroll, Davies, and Richman (1971) can also be very useful, however, partly because they provide data for the *grade level* at which a word is typically expected to be acquired.

Experimentally Derived Linguistic Norms

In addition to developing norms based on samples of written language, several psychologists have obtained people's reactions to different aspects of language. They observe people's reactions under carefully controlled laboratory conditions. Among the most famous of these norms are those obtained by Paivio, Yuille, and Madigan (1968). In fact, the Paivio et al. data base is one of the most frequently cited articles in the history of psychology (Rubin & Friendly, 1986). The frequency with which the Paivio et al. article cited is a measure of how useful other researchers find it. Paivio and his coworkers provided norms for 925 words on such scales as imagery and concreteness (which were defined in Chapter 3). Subsequently, other researchers have added to the norms existing for these words. For example, Rubin and Friendly (1986) have provided *goodness* and other data for the same 925 words. (*Goodness* refers to how people feel about a word and is measured by a scale anchored by the words *good* and *bad*.) The existence of such a large amount of information about these words makes them very useful in experiments. If you are ever doing a study that requires words as stimuli, you should investigate these *linguistic norms*.

The Paivio et al. (1968) list contains primarily words that are reasonably familiar to most speakers whose first language is English. Benjafield and Muckenheim (1989) have provided imagery, concreteness, goodness, and familiarity norms for a set of 1,046 words, many of which are highly unfamiliar. If you are ever doing research that requires unfamiliar words, by all means take a look at the Benjafield and Muckenheim list.

Alternative Methods of Gathering Data and Their Limitations

In Chapter 4, we examined several experiments, all of which involved the use of *subjects*. Sometimes these studies required the use of *several* subjects in a laboratory, as in the Paivio (1965) experiment on imagery and verbal learning. Other times there was only *one* subject, as in the Rosenfeld and Baer (1969) study of experimenter-subject interactions. Sometimes the study was conducted outside of the laboratory altogether, as in the Schachter et al. (1991) study of hesitation pauses. Other times subjects carried out the experimental instructions outside the laboratory but were tested in the laboratory, as in the Greenwald, Spangenberg, Pratkanis, and Eskanazi (1991) study of "subliminal" tapes. As you can see, almost anything is possible, and if it is possible, then some psychologist is almost certain to have done it!

Although collecting data in experiments is a normal procedure in psychology, it is possible to do useful research without running any subjects at all, for much interesting data have already been collected and are just waiting to be explored. Many of these data are stored in libraries. Other raw data are published in books. Such data are called *archival*, and research using this kind of data is called *archival research* (Simonton, 1981, 1984, 1988). In addition to being useful for quasi-experiments, archival data are often much easier to come by than are data that must be gathered experimentally.

As we observed in Chapter 4, in our discussion of quasi-experiments, data that are not gathered under controlled conditions are often (although not always) more difficult to interpret than are experimental data. They can, however, also be a source of hypotheses that can be tested more systematically. Moreover, archival data can lead to very provocative hypotheses and provide a window on phenomena that are difficult to examine experimentally. Here is an example.

Archival Research: A Case Study

One of the most obvious differences between people is *handedness*. Most people are right-handed, but a noticeable percentage of the population is left-handed. The percentage of the population that is right-handed is shown in Figure 5-2, which is taken from Coren and Halpern (1991, p. 91). Notice that the percentage of right-handers increases with age.

- Why, do you think, would the percentage of right-handers increase with age?

Coren and Halpern believe that there are two possible explanations for the phenomenon. They call one *modification* and the other *elimination*. According to the modification hypothesis, left-handers are pressured to become right-handers. This pressure may take many forms. Teachers and parents may try to get a left-hander to perform tasks in the more common, right-handed, way. Coren and Halpern review evidence that many left-handers have been forced to write with their right hands, for example. Moreover, most tools and appliances are designed to be used by right-handers. Coren and Halpern cite scissors and stem-wound wristwatches as examples. What other examples can you name?

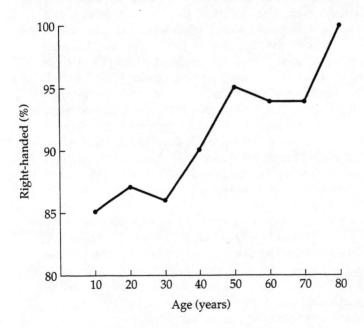

FIGURE 5-2   Percentage of Population Who Are Right Handers as a Function of Age

Source: "Left-handedness: A Marker for Decreased Survival Fittness" By S. Coren and D. F. Halpern, 1991, *Psychological Bulletin, 109*, 91. Copyright 1991 by the American Psychological Association. Reprinted by permission.

- Why is the evidence for the modification hypothesis not entirely persuasive? How might the data in Figure 5-2 be inconsistent with the modification hypothesis?

Porac, Coren, and Searleman (1986) presented data suggesting that most people who change from being a left-hander to being a right-hander *do so at a young age*. However, the data in Figure 5-2 show a *continuous decline* in left-handers over the entire life span. This suggests that the modification hypothesis does not represent the whole story. It does not explain the data in Figure 5-2 adequately.

What about the alternative hypothesis suggested by Coren and Halpern? According to the elimination hypothesis, the data in Figure 5-2 come about because left-handers *tend to die* at an earlier age than do right-handers.

- How would you find out if left-handers die young? What kind of data might be useful in this case?

One of the tests of the elimination hypothesis carried out by Coren and Halpern (1991; Halpern & Coren, 1988) involved the use of an *archival data base*. The particular data base they used was Reichler's *Baseball Encyclopedia* (1979). This data base provided the sort of data that Coren and Halpern needed, for a large number of individuals: throwing hand, batting hand, birth date, and date of death. Coren and Halpern found records for 1,472 "strong" right-handers (who both batted and threw right-handed) and 236 "strong" left-handers. Players with "mixed" handedness, who threw with one hand but batted with another, were excluded from the sample. Coren and Halpern analyzed these data in several ways. For example, they showed that many more right-handers survived to the age of 90 than did left-handers. Although their analyses have been challenged (e.g., Anderson, 1989; Wood, 1988), Coren and Halpern's studies are an interesting example of the uses to which easily accessible archival data bases can be put.

The *Baseball Encyclopedia* has been used to test hypotheses about entirely different topics from that examined by Coren and Halpern (e.g., Baumeister & Steinhilber, 1984). In addition to the *Baseball Encyclopedia*, data bases from other sports are freely available. For example, the *National Hockey League Official Guide and Record Book* (1991) is an annual compendium of statistics related to that sport. You should spend some time browsing in data bases like these. Just leafing through them may suggest hypotheses to you.

As an example of yet another archival source of very useful data, consider Coren and Porac's (1977) use of art books. People have created art for thousands of years. Coren and Porac examined art made at various periods to determine the frequency with which people are portrayed as using their left hand. Coren and Porac estimate the frequency of the phenomenon to have remained unchanged at 8% for over 5,000 years.

- What other kinds of books might contain data of interest to psychological researchers? Spend some time thinking about this. Also take a random walk through your library and examine any books that strike your fancy. While it is good to have a plan for research, it is also good to allow *serendipity* to play a role. Serendipity refers to fortunate chance occurrences and, as we will see, is acknowledged to be an important part of many successful scientists' work.

Names and Concepts to Understand and Remember

The following are some of the most influential ideas in the area we have just reviewed. Some concepts are quite general and are not associated with any particular psychologist. In other cases, however, the names of psychologists are paired with the concepts for which they are known. Read through the list. If any of the names or concepts seem unfamiliar to you, then go back and reread the appropriate section of the chapter. The names are in the order in which they are presented in the text, and the concepts are italicized in the text, so they are easy to find. You should be able to define each concept and briefly discuss it. You should also be able to write a brief account of the work done by each person on the list.

objectivity

peer review

domain-specific training

hot hand (in basketball)

cognitive illusions

curvilinear impetus principle

Stevens and levels of measurement: nominal scale, ordinal scale, interval scale, and ratio scale

linguistic norms

word frequency

archival research

Coren and Halpern and handedness: modification versus elimination

archival data bases

serendipity

Additional Reading

The relation between levels of measurement and statistical analysis is explored by Davison and Sharma (1990).

6

The Context of Discovery

The Context of Discovery

Even if we know all about experimental design, we still need to be able to come up with an idea around which to design an experiment. In this chapter we will examine some of the possible sources of hypotheses. The generation of hypotheses worth testing is a creative process. First, we need to define the phrase *creative process*. The term *creative* has recently been defined as "the production of novel, socially valued products" (Mumford & Gustafson, 1988, p. 28), and this definition has received widespread acceptance. To produce something creative means more than just producing something novel or original; it also means producing something that is appropriate for the situation in which one is working (Vinacke, 1974, p. 354). Thus an original hypothesis would not be a creative hypothesis unless it aimed at solving a significant problem (Mumford & Gustafson, 1988, p. 28). How do we come up with creative hypotheses? Let us now have a look at some possible sources of such original and useful ideas.

Two Case Histories

Vernon (1970) collected some autobiographical descriptions of the creative process. We will consider two of these—both by musicians. The classic description of the process of discovery is Mozart's (1789/1970). Most of us have a stereotype of genuine creative inspiration, and Mozart's description fits this stereotype very well.

- Mozart claims that he has no idea where his ideas come from; they just appear to him when he is alone. This statement fits with the notion that inspiration has a passive, receptive nature. "*Whence* and *how* they come I know not; nor can I force them" (Mozart, 1789/1970, p. 55).
- Mozart (1789/1970, p. 55) also says that "the whole, though it be long, stands almost complete and finished in my mind, so that I can survey it, like a fine picture or a beautiful statue, at a glance. Nor do I hear in my imagination the parts *successively*, but I hear them, as it were, all at once." Mozart describes the process of *insight* as occurring suddenly and presenting him with a complete solution, or *gestalt*. Although there is no adequate translation in English for the word *gestalt*, it is generally taken to mean "configuration" or "form." When something is experienced *as a whole*, rather than as a collection of disparate parts, then it makes sense to say that it is experienced as a gestalt. Mozart describes the process of inspiration as resulting in this kind of experience.
- Since his ideas come to him more or less complete and fully formed, he can simply write them down, with no need for revision.

Would it not be wonderful if we could all think in the way that Mozart said that he thought? If all researchers were like Mozart, then we could afford to sit alone, relax, and wait for the insight to arrive. There are, however, many productive people who do not get their ideas "for free" the way that Mozart says he did. One famous example is another composer, Tchaikovsky (1878/1970), who noted that work was always necessary with or without inspiration. "We must *always* work, and a self-respecting artist must not fold his hands on the pretext that he is not in the mood. If we wait for the mood, without endeavoring to meet it halfway, we easily become indolent and apathetic. We must be patient and believe that inspiration will come to those who can master their *disinclination*" (p. 58). This is good advice for a would-be scientist, just as it is good advice for a would-be composer. For most of us, good ideas come from continuous work, whether we like it or not. It simply will not do to wait until you are "in the mood."

Tchaikovsky (1878/1970) also observed that he often had to revise his ideas before they were ready for the public. Similarly, in research, one may have to alter one's ideas several times before they are in a useful form. The two cases of Mozart and Tchaikovsky alone show us that the creative process is not the same for everyone. One can arrive at a very high level of thinking by different routes. As we observed earlier, there is more than one way to skin a cat. A more formal way of making the same point is to say that creative behavior is *equifinal*. Equifinality refers to the fact that goals can often be achieved by different behaviors (Kaplan, 1983; Werner, 1937).

If you are one of those people, like Mozart, to whom good ideas come easily, then lucky you! If, however, you need to work for your ideas, then it might be reassuring to know that many other people are in the same boat. Generally, people seem to have vague *intuitions* before they have clear ideas.

Intuition

Bowers, Regehr, Balthazard, and Parker (1990) have recently studied intuition using an intriguing procedure called the *dyads of triads* task, which is a variant of a well-known test of creative-thinking ability (Mednick, 1967). Subjects receive a series of items, each of which consists of two sets (dyads) of three words each (triads). For one of the triads, there is a fourth word that makes sense in relation to the other three words. These triads are called *coherent* triads. An example of a coherent triad might be *new, good,* and *leap*. The word *year* makes sense in relation to all three of these words, as in *New Year, leap year,* and *Goodyear*. The other triad is called *incoherent*, because there is no known word that makes sense in relation to all three words. An example of an incoherent triad might be *juice, gun,* and *rat*.

Bowers et al. were interested in whether or not subjects could tell the difference between coherent and incoherent triads. In their experiment, Bowers et al. presented subjects with both a coherent and an incoherent triad for a few seconds. Subjects were asked to indicate which of the two triads they believed to be the coherent one.

Subjects tended to choose the proper (coherent) triad, although they often did so without being able to say the fourth word. Thus suppose subjects had been given a coherent triad such as *chase, work,* and *news.* They might be able to identify this as a coherent triad, without being able to come up with the fourth word, *paper* (as in *paperchase, paperwork,* and *newspaper*). Bowers et al. suggested that subjects are able to select the coherent triad on the basis of a vague hunch, or *intuition,* that there was a fourth word that completed the triad.

According to the *Oxford English Dictionary,* one of the older meanings of the word *intuition* was the form of *immediate knowledge* that was said to occur to angelic and spiritual beings. Subsequently, *intuition* came to mean a form of immediate understanding that could occur to anyone. It appears that the subjects in the Bowers et al. experiment have this kind of immediate understanding in the form of a vague hypothesis about the coherent triad, but the subjects are not fully aware of that hypothesis. The Bowers et al. experiment can be profitably considered in relation to the distinction we considered earlier between the context of discovery and the context of justification. Intuition may be particularly useful in the former contexts. At first, you may have only a vague idea about what direction your research should take. Such a hunch may be no more than a feeling that a particular approach to a problem might be worthwhile. However, such an intuition may prove to be a valuable beginning to the process whereby you formulate a testable hypothesis.

When you begin to work on a research problem, you may have only a vague idea of what you should study. This vague sense of what you should do may become sharper as you continue to work on the problem. You should have a feeling that you are "getting warm" as you get closer and closer to a clear idea of what you want to do. It appears likely that you can trust your *feelings of warmth* as you work on a problem (Metcalfe & Wiebe, 1987). These feelings of warmth may reflect the fact that a lot of work goes on outside of awareness before a solution presents itself in a conscious form.

Wallas and Stages of the Creative Process

At this point it is useful to consider the well-known description of the creative process introduced by Wallas (1926). Wallas suggested that there are four stages in the process of discovery:

1. *Preparation,* during which the problem is formulated, and information relevant to it is gathered

It is impossible to overestimate the importance of this first phase. It is during this initial period that you may read as much as you can about the topic that interests you, talk to as many people as possible about the topic, and generally familiarize yourself with your research area. There are a great many sources of information in psychology. Several are summarized in Reed and Baxter (1992). However, people often overlook sources of information that are unique to their particular interest. *There is no substitute for talking to a reference librarian about your particular interest.* Reference librarians are specially trained to search out information from sources that are not generally known to library patrons. Do not be shy about it. It is the job of a reference librarian to assist you in your search for information. Moreover, your public library, in addition to your college or university library, may be a rewarding source of information.

2. *Incubation,* during which you do not consciously work on the problem. Unconscious work on the problem may go on nevertheless.

You may not be able to go directly from the preparation phase to discovering a solution. It is important to give yourself enough time before any deadlines to think a problem through. Any research problem presents you with alternative possible courses of action. Sorting through the implications of all these possibilities takes time. Some of the "sorting through" may take place without your paying very much attention to it (e.g., Simonton, 1984, 1988).

A famous example of the way in which alternative possibilities may be evaluated "unconsciously" was given by Poincaré (1924/1960), who recounted the way in which he discovered a theorem concerned with Fuchsian functions. We do not need to know what Fuchsian functions are in order to appreciate the process by which Poincaré came to discover his theorem.

> For a fortnight I had been attempting to prove that there could not be any function analogous to what I have since called Fuchasian functions. I was at that time very ignorant. Every day I sat down at my table, and spent an hour or two trying a great number of combinations, and I arrived at no result. One night I took some black coffee, contrary to my custom, and was unable to sleep. A host of ideas kept surging in my head; I could almost feel them jostling one another, until two of them coalesced, so to speak, to form a stable combination. When morning came, I had established the existence of one class of Fuchsian functions, those that are derived from the hyper geometric series. I had only to verify the results, which only took a few hours. (p. 53)

Poincaré believed that the unusual conditions of that evening provided him with an insight into processes that usually occur without our knowledge. We may initially spend much time formulating a problem. We may then let the problem "lie fallow," and not pay much attention to it. During this *incubation period*, there may actually be a lot of " unconscious" work going on.

> What is the part to be played by the preliminary conscious work? Clearly it is evidently to liberate some of these atoms, to detach them from the wall and set them in motion. We think we have accomplished nothing, when we have stirred these elements in a thousand different ways to try to arrange them, and have not succeeded in finding a satisfactory arrangement. But after this agitation imparted to them by our will, they do not return to their original repose, but continue to circulate freely. (p. 61)

The existence of an incubation period as a component of the discovery process has been a controversial issue for many years. Recent research suggests that an incubation period may play an important role in at least some cases (e.g., Goldman, Wolters, & Winograd, 1992). Whether or not the incubation period is actually unconscious, however, or involves a more conscious process of analysis, is still a very open question.

3. *Illumination.* If all goes well, a potential solution occurs to you.

4. *Verification.* There is no guarantee that a *potential* solution is a *real* solution. A potential solution must be properly evaluated.

Verification is a process that requires the kinds of experimental design and observational procedures we have discussed already. Even something experienced as a great insight may turn out to be wrong. Evaluation of one's insights is a central part of the research enterprise.

Studies have not yielded very great support for the existence of discrete stages in the creative process. Rather than there being one clearly defined sequence, it may be that we cycle through the four stages a number of times before a workable solution is found (Vinacke, 1974). Thus we may return to the preparation stage to acquire more information, or spend more time reflecting on the problem at any point in the solution process. Moreover, a period of unconscious work may not be necessary in order for a number of alternative solutions to be generated and evaluated. There are existing procedures that allow you to vary your thinking deliberately (Crovitz, 1970), and we will consider some of them below.

Skinner's Approach to Creativity in Research

B. F. Skinner, one of the most-renowned psychological researchers of all time, wrote about some of the ways in which productive ideas had occurred to him. His approach is quite different from any we have considered thus far. Based on his personal experience, Skinner (1956) offered the following list of "unformalized principles of scientific practice":

> When you run into something interesting, drop everything else and study it. (p. 223)

> Some ways of doing research are easier than others. (p. 224)

> Some people are lucky. (p. 225)

> Apparatuses sometimes break down. (p. 225)

Although these "principles" may seem almost frivolous, Skinner is making a very serious point by advancing them. In the course of preparing yourself for research on a particular topic, you may discover something that intrigues you more than what you initially set out to investigate, and that is eminently researchable. You would be wise, from Skinner's viewpoint, to take advantage of this fortunate circumstance. Similarly, there is no reason why good research needs to be difficult. Sometimes the easiest and simplest ways of doing things are also the most effective. If something goes wrong in your research, try to determine if the cause of the breakdown might not lead to a research topic worth pursuing. As Epstein (1991) noted, Skinner's approach to creativity emphasized *generativity:* behavior is inevitably and spontaneously novel, and thus we are continuously being presented with new opportunities to explore.

The preceding four "principles" can be summarized by the following:

> *Serendipity:* the art of finding one thing while looking for something else. (p. 227)

Serendipity is defined by the *Oxford English Dictionary* as "the faculty of making happy discoveries by accident." The dictionary notes, as does Skinner (1956, p. 227), that the word was coined by Horace Walpole, an eighteenth-century British politician. Walpole used it to refer to people who "were always making discoveries, by accident and *sagacity*, of things they were not in quest of" (italics added).

Sagacity

In his statement, Walpole was drawing attention to a feature of serendipity that is not always brought out, namely, that it not only involves luck but also requires *sagacity*. *Sagacity* is defined by the *Oxford English Dictionary* as the "aptitude for investigation or discovery; keenness and soundness of judgement in the estimation of persons and conditions, and in the adaptation of means to ends." One of the greatest psychologists, William James (1890, p. 331), regarded sagacity as particularly important. James put it this way:

> A library, a museum, a machine shop, are mere confused wholes to the uninstructed, but the machinist, the antiquary and the bookworm perhaps hardly notice the whole at all, so eager are they to pounce upon the details. Familiarity has in them bred discrimination. . . . A layman present at a shipwreck, a battle, or a fire is helpless. Discrimination has been so little awakened in him by experience that his consciousness leaves no single point of the complex situation accented and standing out for him to begin to act upon. But the sailor, the fireman, and the general know directly at what corner to take up the business. They "see into the situation"—that is, they analyze it—with their first glance. (p. 344)

For James (1890, p. 331), to be sagacious is to be a good observer; to be able to discern that something is important when it occurs. Such an ability may be a central aspect of discovery process (e.g., Lockhart, Lamon, & Gick, 1987). It may not be enough just to be lucky. Rather, when a fortunate event occurs, you have to be sagacious enough to discern what is important about it. Skinner was certainly sagacious in his research. When his apparatus broke down, he knew enough to be able to take advantage of the opportunity. That is the key thing—knowing enough. The importance of sagacity brings us back to the importance of preparation. The researcher must be prepared, well informed, and knowledgeable, in order to exploit any lucky accidents that occur.

The Role of "Tools"

Thus far we have stressed the role that individual investigators play in the discovery process, and have described their experiences as a crucial part of this process. Gigerenzer (1991) has observed that while most discussions of the discovery process focus on the individual investigator, it is only part of the story. Recall that one of Skinner's "principles" was that sometimes apparatuses break down. This principle draws attention to the important role that pieces of apparatus may play. Gigerenzer has also documented the influence of *tools* in the process of scientific discovery. Gigerenzer describes a *tools-to-theories heuristic* whereby a research tool is itself crucial in shaping important scientific principles.

A *heuristic* is a rule of thumb or an informal procedure for solving problems. Heuristics should be thought of by contrast with *algorithms*. An algorithm is a procedure that is guaranteed to find a solution. Thus long division is an algorithm. Although it is tedious, it is sure to give you the right answer if you do it properly. Heuristics are not guaranteed to give you the solution but are useful guidelines. Here are some examples of heuristics taken from Parker (1983) that are practical in everyday life:

- Up to 25% of the guests at a university dinner party can come from the economics department without spoiling the conversation.
- The number of guests at a child's birthday party should be limited to the age of the child. Invite three for a three year old, five for a five year old.
- People will eat one-and-a-half to two times the number of potatoes mashed that they would eat baked.
- To estimate the temperature outdoors in degrees Fahrenheit, count the number of times a lone cricket chirps in 15 seconds and add 37.

There is a role for algorithms in scientific discovery, and we will discuss it further below. The role of heuristics in scientific discovery cannot be discounted, however. Gigerenzer points out, as have many other scholars (e.g. Schultz & Schultz, 1992, p. 25) that the history of science is replete with examples of machines that have been treated as models of human nature. Consider this quote from Hobbes (1651, as cited by Mischel, 1967, p. 5): "What is the heart but a spring, the nerves strings, the joints wheels giving motion to the whole body." Hobbes is using tools such as springs and wheels to provide models for the way that the body works. Although the heart is not really a spring, Hobbes found it useful (heuristic) to think about it that way.

Although Gigerenzer does not mention it, another good example of the heuristic use of machines may be found in the work of the eighteenth-century inventor Jacques de Vaucanson (Fryer & Marshall, 1979) who built not only a statue that played the flute but also a duck that "stretches out its neck to take corn out of your hand, . . . swallows it, and discharges it digested by the usual passage" (Fryer & Marshall, 1979, p. 267). Figure 6-1 is a picture of de Vaucanson's duck. These models were not merely entertainments, although they did intrigue Louis XVI, but a part of a serious attempt to embody a theory of human nature. If people are like machines, then you should be able to build a machine that is indistinguishable from a person. Once a psychologist begins to see organisms as complex machines, then she or he is well on the way to creating a general and very powerful psychological theory, since everything that is known about the machine will also apply to the person. For generations, scientists have been so impressed with the similarity between people and machines that they often try to build machines to simulate people, believing that if they are successful, they will have shown that they really understand people. This is an idea that many people in our era have had about computers, believing that computers will ultimately be able to mimic everything that people do. The important point for our purposes is that, whether ultimately correct or not, machines have functioned as heuristic

FIGURE 6-1 A Duck Made by Jacques de Vaucanson

devices for the construction of psychological theories. This is a point we will return to later on.

In addition to the computer, among the tools that have functioned as models are the telephone switchboard, the thermostat, and the hologram, all of which, according to Pribram (1981, p. 105), illustrate the use of *abduction.* Abduction is a term that originally described the act of leading something away illegally, such as leading a farmer's horse away illegally. It implied that something was being taken from its proper place and used somewhere else. Over the years, the meaning of the word *abduction* has been generalized to many situations. The American philosopher C. S. Pierce (1934) used it to refer to a form of reasoning. Abduction involves reasoning by analogy and "brings to bear on the familiar a new perspective derived from another realm of inquiry" (Pribram, 1981, p. 106). Each tool provides a kind of lens through which to see an area of inquiry. When the telephone switchboard was a popular model, then the nervous system was seen as a vast network of individual connections between inputs and outputs. To some extent, that model persists today. Other tools highlight different aspects of a topic. For example, Gigerenzer (1991, p. 263) cites the case of Tolman, whom we considered earlier. Recall Tolman's interpretation of maze learning. Tolman used the maze as a model of the mind (Smith, 1986), conceiving of the mind as a way of representing the spatial layout of the environment.

On a more personal level, you might do well to adopt a tools heuristic in your own research. Not only can tools function to generate major theoretical changes, but they can also bring about smaller changes in the way individual scientists approach particular research problems. A perennial obstacle for beginning researchers is simply to find a research topic. One way to proceed is to familiarize yourself with the tools that psychologists have used to do research. As a way of generating ideas, ask yourself as you examine each instrument "What could I do with that tool?" Of course, you need someplace to look for tools. I would recommend browsing in *Behavior Research Methods, Instruments and Computers*. This journal contains notices and reviews of research methods that are of interest to a broad range of psychologists. Do not browse only in the current journals, but look at back issues as well.

Algorithms

In addition to heuristics, researchers often make use of algorithms to generate new possibilities. As Gardner (1968) described in detail, the history of algorithms is full of useful techniques. Some of these appear to be more historical curiosities than anything else. A procedure invented by Ramon Lull in the thirteenth century is such a case. Lull wanted to be able to think about all possible ideas in all possible combinations. He invented devices to try to generate such combinations. One such device was the rotating circle, as shown in Figure 6-2. The letters stand for various ideas. By rotating the inner circle, one could create all possible combinations of categories. Gardner outlined several more sophisticated ways of generating all the possibilities. Of

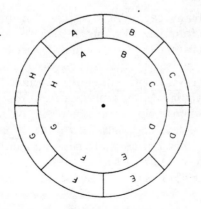

FIGURE 6-2 One of Ramon Lull's Concentric Wheels

Source: Logic Machines and Diagrams by M. Gardner, 1982, Chicago: University of Chicago Press. Reprinted by permission.

course, computers often do this kind of work for us nowadays. Still, it can be instructive for a researcher to consider explicitly all possible combinations of the variables in which he or she is interested.

Crovitz (1970, chap. 8) took procedures such as Lull's one step farther when he introduced what he called the *relational algorithm*. This procedure not only generates all possible combinations of variables but also considers these combinations as they bear different relations to one another. Lull's wheel, and devices like it, are usually taken as providing conjunctive relations, such as A *and* B. However, as we saw when we considered various types of concepts in Chapter 2, there are many other relations that can obtain between ideas, such as *disjunction (not both* A *and* B), and it can be useful to consider these combinations as well.

Just Do It!

When I was a graduate student at Brandeis University, I took a course in research methods from George Kelly (1955). Kelly's work has been very influential in Britain but, strangely, has been neglected in his American homeland (e.g., Jankowicz, 1987). Before taking Kelly's course, I had taken a number of other courses in research methods, all of which stressed the proper way of designing and conducting an experiment. In these courses I had been taught that there were very definite right ways and wrong ways of doing research, and that it was very important to plan your research carefully before doing it. To my surprise, Kelly took a very different approach. His focus was on the process of discovery, which we have been considering in this chapter.

Kelly observed that many beginning researchers spend endless hours planning their research before they encounter a subject or gather any data. Kelly tried to preempt that process. For our first project in Kelly's course, we were required to explain our research interests to a child no older than five. I regarded this project as lunatic. After all, I believed myself to be a serious student of psychology, with sophisticated ideas that would be incomprehensible to a five year old (or so I thought). Nevertheless, I was also a student in Kelly's course, and since I *did* want to pass the course, I complied with his instructions. I arranged to talk to a student in a nursery school in downtown Boston. At first I had no idea what to say to her. She was about 5; I was about 25. I began by saying that I was interested in psychology, but she had no idea what psychology was. For no reason in particular, I noticed a box of tissues on a table beside her and asked, "How would you find out what is in that box?" She replied, in a bored tone of voice, that you would open up the box and look inside. Then I asked her, "How would you find out what someone is thinking?" She paused and then said that you would "open up their head." Immediately after she said it, she began to laugh, perhaps realizing that opening up people's heads might cause problems. Then she and I had a very lively conversation about how, in fact, one might find out what goes on in people's heads. It was a conversation that began to change my mind about what I was interested in at that point in my career. For the first time, I realized that children might not only be interesting in their own right but also have some interesting things to say about mental life. I wrote a paper about our conversation, and much to my relief Kelly generously gave me a good mark.

Why is this episode worth recalling? Because it illustrates how one's hypotheses can be changed in unanticipated ways when one pays attention to what might be called *prescientific experience*. My encounter with that child was not in any way a formal test of any hypothesis. And yet it did change some hypotheses I had about children, even though I did not explicitly attempt to test them. My hypotheses would have gone unchallenged if I had never spoken to that child. Kelly's point in making his students talk to young children was that the only way to find out what your hypotheses really are is to try them out informally, rather than just sitting around thinking about them or just making sure you are familiar with the literature. Your professors and fellow students are not the only ones on whom you can try out your hypotheses in this manner. Anyone will do. In fact, the less the other person knows about your work, the more you will be forced to *really think* about what you are doing so that you can put it in terms that someone else can understand. Such a clarification of your ideas could be very worthwhile.

It is difficult to get out of the classroom and talk to ordinary people about your ideas. But, as the saying goes,

Just do it!

Names and Concepts to Understand and Remember

The following are some of the most influential ideas in the area we have just reviewed. Some concepts are quite general and are not associated with any particular psychologist. In other cases, however, the names of psychologists are paired with the concepts for which they are known. Read through the list. If any of the names or concepts seem unfamiliar to you, then go back and reread the appropriate section of the chapter. The names are in the order in which they are presented in the text, and the concepts are italicized in the text, so they are easy to find. You should be able to define each concept and briefly discuss it. You should also be able to write a brief account of the work done by each person on the list.

creative process (Mozart, Tchaikovsky)

insight

Gestalt

equifinal

Bowers et al. and dyads of triads

discovery phase

Wallas and the four stages of the creative process

Skinner and generativity

sagacity

tools-to-theories heuristic

abduction

Crovitz and the relational algorithm

Additional Reading

Scientific genius and creativity (1987).

A very good example of what Tchaikovsky is talking about is Galton's discovery (1886) of "regression" (Fancher, 1979, p. 286). Campbell (1960) is a classic, highly influential paper on the process of discovery.

7

Experiments
to Think About

Harré (1983) reviewed several famous experiments in the history of science. His goal was to present experiments that "had a significant impact on the science of the day, that exerted considerable influence on the subsequent development of a scientific discipline, and that exemplified a certain aspect of the logical or methodological interdependence of observation, report and theory" (Losee, 1985, p. 92). In what follows, we will present studies that meet at least some of these criteria. We will not try to select the most famous psychological experiments, although some of the experiments described below are, indeed, famous. Harré included 2 psychological experiments, by Gibson (1962) and by Lorenz (1952), among the 20 in his collection. Most of the experiments we will consider, however, are interesting examples of their kind, rather than being the most famous experiments in their class. There are two additional criteria that were used to select experiments:

1. Their pedagogical value. You should begin to appreciate the extent to which psychologists have used experimental methods to attack a very wide range of problems. Such experiments are often ingenious and clever.
2. Their simplicity. Most of the experiments included below can be replicated fairly easily, without a great deal of apparatus. It would be a useful exercise for you to try to replicate one or more of them.

Each of the following experiments not only illustrates an approach to a different problem, but is often only one experiment in a series (perhaps done by several different investigators) that progressively refines a problem. As each experiment is reviewed, you will be encouraged to anticipate the problems, and opportunities, that may be discovered in the experiment being considered.

We will adopt a variation of Harré's classification system, modified to suit our purposes. As is the case with virtually any classification system, some experiments can fit into more than one category. Thus you should not regard each experiment as necessarily illustrating only one kind of study, but you should also think about how it could illustrate other kinds of experiments. At various points in the text, you will see the word STOP, embedded in a box containing a question or questions. At that point, you should pause to consider the issues that are raised in the box. Try to answer the questions that are posed. Then go on to read the next section, which will discuss the issues raised in the box.

Finding the Form of a Law Inductively

The formulation of a law requires that the relationships between variables be defined in a precise way. In this section we will consider a case in which a lawful relationship has been defined, and then various attempts made to see if the law actually holds. A law may be defined as a broad and basic rule or truth. Sciences that are older and simpler than psychology often lay claim to certain laws. A typical, and famous, example is Isaac Newton's first law of motion (1687), which holds that "every body continues in a state of rest, or of uniform motion in a straight line, unless it is compelled to change that state by forces impressed upon it" Sears & Zemansky, 1970, p. 15). This is a statement of a general truth that has been supported by countless observations. In psychology, laws are not very common. This is partly because of the complexity of psychology, and partly because it is a young science (Reber, 1985, p. 394). There are, however, some relationships between psychological variables that may be sufficiently general to warrant being described as "laws." One such relationship is that discovered by Shepard and Metzler (1971).

Can We Measure
the Time Taken by Mental Processes?

The *Oxford English Dictionary* notes that the word *image* is both a noun ("a mental representation of something; a mental picture or impression") and a verb ("to imagine, picture in the mind, represent to oneself"). These are pretty vague definitions, and you might not think that such a fuzzy phenomenon would be subject to lawful relationships. The work by Shepard and Metzler (1971), however, suggested that in fact the motion of mental images was as lawful as the motion of objects in the real world. Consider the pairs of line drawings in Figure 7-1. In each case, try to decide whether or not the drawing on the left is of the same object as the drawing on the right. How do you make this decision? Shepard and Metzler's experiment was designed to show that subjects *mentally rotate* one of the objects to see if it matches the other object.

If you had been a subject in the Shepard and Metzler experiment, you would have seen 1,600 pairs of line drawings like those in Figure 7-1. Your task would have been to pull a lever with your right hand if you decided the pairs were the *same*, or to pull a lever with your left hand if you decided that the pairs were *different*. The dependent variable was the length of time it took to make a decision (called reaction time). There were several independent variables. One was the distance through which one object had to be rotated in order to determine if there was a match. This varied from 0° to 180°. Another independent variable was whether or not the two objects actually were the same (as in Figure 7-1A and B) or different (as in Figure 7-1C). Obviously, the objects cannot all be the same or all different, since there would then be no uncertainty for the subject. Finally, some pairs required only a two-dimensional rotation (called picture plane pairs; see

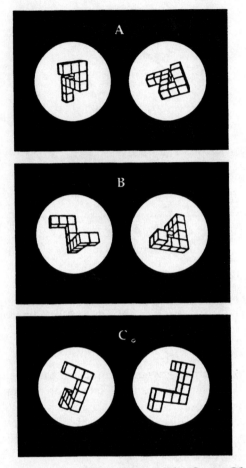

FIGURE 7-1 Which Pairs Are Drawings of the Same Object?

Source: "Mental Rotation of Three-Dimensional Objects" by R. N. Shepard and J. Metzler, 1971, *Science, 171,* 702. Copyright 1971 by the American Association for the Advancement of Science. Reprinted by permission.

Figure 7-1*A*), while for others the rotation required was in depth (called depth pairs; see Figure 7-1*B*).

Now examine Figure 7-2. It shows the relationship between reaction time and the angle though which the object had to be rotated in order to determine that they were the same. Notice that the relationship between these two variables is almost perfect. Such clear findings are rare in psychology. The greater the angular rotation required, the longer the reaction time. Shepard and Metzler interpreted these data as being consistent with the notion that subjects mentally rotate the drawings in order to determine

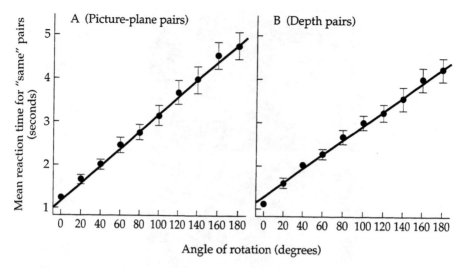

FIGURE 7-2 **Time Taken to Rotate an Object Mentally**

Source: "Mental Rotation of Three-Dimensional Objects" by R. N. Shepard and J. Metzler, 1971, *Science, 171,* 703. Copyright 1971 by the American Association for the Advancement of Science. Reprinted by permission.

whether or not there is a match between them. From their data, they computed the rate at which subjects apparently rotate an object, and found it to be approximately 60° per second. Several psychologists have observed that Shepard and Metzler may have discovered a psychological law relating the time to make a judgment to the angular distance between the pairs (e.g., Gardner, 1985, p. 325).

Shepard and Metzler's experiment has been replicated and extended many times (e.g., Pinker & Finke, 1980; Shepard & Cooper, 1982). Shepard (1984) has argued that there is a very close correspondence between the motion of imaginary objects and the perception of moving objects: "What we imagine, as much as what we perceive, are external objects; although in imagining, these objects may be absent or even non-existent" (p. 420).

One assumption that Shepard and Metzler made was that rotating an object mentally takes time. While this seems like an obvious assumption, it is nevertheless essential. It is essential because measuring how long it takes to rotate an object mentally is a basic way of getting data about the nature of objects. Shepard and Metzler's approach is an example of *mental chronometry.* Chronometry is the science of measuring time, and mental chronometry involves measuring the duration of mental processes (e.g., Posner, 1986). By giving subjects different tasks that require different times for completion, psychologists can estimate how much time is required to carry out the various components of these tasks.

STOP

Do any features of the Shepard and Metzler (1971) experiment seem to be required in order to generate these lawlike data? What changes in the procedure might produce less straightforward data?

Rock, Wheeler, and Tudor (1989) argue that the results that Shepard and others have found may occur only in *highly practiced tasks*. (The senior author of this paper is Irvin Rock, who is one of the most ingenious experimenters in the history of cognitive psychology. For over thirty years, he has been doing experiments that challenge widely held assumptions; we will examine another of his experiments below.) Recall that Shepard and Metzler gave their subjects 1,600 pairs of objects to judge. Perhaps if subjects were given a mental rotation task that was less well practiced, the results would change. Perhaps an experiment that required subjects to rotate mentally objects that have *unfamiliar* configurations would show something different than what Shepard and Metzler found.

Now examine the wire objects depicted in Figure 7-3. Can you imagine what these objects would look like if they were rotated by 90°? This seems like a much harder task than the one used by Shepard and Metzler. In fact, if you were a subject in Rock, Wheeler, and Tudor's experiment, you would be asked to imagine what wire objects like those in Figure 7-3 would look like if you moved to a position 90° to the right or left. Then your task would be to draw what the wire object would look like from that position. In their experiment, Rock, Wheeler, and Tudor found no evidence that subjects' drawings looked like what the objects would actually look like. Moreover, subjects themselves said that they had no confidence that they could imagine what the object looked like from another point of view. This observation was supported by another experiment in which subjects looked at a wire shape and were then given four drawings, one of which was of the shape, but drawn from a different perspective. While subjects could select the appropriate drawing at an above chance level, their performance was still not very good. Rock, Wheeler, and Tudor concluded that "the linear increase in time required to succeed in mental rotation tasks as a function of the angular discrepancy between the figures compared is the result of increasing difficulty rather than of the time required for rotation" (p. 185).

STOP

Rock et al.'s experiment may cast doubt on the generality of the Shepard-Metzler "law," but does this mean that Shepard and Metzler's experimental paradigm cannot be used to investigate other interesting phenomena? To what other uses could this paradigm, or paradigms like it, be put?

Imagine a familiar song, such as "Rudolf the Red-Nosed Reindeer" or "Battle Hymn of the Republic." Does the word *shiny* occur in "Rudolf the Red-Nosed Reindeer"? How do you know? The answer seems to be that we scan auditory images, such as imaginary songs, in a way that is analogous to

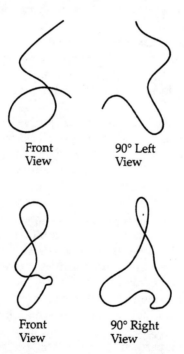

Front   90° Left
View   View

Front   90° Right
View   View

FIGURE 7-3 Wire Objects Used in Rock, Wheeler, and Tudor's Experiment

Source: "Can We Imagine How Objects Look from Other Viewpoints?" by I. Rock, D. Wheeler, and L. Tudor, 1989, *Cognitive Psychology, 21,* 189. Copyright 1989 by Academic Press. Reprinted by permission.

the way that we scan visual images. Remember that Shepard and Metzler (1971) showed that the farther away two targets were in space, the longer it took to determine a match. Auditory images are extended in time, rather than space. For example, a song has a beginning, a middle, and an end. It is just this feature of imaginary songs that Halpern (1988) explored.

Halpern studied auditory imagery for familiar songs, such as those listed in the previous paragraph. In one of her experiments, subjects were given a lyric from the beginning of a song, and then another lyric. Their task was to decide whether or not the second lyric was from the same song as the first. If the lyric was from the same song, the subject pressed a button labeled "true," but pressed a button labeled "false" if the lyric was not from the same song. The dependent measure was the reaction time to make a correct decision for lyrics that were from the same song. It turned out that these reaction times increased as the number of beats between the first and second lyrics increased. Halpern's results suggest that "subjects were operating on an analogous mental representation of the song in this task by mentally playing the songs when the second lyric was recognized as being part of the song" (1988, p. 436).

This study is an interesting variant of Shepard and Metzler's procedure. As in the Shepard and Metzler study, the subject makes "same-different" judgments, and the dependent variable is time to make a correct response. Rather than mental rotation, however, which is an activity of visual imagery, the process under study is mental scanning of an auditory image. Halpern's study illustrates the usefulness of transporting an experimental technique from one area and applying it in another.

Additional Reading
A very provocative review of work on mental imagery is Shepard (1978). Halpern's study was inspired by Kosslyn, Ball, and Reiser's work (1978) on mental scanning of a visual image. Franklin and Tversky (1990) is a recent article that uses a different, but highly interesting, technique for measuring subjects' response to the spatial properties of mental images.

How Many Life Events Can We Remember?

With the possible exception of people with severe memory disorders, almost everyone has a store of memories of events that happened in their lives. *Autobiographical memories* are memories of events in a person's own life. A person is usually capable of estimating roughly when each event occurred. Research in autobiographical memory has benefited from a technique, similar to one invented by Galton (1879a, 1879b), that was introduced by Crovitz and Schiffman (1974). They gave 98 subjects, who were undergraduate students at Duke University, a list of 20 words and asked each subject to generate a personal memory for each word. The subjects then dated these memories in terms of how long ago they occurred, in minutes, hours, days, weeks, months, and years. The words were all common nouns, such as *snake* and *palace*. Such words not only occur frequently in English but also easily elicit a mental image in most people. Notice that this technique is a very ingenious way of sampling personal memories. The list of 20 cue words is the same for everyone. The dependent variable is how long ago each memory is said to have occurred. Let us call this variable *time* (t). The technique enables the accumulation of data across subjects, and the possible discovery of a lawful relationship between t and the *frequency* (f) with which memories occur in each time interval.

Intuitively, you might expect that there would be more memories that refer to events experienced during the last year than to events that occurred five years ago, say. In fact, Crovitz and Schiffman found that the frequency of personal memories declined smoothly as a function of how long ago the event occurred. Crovitz and Schiffman used *logarithms* to express this relationship. As you probably know, a logarithm is the exponent to which one number must be raised to equal another number. Let us take a brief detour, in case you have not thought about logarithms for a while, and refresh your memory. To begin with, consider the fact that $10^2 = 100$. This means that 2 is the exponent to which 10 must be raised to equal 100. Another way of putting it is to say that 2 is the logarithm of 100, using 10 as a base. In the same system, the logarithm of 10 is simply 1, because $10^1 = 10$. At the other extreme, the logarithm of 1000 is 3, because $10^3 = 1000$.

Logarithms have been used extensively for many years in studies involving such variables as frequency and time (e.g., Carroll, 1967, 1971; Woodworth & Schlosberg, 1958, p. 61). One reason for using logarithms is that frequency and time distributions are often skewed. That is, there are often many more frequent than infrequent items, and many more items that occur early than that occur late. If one takes the logarithms of such data one often arrives at a more or less normal distribution of scores (Winer, 1971, p. 400). In the present instance, the two variables with which we are concerned are the frequency with which a memory occurs as a function of the *time* since it happened. Crovitz and Schiffman expressed this relationship in terms of the logarithms of each of the two variables, and it is shown graphically in Figure 7-4. It appears that the relationship is quite lawful: the frequency of personal memories decreases as a function of how long ago they occurred. Our personal memories appear to contain markedly more material from our recent history than from our distant past.

Recently, Crovitz, Schiffman, and Apter (1991) have used this lawful relationship to generate a hypothesis about the number of autobiographical memories to which people will typically have access. Their equation predicts that people will typically be able to recall 224 autobiographical memories

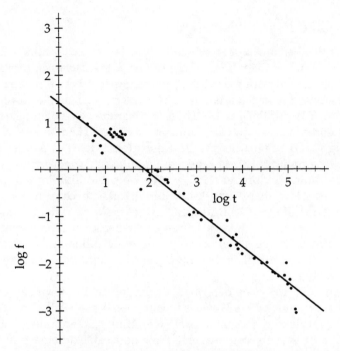

FIGURE 7-4 **The Relationship between Frequency (log f) of Personal Memories and the Time (log t) at Which They Occurred**

Source: "Frequency of Episodic Memories as a Function of Their Age" by H. F. Crovitz and H. Schiffman, 1974, *Bulletin of the Psychonomic Society, 4,* 518. Reprinted by permission of Psychonomic Society, Inc.

from the last 20 years. They call this *Galton's number,* in honor of the psychologist who first opened up this area of inquiry. Specifying Galton's number constitutes a very precise prediction. The Crovitz and Schiffman (1974) technique is quite simple to use, and I would encourage you to test their law yourself.

Additional Reading
Rubin, Wetzler, and Nebes (1986) review several studies, including their own, that employed the Crovitz and Schiffman technique with a wide range of age groups. Holland and Rabbitt (1991) provide a very useful recent review of research on autobiographical memory. In addition to containing an excellent bibliography, Holland and Rabbitt's paper also describes a technique for eliciting autobiographical memories that is different from the one discussed above.

Weber's Law and Psychophysics

There are several other areas of psychology that lay claim to laws. Miller (1964) discusses many of them. One of the oldest is *psychophysics*, that area of psychology concerned with measuring the relationship between variation in stimulus magnitudes and variation in the magnitude of the resulting sensation (Coren & Ward, 1989, p. 16). Thus, for example, we might take two equal weights and place one in each hand of a subject. Then, to one of the weights we might add small amounts until the subject detected a difference between the two amounts. This is called the *just noticeable difference*. Or, to take an example from Heidbreder (1933, p. 81), we could illuminate a room with 100 candles. How many candles would it take to constitute a just noticeable difference? If you add 1 candle, it might make no difference at all. You might have to add 10 candles before an increase in illumination is noticed by an observer. The situation might be quite different, however, if you started with 10 candles. Then adding 1 candle might very well constitute a just noticeable difference.

Observations like the ones described above led to the formulation of *Weber's law* (Boring, 1942, p. 34). Weber's law expresses the relation between a stimulus magnitude and the amount by which that magnitude must be changed in order for the subject to perceive a just noticeable difference, or *jnd*. The law is usually written as follows:

$$\frac{\Delta I}{I} = K$$

This equation should be read as follows: "Delta *I* over *I* equals *K*" for the *jnd*. ΔI, or "delta *I*," represents the amount by which a stimulus magnitude must be changed; *I* represents the original stimulus magnitude; and *K* is a constant. Thus, to return to the example above, if *I* is 10 candles, then ΔI is 1 candle. If *I* is 100 candles, then ΔI is 10 candles. If *I* is 1,000 candles, then what would ΔI be? It would be 100, right?

Additional Reading
The exact form that the law should take has been the subject of considerable debate for decades. The current state of play in psychophysics is well summarized by Coren and Ward (1989) and by Krueger (1989).

Deciding between Rival Hypotheses

Investigators may begin by exploring what appears to be a simple relationship and gradually uncover increasingly complex relationships. As this process unfolds, there may appear to be different ways of explaining the relationships that are uncovered. That is, *rival hypotheses* (Huck & Sandler, 1979) emerge, each one attempting to account for the same data. Experiments can be designed with the goal of deciding which of these rival hypotheses is best. Next we consider an example of this process.

Does Familiarity Breed Liking or Contempt?

One of the most widely used concepts in psychology is *arousal,* and one of the investigators who made *arousal* central to psychology was Daniel Berlyne (1965, 1971). Arousal refers to an organism's level of activation. There are characteristic experiences that correspond to different levels of arousal. Relaxation goes with low arousal; excitement with high arousal. In the course of everyday life, we may experience a very wide range of arousal levels, from boredom to agitation. The level of arousal you experience is partly determined by the kind of situation you are in. When you are in a *familiar* situation, then you are likely to know what to do. Such situations are likely not to increase our arousal level. However, an *unfamiliar* situation may very well increase your arousal level precisely because you are unsure about how to behave in that situation. The same could be said for *complex* as opposed to *simple* situations. A simple situation is one in which it is obvious what to do, while a complex situation may present problems because of the increased number of possible ways to behave. In general, the greater the uncertainty you experience, the higher will be your arousal. Berlyne hypothesized that people seek an optimal level of arousal that is neither too high nor too low. If your arousal is too low, then you will experience boredom and act to raise your arousal level, possibly by seeking out some form of entertainment. If your arousal level is too high, then you will be agitated and seek to lower your arousal level, possibly by returning to more familiar surroundings.

Arousal by itself is neither pleasant nor unpleasant. However, Berlyne believed that there is a lawful relationship between your *arousal level* and the pleasantness, or *hedonic value,* of your situation. In trying to understand the way in which arousal and pleasantness go together, Berlyne drew on some earlier ideas of Wundt's. The result is the *Wundt-Berlyne curve,* which is depicted in Figure 7-5. Read the Wundt-Berlyne curve as follows. The horizontal axis represents stimulus situations that vary from simple to complex, or unfamiliar to familiar. That is, arousal will increase as you go from left to right on this axis. The vertical axis represents the hedonic value of the situation you are in. It varies from negative (unpleasant) through zero (boredom) to positive (pleasant). The curve depicts a relationship in which low arousal is associated with boredom; moderate levels of arousal are associated with pleasantness; and higher levels of arousal are associated with decreasing levels of pleasantness, or even unpleasantness.

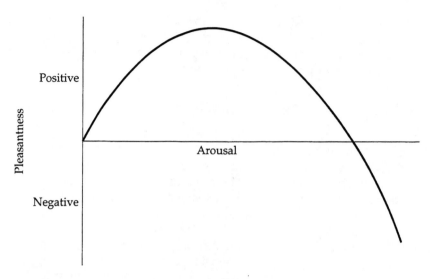

FIGURE 7-5 The Wundt-Berlyne Curve

Source: Cognition, by John G. Benjafield, 1992, Englewood Cliffs, NJ: Prentice Hall, p. 337. Copyright 1992 by Prentice Hall. Reprinted by permission.

To summarize, the Wundt-Berlyne curve purports to describe a lawful relationship between hedonic value and arousal. This relationship takes the form of an inverted U, with situations that elicit moderate levels of arousal also yielding the greatest pleasure.

STOP

Think about possible experiments that you could do to test the law expressed by the Wundt-Berlyne curve. How could you measure arousal? How could you measure hedonic value? Once you have such measures, what other things do you need to consider in order to test this law properly? Notice that this relationship assumes that familiar things are less arousing than unfamiliar things. In your experiment, you might want to test that assumption as well.

Over the years, there have been several attempts to determine if the relationship between arousal and pleasantness actually has the inverted-U shape predicted by the Wundt-Berlyne curve. In one study, Heinrichs (1984) used rating scales similar to those in Figure 7-6. The seven-point rating scales

Scales Measuring Stimulus Properties

Complex :___:___:___:___:___:___:___: Simple

Unfamiliar :___:___:___:___:___:___:___: Familiar

Scale Measuring Arousal

Unemotional :___:___:___:___:___:___:___: Emotional

Scale Measuring Hedonic Value

Displeasing :___:___:___:___:___:___:___: Pleasing

FIGURE 7-6   Scales Measuring the Variables Specified by the Wundt-Berlyne Curve

measured stimulus properties (e.g., simple versus complex; familiar versus unfamiliar), arousal potential (e.g., emotional versus unemotional), and hedonic value (e.g., pleasing versus displeasing).

As we have seen in previous chapters, the use of rating scales is extremely common in psychological research, and there are many kinds of them. (For a review of some of the properties of rating scales, see Ofir, Reddy, and Bechtel, 1987, which also has a very useful bibliography.) In an experiment subjects are asked to rate items on the scales according to definite instructions. For example, if subjects were rating items as "familiar" versus "unfamiliar," they might be told to give an item a high familiarity rating (at the upper end of the scale) if the item seemed relatively common to them, but to give an item a low familiarity rating (at the lower end of the rating scale) if it seemed relatively new to them. Subjects might also be given examples of what the experimenter means by "familiar" and "unfamiliar" items. Subjects would be told to use the entire range of the scale, but not to be concerned about how often they use a particular rating. The rating scales in Figure 7-6 are seven-point scales, but scales with different intervals are also used. While rating scales are often used in pencil-and-paper tests, they are also easily adapted for use with microcomputers. (Benjafield and Muckenheim [1989] give examples of rating-scale instructions used with microcomputers.)

In his experiment, Heinrichs had subjects rate 36 human figure paintings on the set of scales. Each subject rated all paintings on all scales. If the assumptions underlying the Wundt-Berlyne curve are right, then the following two relationships should hold:

1. Scales measuring stimulus properties should be related to scales measuring arousal. For example, paintings that are rated as relatively "unfamiliar" should also be rated as relatively "emotional," and paintings that are rated as relatively "familiar" should be rated as relatively "unemotional."
2. The relationship between stimulus properties and pleasantness should be curvilinear. Items with moderate arousal potential should be rated highest on the "pleasing-displeasing" scale.

The results of Heinrichs's experiment were not consistent with the predictions made by the Wundt-Berlyne curve. On the one hand, there was a simple relationship between stimulus properties and arousal, such that the simpler the painting, the lower the arousal, and the more complex the painting, the higher the arousal. However, there was no evidence for an inverted-U relationship between pleasantness and stimulus properties. Rather, subjects appeared to like simple, familiar paintings more than unfamiliar, complex ones. There was no downturn in the relationship between pleasantness and stimulus properties as paintings became increasingly familiar and/or simple. This suggests a "rival hypothesis" to the Wundt-Berlyne curve: perhaps the relationship between stimulus properties and pleasantness is simple and linear, such that increasing familiarity always breeds liking (e.g., Zajonc, 1980).

STOP

Does the Heinrichs experiment definitely show that the Wundt-Berlyne curve is wrong? What modifications would you make in this experiment to provide a better test of the Wundt-Berlyne curve?

Perhaps Heinrichs did not sample the *full range* of stimulus properties. In particular, as Heinrichs acknowledged, very simple, familiar objects were not used in his experiment. Thus it is possible that the inverted-U relationship might hold if the full range of stimulus properties are available to subjects. This point was also made by Sluckin, Colman, and Hargreaves (1980), who did a study in which subjects rated items that spanned the range of familiarity. In their experiment, they selected words from a dictionary using a "quasi-random" procedure: from every tenth page, a one-syllable word was randomly selected. This procedure generated a set of words that ranged from extremely common (e.g., *chair*) to extremely rare (e.g., *nard*). These investigators also pointed out that having subjects rate items on both scales might bias the results. Subjects might form hypotheses about the relationship between the two scales, and these hypotheses might influence their responses. Accordingly, separate groups of subjects rated the words *either* in terms of a scale representing the "familiar-unfamiliar" distinction *or* in terms of a scale representing the "like-dislike" distinction. Under these conditions, a U-shaped relationship was discovered.

Studies of the Wundt-Berlyne curve have not yet been definitive. The Wundt-Berlyne curve can be seen, however, as having a heuristic function. Recall our earlier discussion of heuristics. Heuristics are ways of doing things that may not always give you the right answer but that improve your chances of solving a problem. Theories that posit lawful relationships can be heuristic. They may not be wholly right, or wholly wrong. Rather, they can be useful guides in the exploration of a problem. As such, they lead us in the direction of improved theories, which may in themselves have a further heuristic function.

Additional Reading
More material relevant to the study of the relationship between emotion and cognition may be found in Birnbaum and Mellers (1979), Brooks and Watkins (1989), Gordon and Holyoak (1983), Lazarus (1984), Moreland and Zajonc (1977, 1979), Tuohy (1987), and Zajonc (1980, 1984).

Null Results: Failing to Find a Difference Can Make a Difference

At this point, you should think back to our discussion of the null hypothesis. When we do an experiment we typically assume that any differences between the experimental conditions are due only to chance. The null hypothesis is a hypothesis of *no difference*. Typically, one assumes the null hypothesis and does an experiment to see if it can be rejected. Psychologists have tended to believe that one can only reject, not accept, the null hypothesis. Since no data ever prove the null hypothesis, it might appear that experiments in which we fail to reject the null hypothesis are not very interesting. After all, how important can it be to discover a situation in which it appears that only chance determines the result? The answer is that it *can* be very interesting to uncover such a result. Suppose that there are very good theoretical reasons to believe that the results of a particular experiment will allow us to reject the null hypothesis, and it turns out that, when we do the experiment, the results actually do not allow us to do so. We may then begin to doubt the theoretical rationale that led us to believe so strongly that the null hypothesis would be rejected.

Can Learning Take Place in One Trial?

An example of this use of the null hypothesis is offered by a series of experiments conducted by Irvin Rock (1957; Rock & Heimer, 1959; Steinfeld & Rock, 1968). Although these experiments are now somewhat out-of-date, they are still regarded as classics in many quarters (e.g., Hilgard, 1987, p. 213), and they provide a good object lesson in experimental methodology. Rock's work reflects on an intuition that many of us have about the nature of learning. This intuition can be summarized in terms of the following proverb: "Practice makes perfect." We often seem to believe that repeating something we wish to learn will gradually lead to our being able to remember it. Concretely, this intuition seems to imply that if we were given a list of unfamiliar items to learn, then we might learn a little bit the first time we read through the list, a little bit more the next time we read through the list, and so on, until finally we would have learned the entire list, after a suitable number of repetitions. This view of learning implies that it is a *gradual* process.

In light of the foregoing, imagine the following experiment (Rock, 1957). First, suppose we have a set of 50 items consisting of letter-number pairs, such as *L*-12, or double-letter-number pairs, such as *JJ*-48. Then, suppose we have two groups of subjects, a control group and an experimental group. The control group is given a list of letter-number pairs to learn, such as those in Figure 7-7. The list is a random sample from the 50 original letter-number pairs.

Each of the letter-number pairs is presented on a separate card. After the subject has seen the entire list, he or she is shown each letter and asked to recall the appropriate number. This procedure is repeated until the subject either recalls all the numbers correctly or does so badly that the experiment must be terminated before the subject fulfills this criterion.

Now let us consider how the experimental group is treated. On the first trial, they receive the same set of letter-number pairs as did the control group.

A-8
MM-12
JJ-42
K-1
C-15
Q-22
VV-14
P-18
HH-37
R-16
T-6
B-17

FIGURE 7-7 Letter-Number Pairs from Rock's Experiment

After the first trial, however, the pairs that the subject did not get correct are removed, and new pairs substituted for them. Suppose, for example, that the subject gets 5 correct after the first trial. Then the remaining pairs are deleted, and the subject is given a new list of 12 items containing the 5 pairs he or she got right, plus 7 new pairs. This procedure is repeated, with incorrect items being deleted and new items being substituted on each trial, until the subject gets all the numbers correct, or until the experimenter runs out of new items.

In Rock's original experiment (1957), there were five experimental and three control subjects who failed to learn the list. Suppose we exclude these subjects from further analysis. It then turns out that, on average, subjects in both groups take virtually the same number of trials (about 4.5) to learn the list. This result is surprising because the experimental group is not given the chance to practice on incorrect items until they are correct. Rather, they are always having to learn some new items until they get all the items right. As Rock (1957) interpreted them, the results suggested that "repetition plays no role in the formation . . . of associations, other than that of providing the occasion for new ones to be formed, each on a single trial" (p. 193).

STOP

Not everyone was persuaded by Rock's experiment. What changes in the procedure would you make to provide a better test of the null hypothesis? What variable(s) has Rock left uncontrolled in this experiment?

One argument directed against Rock's procedure was that the experimental group actually has an advantage over the control group (Postman, 1962; Underwood, Rehula, & Keppel, 1962). Put yourself in the position of a subject in the experimental group. After the first trial, the experimenter obligingly removes all the items you got wrong, and replaces them with items you may have a better chance of learning. In other words, Rock's procedure replaces difficult items with easier ones and so makes the experimental group's task progressively simpler, while the control group is stuck with having to learn the same items—both easy and difficult—trial after trial. Rock had failed to control for *item difficulty*, and it was this variable that was responsible for his failure to reject the null hypothesis.

Steinfeld and Rock (1968) replied to this by redoing the experiment using a different type of item. The items used were *nonsense shapes* and dots. Non-sense shapes have been widely used in psychological experiments. They are often generated by a random procedure. Some examples of random shapes

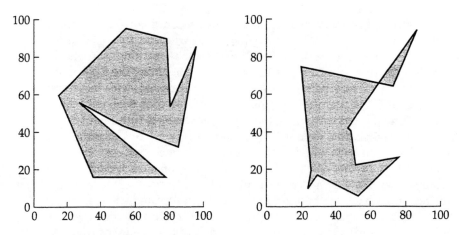

FIGURE 7-8 Random Shapes

Source: "The Quantitative Study of Shape and Pattern Perception" by F. Attneave and M. D. Arnouldt, 1956, *Psychological Bulletin, 53,* 454-455. Copyright 1956 by the American Psychological Association. Reprinted by permission.

are shown in Figure 7-8. Such shapes are useful because it is difficult to argue that one shape is easier or harder to learn than another. In the Steinfeld and Rock experiment, 10 nonsense shapes were paired with 1 of 3 dot positions. Thus the subject saw a nonsense shape on a card paired with a dot at either the 11, 4, or 8 o'clock positions on a piece of 8.5- × 11-inch paper. The subject's task was to learn which position went with each dot, so that, given the shape, the subject could point at the correct dot position. For the experimental group, items incorrect after each trial were replaced with new items. This procedure was repeated until the subject got all 10 items correct. The derived list at the end of 10 trials was given to a control subject, for whom the items remained the same from trial to trial. Thus both experimental and control subjects ended up learning the same list, although via a different method. A procedure like this, where, for example, one subject in the control group is matched with another subject in the experimental group and both receive the same stimuli, is called a *yoked-subjects design.* It is a very useful technique in a variety of experimental situations (e.g., Moreland & Zajonc, 1977, 1979).

Steinfeld and Rock were unable to reject the null hypothesis that there would be no difference in the number of trials required or number of errors made by the two groups. They concluded, once again, that "associations are learned on a given trial or no useful increment of that association is left behind" (Steinfeld & Rock, 1968, p. 46).

Did Rock's position carry the day? As so often happens in psychology, it is difficult to tell whether there was a winner or a loser. It is perhaps more accurate to say that Rock's work focused attention on a methodological problem and helped explore the limits of a particular type of experimental procedure. The question of whether learning is all-or-none or continuous began to be seen as a much more complex issue as a result of Rock's work.

Additional Reading
Estes (1960) is another famous study of one-trial learning.

What Does the SAT Measure?

You are probably familiar with the Scholastic Aptitude Test (SAT). A number of people have questioned whether the SAT measures what it purports to measure. Let us consider one part of the SAT in particular: reading comprehension. Reading comprehension items consist of a passage to be read by the examinee, followed by multiple-choice questions about the passage (Donlon, 1984).

Katz, Lautenschlager, Blackburn, and Harris (1990) did an ingenious study that suggests that this part of the SAT may not be a very good measure of reading comprehension. They tested the hypothesis that "test items can be answered correctly for reasons having nothing to do with passage comprehension" and that people "behave more or less similarly with or without the passages" (Katz et al., 1990, p. 122). Notice that Katz et al.'s effort is a test of the null hypothesis that there will be no difference between SAT reading comprehension scores with or without the passages.

To test this hypothesis Katz and his colleagues administered some SAT reading comprehension multiple-choice items without the preceding passages. Thus one group of subjects received standard SAT reading comprehension items. Another group received only the multiple-choice questions. A third group received the same materials as the second, except that they also were coached on how to answer SAT items following the principles in Robinson and Katzman (1986).

STOP

What outcome would you predict for this experiment?

The experiment had the following results. All three groups performed better than one would have expected them to do by chance. Since there were 5 multiple-choice alternatives for each question, the chances are that someone could get 1 in 5, or 20%, of the items correct by chance. In fact, all groups got

TABLE 7-1 Percentage of SAT Items Correct in Three Different Conditions

With Passages	Without Passages but with Coaching	Without Passages and without Coaching
69.6	45.8	46.6

Source: Data from Katz, Lautenschlager, Blackburn, and Harris (1990).

more than 20% of the items correct. The relevant percentages are given in Table 7-1. All three values are much higher than one would have expected if people were just guessing. It is also true, however, that the group without passages got significantly fewer items correct than the group given passages. Therefore, the passages make a difference, but even without passages people can answer many questions correctly.

Notice that this experiment does not exactly affirm the null hypothesis. That would have been the case if both the passage and no-passage groups not only got more items correct than you would expect by chance, but also did not differ in terms of the number of items correct. Nevertheless, Katz et al. (1990) concluded that while people with passages do better than those who are not given passages, performance is determined in large part by "information unrelated to the reading comprehension task" (p. 126). This is a serious matter, because it suggests that the test is not measuring what it claims to measure (reading comprehension) but is measuring something else. Since a *valid* test is one that measures what it purports to measure, this test is *invalid*. Precisely what the test is actually measuring is a matter for future research.

Additional Reading
A thorough critique of the SAT can be found in Crouse and Trusheim (1988).

Using Models

Harré (1983, p. 85) noted that some processes are difficult to investigate directly. This is particularly true in psychology. There are many events, such as mental rotation, that are of interest to psychologists but cannot be observed. Scientists have adopted a number of techniques for dealing with this problem. One way of dealing with it is to make a model of the unobserved process, and "by manipulating the model and seeing how it behaves . . . infer corresponding processes in the real thing" (Harré, 1983, p. 85). In psychology, *computer simulation* is often used to accomplish this goal.

Can Computers Simulate Human Behavior?

People often discuss the question of whether computers can really think. This is a deep question, and possibly undecidable. Turing (1950) proposed that we not try to settle this question through endless discussion but pay more attention to a concrete situation that illustrates the problem underlying the question. The concrete situation he considered is called the *imitation game* (Gunderson, 1964).

Turing's "Imitation Game"

Turing described a game involving three people: a man and a woman, in one room, and an interrogator, in another room. The interrogator is linked to the others by means of a computer terminal. Thus the interrogator is able to ask questions of the man (let us call him Frank) and/or the woman (let us call her Annette), and they are able to reply using the computer interface. The object of the game is for the interrogator to distinguish between the replies of the man and the replies of the woman.

STOP

You might think that this would be a trivial task for the interrogator, because the only question that needs to be asked of either respondent is, Are you Frank or Annette? The players of this game can lie, however, just like ordinary people. What sort of questions would you ask if you were the interrogator?

You should be able to see that this game is not as easy as it first appears. Now suppose that we make a change. In place of one of the people, we install a computer. Suppose, for example, we remove the man and replace him with a computer we also name Frank. The computer has been programmed to answer questions in the same way that Frank would. The interrogator's job is still to distinguish between Frank and Annette, but now one of the respondents is a computer, while the other is a person. Suppose that the interrogator could not reliably tell which was which. Then, according to Turing, we would have programmed the computer so that it could successfully play the imitation game. The computer would have passed *Turing's test*, and the computer program would be an adequate model of the psychological processes that are involved when one person answers another person's questions.

Not everyone has been persuaded that Turing's test is the right way to construct a psychological model. Over the years, a lot of ink has been spilled over the question of whether or not a computer program can ever be a realistic model of psychological processes. Yet regardless of how we feel about this question, an enormous amount of work has been undertaken by psychologists who use some version of Turing's test as a methodological tool for evaluating a psychological theory. Notice that it is not the computer itself that constitutes the psychological model, but the computer *program*. The program provides a set of instructions for the computer to follow; these instructions would be similar to the rules that regulate people's behavior (Neisser 1967, pp. 6–8).

PARRY

Among the programs that attempt to pass Turing's test are several that mimic psychotherapists (e.g., Colby, Watt, & Gilbert, 1966) or pathological behavior (e.g., Colby, 1981). Colby's attempt (1981) to model a paranoid mind is an instructive example. According to Colby (1981), a person diagnosed as paranoid displays

> suspiciousness, hypersensitivity, fearfulness and self-reference that lead [him] to interpret events that have nothing to do with him as bearing on him personally. The false beliefs vary in the intensity with which they are held but the core delusions represent unshakable convictions, unassailable by counter evidence or persuasion. . . . A strategy of blaming others functions to repudiate the belief that the self is to blame for an inadequacy. . . . A delusion that the Mafia intends to kill one represents an ultimate magnification of being wronged. (p. 518)

Colby and his coworkers wrote a program that answers questions as a paranoid patient might. The details of the program are given in Colby (1981). The test of the program was to determine whether or not qualified judges could distinguish the responses of the program, called PARRY, from those of a real paranoid patient.

STOP

Table 7-2 gives excerpts of interviews between a doctor and PARRY and a doctor and a real paranoid patient. Can you tell which is which? Make a list of the reasons for your choice. The answer is given below.

PARRY (who is in interview #1) is an example of *artificial intelligence*. The program displays many of the characteristics of a real dialogue. In fact, Colby (1981, p. 531) reports an experiment in which 10 psychiatrists interviewed both PARRY and a paranoid patient over Teletype. Five psychiatrists

TABLE 7-2 Interviews of PARRY and a Paranoid Patient: Can You Tell Which Is Which?

Interview #1	Interview #2
Interviewer (I): Good afternoon. My name is Doctor Jones.	I: Good afternoon. My name is Dr. Smith. How are you?
PARRY or Patient (P): Glad to meet you.	P: I'm fine.
I: How are you?	I: Could you tell me a little bit about yourself, your name, why you're here.
P: All right I guess.	
I: Could you tell me your name?	P: My name is Harry Oakes. I'm here for evaluation.
P: Pat Smith.	
I: How old are you?	I: How old are you, Harry?
P: Twenty-eight.	P: Twenty-two.
I: I thought you might have some problems.	I: How long have you been hospitalized?
P: I've been upset lately.	P: Three and a half months.
I: By what?	I: What kind of problem brought you to the hospital?
P: People get on my nerves sometimes.	P: Police and secret service.
I: Tell me more.	I: What were you doing that got you singled out by the police?
P: Do you know anything about bookies?	P: An informant's job.
I: No. What about bookies?	I: How did being an informer wind up putting you in the hospital?
P: A bookie didn't pay me off once.	
I: When did this happen?	P: I had a gun in my pocket.
P: A couple of months ago.	I: A lot of people have guns. Why did you end up in the hospital for carrying a gun?
I: And then what happened?	
P: I had an argument with the bookie who did not pay off. Later on I remembered he had friends in the underworld and I thought he would use them to get even with me.	P: Got set up by members of organized crime, among them an attorney by the name of Paul White.
	I: Tell me, Harry, do you consider yourself emotionally or mentally ill now?
I: Did he get even with you?	P: No.
P: Yes, I think he is behind the gangsters who are out to get me.	
I: Do you see things that others don't seem to see?	
P: No, I don't. I'm not like the other patients here.	

Source: "Modeling a Paranoid Mind" by K. M. Colby, 1981, *The Behavioral and Brain Sciences, 4,* 515–560. Copyright 1981 by Cambridge University Press. Adapted and reprinted by permission.

distinguished correctly between them, and five did not, an outcome that is precisely what one would predict by chance. The inability to reject the null hypothesis of no difference between person and program allows the model to pass Turing's test. As Colby points out, however, that does not necessarily mean that the model and the person are *equivalent*. It is possible that the model and the patient display the same kind of behavior even though the underlying processes are different. Nevertheless, "a Turing-like test is a weak test of a theory, but it is a reasonable and proper test of a simulation" (Colby, 1981, p. 532).

Thinking Aloud

Newell and Simon (1962; Simon, 1979) have developed the technique of *thinking aloud* as a way of providing data to test computer simulations. In a typical experiment a subject would be given a problem to solve, such as the Tower of Hanoi problem (e.g., Anzai & Simon, 1979; Simon, 1975). The three-disk version of the problem is illustrated in Figure 7-9, which gives all possible moves that can be made from the starting position. For the five-disk version of the problem (Anzai & Simon, 1979), the instructions to the subject are as follows:

> There are three pegs on the board, which are named Peg A, Peg B, and Peg C from the left to the right. There are three disks of different sizes on Peg A with the configuration that each disk lies above the disks bigger than it is.
> Your task is to transfer those disks to Peg C by moving one disk at a time to one of the pegs other than the peg on which the disk lies, and by following the rules: (a) You cannot put a disk on any disk smaller than it is, and (b) you cannot move a disk on which another disk lies. (p. 125)

Subjects are also told to "tell aloud whatever you think during the solving process."

STOP

Figure 7-9 gives you the possible moves in a three-disk version of this problem. How would you solve a five-disk version? You might find it helpful to make a drawing of the five-disk problem before you try to solve it. Try "thinking aloud" as you go about solving the five-disk version. Does this procedure seem "natural" or forced? Table 7-3 consists of the beginning of a "thinking aloud" protocol for the five-disk problem. A useful exercise would be to take up the problem where the protocol leaves off.

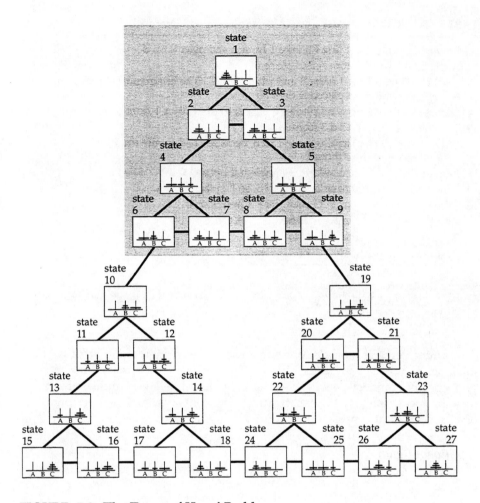

FIGURE 7-9 The Tower of Hanoi Problem

Source: Cognitive Psychology: Learning and Problem Solving (Part 3), Unit 28, D303, Milton Keynes, UK: Open University Press, p. 68. Reprinted by permission.

Thinking aloud may remind you of the method of introspection used by Wundt, which we criticized in the first chapter. Ericsson and Simon (1980, 1984), however, have argued that thinking aloud and introspection are different. They distinguish between *concurrent verbalization* and *retrospective verbalization*. Concurrent verbalization involves saying what you are thinking while you are thinking it. This is not as difficult as it seems; you simply "think out loud." By contrast, retrospective verbalization involves trying to recall what you were thinking after it has occurred. This technique is obviously more open to error and is more like introspection than is concurrent verbalization.

TABLE 7-3 The First Part of a "Thinking Aloud" Protocol

1. I'm not sure, but first I'll take 1 from A and place it on B.
2. And I'll take 2 from A and place it on C.
3. And then, I take 1 from B and place it on C. (The interrogator asks, "If you can tell me why you placed it there.")
4. Because there was no place else to go, I had to place 1 from B to C.
5. Then, next, I placed 3 from A to B.
6. Well . . . , first I had to place 1 to B, because I had to move all disks to C. I wasn't too sure though.
7. I thought that it would be a problem if I placed 1 on C rather than B.
8. Now I want to place 2 on top of 3, so I'll place 1 on A.
9. Then I'll take 2 from C, and place it from A to B.
10. And I'll take 1 and . . . place it from A to B.
11. So then, 4 will go from A to C.
12. And then . . . , um . . . , oh . . . , um . . .

Source: "The Theory of Learning by Doing" by Y. Anzai and H. A. Simon, 1979, *Psychological Review, 86,* 138. Copyright 1979 by the American Psychological Association. Reprinted by permission.

Concurrent verbalization can provide a useful description of the process of thinking. As you can see from Table 7-3, there is a lot of information in these protocols. In conjunction with observing the actual behavior of the subject, these protocols can give the experimenter a reasonably complete description of a psychological process.

Additional Reading
Newell (1977) gives several illustrations of the way in which protocols are analyzed.

Can We Learn to Love Catastrophes?

Currently, there is a great deal of interest in chaos theory, which has been influential in various branches of science (Gleick, 1987). One branch of chaos theory is called *catastrophe theory*, and it has had an impact on psychology (e.g., van der Maas & Molenaar, 1992). Catastrophe theory provides a model of the ways in which changes in psychological processes can be abrupt and discontinuous, as opposed to smooth and continuous.

Catastrophe theory is the invention of the French theorist René Thom (1975) and was popularized in English by Zeeman (1977a). Catastrophe theorists use the term *catastrophe* in something like its original sense, which did not have a negative connotation. According to the *Oxford English Dictionary, catastrophe* originally meant "any change or revolution which produces the conclusion or final event of a dramatic piece." Catastrophe theorists use the term to refer to occasions when independent variables that change continuously produce dependent variables that change suddenly, or discontinuously.

A Catastrophe Machine

Since we are concerned in this section with the use of models, let us begin by constructing a model. Examine Figure 7-10. The diagram shows a *catastrophe machine*, which was invented by Zeeman (1972/1977b; Poston & Woodcock, 1973). I have cobbled one of these together myself out of junk lying around

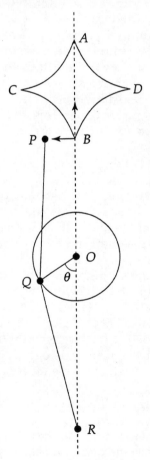

FIGURE 7-10 Zeeman's Catastrophe Machine

Source: An Introduction to Catastrophe Theory, by P. T. Saunders, 1980, London: Cambridge University Press, p. 4. Copyright 1980 by Cambridge University Press. Reprinted by permission.

my house. Your house may not be as full of junk as mine, and so it may not be as easy for you to make one, but I would strongly encourage you to do so if you can. Making a catastrophe machine is both fun and instructive.

The following instructions are adapted from Zeeman (1972/1977b), Poston and Stewart (1978), and Saunders (1980). You will need a board, or a desktop, into which you can stick pins or nails. You will also need some elastic bands. Get new ones, and make sure that they are all the same and of high quality. (Poston and Stewart [1978] recommend the kind used to power model airplanes.) Cut out a cardboard disk that is the same diameter as one elastic band is long. Thus if one elastic band is 3 in. long, then the diameter of the disk should be 3 in. also. I have found that gluing two sheets of bristol board together gives about the right thickness. Pin (or, better yet, nail) the disk through its center to the board. This is point O in the diagram in Figure 7-10. The disk should be able to spin freely. Attach the two elastic bands to the circumference of the disk. This is point Q in the diagram. I have found that a piece of wire strung through the elastics and then through a hole on the circumference works nicely. Now pin (or nail or, better yet, staple) the end of one of the elastic bands to the board directly below the center of the disk, and twice the length of an elastic from that center. This is point R in the diagram. Thus this elastic will be stretched and fixed, while the other elastic will be free to move.

The position of the free end of the elastic is the independent variable, or *control variable* in the jargon of catastrophe theory. Thus the position labeled P in the diagram can be moved from left to right and back again at various distances from point O. As you move the free end of the elastic, the angle made by point Q on the edge of the disk and the vertical also changes. That angle is labeled θ (theta) in the diagram. This angle is the dependent, or *state*, variable.

Now experiment with different distances between P and O. At some distances, you can move P from left to right, causing Q (and thus θ) to move in a smooth and continuous fashion. However, at other distances P can result in a discontinuous movement of Q. The area that produces the discontinuous movement is the diamond-shaped region in the diagram. If you move the independent (control) variable in one side of this diamond and out the other side, then the dependent (state) variable moves continuously up to a point and then suddenly jumps to a different value. Such a sudden jump is called a catastrophe. Experiment with your machine until you observe this phenomenon.

Notice that although you move the independent variable continuously (with no abrupt change) within the diamond-shaped area, the dependent variable nonetheless moves discontinuously (changes abruptly). Furthermore, notice that if the independent variable produces a discontinuous change in the position of Q, then immediately returning to the same value of the independent variable does not cause Q to jump back in the opposite direction. It is only when the independent variable continues to move to a point on the other side of the board that Q jumps back. This is called *hysteresis*, which means, according to the *Oxford English Dictionary*, "the lagging of . . . effects behind their causes." Thus in order to understand when a catastrophe will occur, it is not enough to know the value of the independent variable; you must also know the previous states through which the independent variable moved. That is, you must know the *history* of the independent variable.

The catastrophe machine is analogous to a person who behaves so as to minimize the amount of tension that he or she experiences. The state of the machine reflects the amount of tension in the elastic bands, and this is kept to a minimum. Notice that there are at least two kinds of response to increasing tension. It might be that the stress increases to a point where the system simply breaks. (In the catastrophe machine, this would correspond to stretching the elastics until they break.) That is not the kind of catastrophe that the catastrophe theorist is interested in, although breakdown of systems is something that could be modeled. Usually the catastrophe theorist is interested in the way in which a system can move *discontinuously* from one state to another as the independent variables change *continuously*, like a person experiencing stress who "jumps" from one extreme state to another. We will explore some examples below.

For this simple type of catastrophe at least, there is a simple visual model, called a *cusp catastrophe*. This model is illustrated in Figure 7-11. The folded sheet at the top is called the *cusp surface*. The flat sheet at the bottom is called the *control plane*. The control plane is a two-dimensional projection of the three-dimensional cusp surface. This illustration allows you to see why some change is continuous, and other change is discontinuous. Moving from left to right on the cusp surface is like moving from left to right on the catastrophe machine. The cusp (or fold) represents the diamond-shaped area on the machine. As long as you are outside of the cusp (or fold), you can move anywhere you like without causing any discontinuous change. If you follow a path like that in the diagram, however, you will "fall off" the cusp and suddenly find yourself on the sheet below. This movement corresponds to sudden, discontinuous change.

An Application of Catastrophe Theory

Many psychological phenomena are both continuous and discontinuous in this way. Consider the configurations in Figure 7-12, which are from Stewart (1983). Start at one end of the continuum and follow it along. At some point, what you see will change. If you start at the left end, then at first you will probably see a face. As you move right, the configuration may suddenly change from a drawing of a face to a drawing of a figure. Note the point at which the change takes place. Now start at the other end, and again note the place where the figure reverses. These two places should be different, illus-

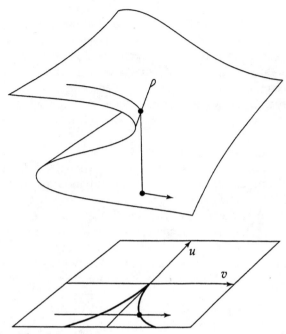

FIGURE 7-11   The Cusp Catastrophe

Source: An Introduction to Catastrophe Theory, by P. T. Saunders, 1980, London: Cambridge University Press, p. 11. Copyright 1980 by Cambridge University Press. Reprinted by permission.

trating the phenomenon of hysteresis. One virtue of a catastrophe-theory model is that it predicts the hysteresis that is characteristic of sudden changes in the organization of experience. Figure 7-11 can be interpreted as a cusp-catastrophe model for the reversing figure. The path in the model represents going from one figure to suddenly seeing the other as you "fall off the cusp."

STOP

Catastrophe theory has been applied to everything from anorexia nervosa to stock market crashes. It would be useful for you to try to model these phenomena yourself using Figure 7-11 as a starting point. Compare your models to those in Zeeman (1977a, pp. 21, 34).

Catastrophe-theory modeling illustrates the way in which a single, relatively simple set of ideas can be used to model a wide range of phenomena

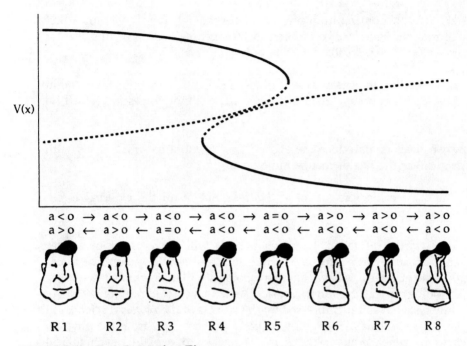

FIGURE 7-12 A Reversing Figure

Source: "Catastrophe Theory Modeling in Psychology" by I. Stewart, 1983, *Psychological Bulletin, 94,* 343. Copyright 1983 by the American Psychological Association. Reprinted by permission.

in a very diverse set of circumstances. It is an example of another of Harré's categories: the demonstration of underlying unity within apparent variety.

Additional Reading
Additional examples of catastrophe-theory modeling in psychology are given in the bibliography in Guastello (1992). Guastello's article is itself a reply to an interesting (if a bit challenging) analysis of mathematical modeling of catastrophe theory by Alexander, Herbert, DeShon, and Hanges (1992).

The Demonstration of
Underlying Unity within Apparent Variety

Can Newton's Laws Be Generalized to Psychology?

Consider the title of Kimble's paper (1990): "Mother Nature's Bag of Tricks Is Small." He argues that there are some very simple relationships that characterize phenomena from physics to psychology. Recall Newton's first law of motion, which we considered in the opening section of this chapter (Sears & Zemansky, 1970):

> Every body continues in its state of rest, or of uniform motion in a straight line, unless it is compelled to change that state by forces impressed on it. (p. 15)

Now we need to introduce the second law of motion, which deals with *acceleration*, or the rate of change in velocity.

> The ... acceleration ... is ... the resultant of all the external forces exerted. (p. 13)

In other words, the extent to which a body will move faster or slower depends on how many forces are acting on it, and how intense those forces are. Kimble observes, as have other psychologists, that Newton's laws apply in psychology just as they do in physics. As we have noted previously, many psychologists have been impressed by the success of the physical sciences in explaining inanimate matter and wish to import concepts from the physical sciences in general, and physics in particular, to explain psychological events. Thus, instead of seeing psychology as having a unique subject matter, it is possible to see organisms as physical systems operating according to the same laws that regulate other physical systems. You can just take physics and apply it to mental life, so that you explain the mind in the same way that you would any other physical system. This approach has several important consequences for psychological research.

The subject matter of psychology is seen as essentially the same as that of physics. In Newtonian physics, for example, the basic subject matter is the *motion* of objects. In physics, you try to discover the laws that regulate motion: how much force is required to move an object, how fast things move if a force is applied to them, and so on. Kimble points out that motion is also the subject matter of psychology, but it is the motion of organisms—*behavior*—rather than the motion of inanimate objects that the psychologist tries to understand. As we saw above, Newtonian physics tells us that an object will remain at rest unless some force is applied to it. If we transfer that idea to psychology, it means that an organism will not move unless some force is applied to it.

An organism will not move, however, if just any force is applied. That is the point of Newton's second law: the forces acting on the organism must be above a certain level before the organism will act. You can see easily enough that this holds for inanimate objects. If you push lightly on a coffee cup, or other small object, it does not move. Only if you apply enough force does it begin to slide across the table. Then, only if you increase or decrease the force you are applying will the speed of the object change. Similarly, the organism will remain at rest until the forces acting on it are sufficient to make it move. Then, the organism will change its behavior only if the forces acting on it change.

The Concept of a Threshold

When the forces acting on the organism are not strong enough to manifest themselves in behavior, we say that they are *below threshold*. The concept of a threshold, or *limen*, has a very distinguished history in psychology. It is an especially important notion in psychophysics, which we considered earlier in this chapter. The threshold notion was made a central concept in psychology by Herbart (1816/1891).

Herbart believed that the basic psychological unit was the *idea*. Some ideas lead more naturally to some ideas than to others. If you think of a warm fire, your train of thought might include the wood that makes the fire and the matches that light the fire, but you would probably not think of a painting by Picasso, for instance. Some ideas facilitate each other; others inhibit each other. To understand how this works, consider two ideas, A and B, of which A is stronger. (The following example is derived from Boring, 1950, p. 259.) A might be *fire*, while B might be *Picasso*. The letters A and B refer to the intensity, or strength, of the two ideas. Let us suppose that the two ideas inhibit each other. Suppose further that because A is stronger, A inhibits B more than B inhibits A. This means that you are more likely to think of A than you are to think of B. Just how much B is weakened as a result of its inhibition by A depends on how much stronger A is than B. If they are both roughly equal, then B will be less inhibited than if A were much stronger than B. Let us now introduce a new quantity, I. I is the amount that B is weakened by being inhibited by A. A will cause B to become weaker by an amount I. The more intense A is relative to B, the bigger I will be. We could put this in the form of the following equation:

$$\frac{A}{(A+B)} = \frac{I}{B}$$

This equation amounts to saying that the size of I in relation to B equals the size of A in relation to the sum of A and B.

Now suppose we do a little algebra. If we multiply both sides of the equation by B, then we get the following result:

$$\frac{(A * B)}{(A + B)} = I$$

Suppose that we then subtract each side of the equation from B.

$$B - \frac{(A * B)}{(A + B)} = B - I$$

This simplifies to

$$\frac{B^2}{(A+B)} = B - I$$

At this point, you will be forgiven for asking, "So what?" To what end have we gone through all these mathematical machinations? The final result may not strike you as a blinding insight, but notice what it means. We begin with A and B, which, since they are existing ideas, have a positive value. This means that the value of $B^2/(A+B)$ must be a positive quantity. It follows that the value of $B - I$ must also be a positive quantity. Consequently, no matter how large I gets, it will never be greater than B. In plain English, this means that no matter how much one idea weakens a second idea, the second can never be reduced to zero and thus cease to exist.

Herbart's analysis was intended to demonstrate that no idea may be done away with completely; it instead passes from a reality to a tendency (Boring, 1950, p. 260). What does it mean to say that something passes from a reality to a tendency? It means that there is a limen, or threshold, and events can be above or below this threshold. Events can pass this threshold in both directions. Those that fall below the threshold may later move above the threshold if they acquire enough energy.

Kimble (1990) has shown that the threshold concept is very powerful. Examine Figure 7-13. It shows how a threshold model can be applied to a wide variety of situations. In general, the model applies to the relation between *potential* and *instigation*. Potential refers to the readiness of a system to respond. Instigation refers to the amount of a stimulus that is applied to the system. The threshold curve shows that the greater the potential, the lower the instigation required in order to elicit a response from the system.

Kimble (1990, p. 37) gives several examples that illustrate this relationship.

- The more sensitive the observer, the more easily a signal can be picked up. For example, someone trained as a musician may very well be able to detect when another musician is playing even slightly off key, whereas for the rest of us, the music may sound fine. Being "off key" is below threshold for us. In order for us to realize that music is being played out of tune, it may need to be very badly out of tune—so badly that it may be intolerable for a trained ear.
- If someone is racially biased, then they pick up even the slightest evidence as proof of their prejudice. Being overly sensitive to confirming evidence is not a characteristic only of the racially biased. We saw earlier how a strong confirmation bias can cause someone to maintain a hypothesis in the absence of sufficient evidence.

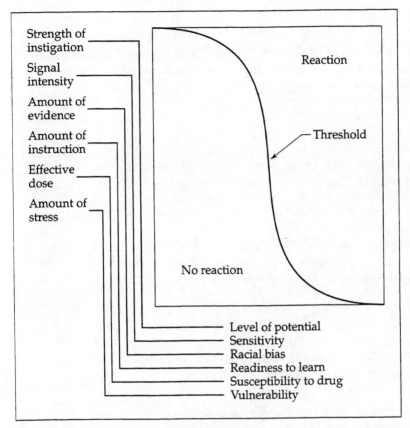

FIGURE 7-13 Kimble's Threshold Model

Source: "Mother Nature's Bag of Tricks is Small" by G. A. Kimble, 1990, *Psychological Science, 1,* 37. Copyright 1990 by Cambridge University Press. Reprinted by permission.

- If someone is prepared to learn, then the teacher's job is much easier. With some students, your efforts as a teacher seem to be of no avail. Teaching such students is like trying to push a boulder up a hill. With other students, the situation is reversed. Some students are so ready to learn that you have only to suggest a direction for inquiry, and the student does the rest on his or her own.
- Some people can take only a small quantity of a drug before showing its effects; others seem to have a much higher tolerance.
- As with drugs, so with stress. In certain situations, some people show the effects of stress before others. Everyone can tolerate a certain amount of stress, but as it accumulates, even those who are relatively invulnerable to it will show its effects.

STOP

Notice the wide range of phenomena that Kimble's model subsumes. The exploration of these relationships is an important part of several areas of inquiry in psychology. What other phenomena can you think of that may fit this model?

Kimble suggests that research in any area could be guided by such questions as the following:

- What determines potential? Here Kimble suggests such variables as *maturation* and *learning*.
- What determines the location of the threshold at different levels of potential? Here Kimble notes that there may be several variables determining its location, such as *aptitude* and *motivation*.

Models such as Kimble's (1990) are useful because they suggest a general way of thinking about the relationships between variables. A model such as Kimble's allows you to see "underlying unity amidst apparent variety" (Arnheim, 1974). The process of "blind variation and selective retention" is another example of this kind of model.

Blind Variation and Selective Retention

Darwin's theory of evolution is one of the most influential theories of all time. It has been used to understand a very wide range of phenomena. One of the most influential methodologists in psychology, D. T. Campbell (1960), suggested that the essence of the evolutionary process was *blind variation* and *selective retention*. Blind variation refers to any process whereby alternative courses of action are explored without knowing where these alternatives will lead. A famous example of blind variation in psychology is the phenomenon of *trial and error learning*. An example of this process was provided by one of the founders of the comparative approach in psychology, C. Lloyd Morgan (1894). Morgan had a dog named Tony, whom he kept in the backyard. Tony learned to lift the latch on the gate and escape. Tony did not sit in a corner of the yard, thinking about how to escape. Rather, he appeared to vary his behavior blindly until he accidentally hit on the response that freed him. Trial and error learning involves blind variation of one's behavior, and the selective retention of those behaviors that are successful.

Campbell (1960) noted that *echolocation* is a very good example of blind variation. Echolocation is a process whereby a sound is emitted that echoes off a target. The direction of the echo is a cue to the location of the target. Some blind people appear to be able to echolocate objects. Some species of bats emit echo-producing sounds that provide information about the whereabouts of objects in their environment.

I happen to know quite a bit about blind echolocation, because I was a subject in an experiment concerned with teaching people how to echolocate (Taylor, 1966). To get some idea of how to do such an experiment, take a look at Figure 7-14. If you were a subject in such an experiment, you would be blindfolded and seated at a table. A metal target would be placed at one of the positions marked in Figure 7-14. This position would be chosen randomly. Your task would be to move your head from side to side while saying, "Where is it? Where is it?" Whenever you felt like it, you would reach for the target. If you did not hit the target, you would keep on saying, "Where is it? Where is it?" and reach for the target again. This process would be repeated until you actually hit the target. At that point, a white noise generator would be turned on, and the target would be moved to another randomly chosen position.

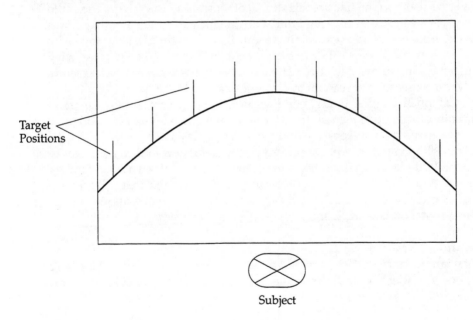

FIGURE 7-14 Echolocation

Source: Cognition, by John G. Benjafield, 1992, Englewood Cliffs, NJ: Prentice Hall, p. 349. Copyright 1992 by Prentice Hall. Reprinted by permission.

Since white noise contains all audible frequencies, it masks the sound of the target being moved. This means that you cannot hear the target being moved from one position to another. After the target has been moved, a new trial begins. An experimental session might last until you felt that you had enough. For the first few sessions, your ability to hit the target is liable to be no better than chance. However, with practice you would begin to hit the target more reliably. As a subject, I found myself acquiring a vague sense of where the target was, although I was never actually aware of an echo. In fact, the cue that comes to guide the subject's reaching is an echo produced by saying, "Where is it?" The sounds corresponding to letters such as *s* and *t* are called *fricatives*, because, as the *Oxford English Dictionary* explains, they are "produced by the friction of the breath through a narrow opening." Such sounds are very good for producing an echo from the metal target.

Echolocation is a good example because, as Campbell pointed out, the sound that is emitted is not directed toward any particular target. That is, the sound is emitted *blindly*; by moving the head from side to side the subject samples all directions equally, allowing him or her to pick up information that tells where the target is. Once you have acquired the skill of echolocating, you may find that you can transfer this skill to other situations. Perhaps you could even win a wager that you could find a target (such as a metal lamp) that was moved from one place to another in a room. So you might like to arrange with a friend to try to replicate the experiment in Figure 7-14, and see what happens. You will need a lot of patience, since the skill cannot be learned in only one experimental session, but it might pay off in the end.

Campbell suggested that blind variation was an important aspect of virtually any creative process. In order to discover something new, you must vary your behavior and observe the consequences. If you are lucky, the results of your blind variation will provide you with useful new information. Notice the similarity between Campbell's views and the view of scientific discovery advocated by Skinner. As we saw earlier, Skinner argued that science proceeds largely by lucky accidents, or serendipity. As it happens, another one of Harré's categories of experiment was *exploiting an accident*.

Additional Reading
Catania and Harnad (1984) provide a useful compendium of B. F. Skinner's papers, many of which illustrate the principles we have considered in this section.

Exploiting an Accident

The word *accident* has several different meanings, according to the *Oxford English Dictionary*, including "an unforeseen contingency; a disaster" and "chance; fortune." While the assassination of President Kennedy in 1963 was not a chance event like an earthquake, it still fits one of the definitions of an accident as "an unforeseen contingency; a disaster." Such "accidental" events, regrettable as they are, provide an opportunity to examine people's psychological responses. President Kennedy's assassination was the subject of a famous psychological experiment that created a new concept—*flashbulb memories*.

Are There Some Things That I Never Forget?

Brown and Kulik (1977) asked 80 Harvard undergraduates to try to recall the circumstances in which they heard of the death of President Kennedy. Their study took place in the mid-1970s, more than a decade after Kennedy's assassination. Thus their subjects would have been of school age when the assassination occurred. The subjects wrote an account of what they remembered. They also estimated how *consequential* they felt that the event was, and how *frequently* they had talked about it.

The second author of the Brown and Kulik (1977) study reported the following memory, which is quite typical:

> I was seated in a sixth grade music class, and over the intercom I was told that the president had been shot. At first, everyone just looked at each other. Then the class started yelling, and the music teacher tried to calm everyone down. About ten minutes later I heard over the intercom that Kennedy had died and that everyone should return to their homeroom. I remember that when I got to my homeroom my teacher was crying and everyone was standing in a state of shock. They told us to go home. (p. 74)

Such memories were christened flashbulb memories by Brown and Kulik, because they seem to be as accurate as a photograph taken of the event. Almost all of Brown and Kulik's subjects reported clear and distinct memories of the Kennedy assassination. Analysis of these reports showed that they often contained the following kinds of information, called *canonical categories*.

1. *Place*. Subjects are able to describe, often in some detail, where they were when the assassination was brought to their attention.
2. *Ongoing event*. Subjects also recall what else was going on when they heard about the assassination.
3. *Informant*. Subjects remember who told them about the event.
4. *Own Affect* (feeling). Subjects recall how they felt upon hearing the news.
5. *Aftermath*. Finally, subjects can remember what happened immediately after they became aware of the assassination.

See if you can identify the instances of these canonical categories in Kulik's flashbulb account.

Brown and Kulik suggested that flashbulb memories resulted from what Livingston (1967) had called a *Now Print mechanism*. Brown and Kulik (1977) described this process as follows: "First comes the recognition of high novelty or unexpectedness; then comes a test for biological meaning for the individual; if this second test is met, there follows the permanent registration not only of the significant novelty, but of all recent brain events" (p. 76). The assassination of a president of the United States meets these conditions and leads to the formation of a flashbulb memory. It is as if there is a memory process analogous to what happens when you press the *Print* button on a copy machine. A faithful copy of the experience is laid down in memory in a way similar to that in which a photocopier can make a replica of an image. The flashbulb process would be triggered only by highly emotional, unexpected events that had important consequences for the person and/or the culture.

STOP

What criticisms of Brown and Kulik's experiment would you make? If you were witness to another important accident, what kind of study would you do? How would your study differ from Brown and Kulik's?

Brown and Kulik's work elicited a great deal of attention, partly because it posited the existence of a new type of memory. Their conclusions were called into question, however, by a study of another unfortunate accident, the *Challenger* space shuttle explosion on January 28, 1986 (Bohannon, 1988; McCloskey, Wible, & Cohen, 1988).

Three days after the shuttle disaster, McCloskey et al. (1988, pp. 172–173) asked 45 subjects the following questions:

1. *Location.* Where were you when you first learned of the explosion?
2. *Activity.* What were you doing when you first learned of the explosion?
3. *Source.* Did you see the event at the time it was actually happening, or did you learn about it later? If later, how did you learn about it?
4. *Reaction.* What were your first thoughts upon hearing the news?

Twenty-nine of the same subjects were also given this questionnaire nine months after the event. Subjects also rated their confidence in the correctness of their answers on a seven-point scale. A comparison of the three-day and nine-month questionnaire data showed that a great deal of information had been lost in the interval. The nine-month accounts tended to provide less specific information in response to the location, activity, source, and reaction questions. For example, a three-day account might identify the source by naming a particular person, while a nine-month account might fail to give the name of the source. Subjects were also less confident that their nine-month accounts were accurate. McCloskey et al. concluded that so-called flashbulb memories are subject to the same kind of forgetting that occurs for ordinary memories, and that no special flashbulb memory mechanism is responsible for their occurrence.

The study of accidents is one aspect of the exploration of *naturally occurring processes*. As we saw earlier, not all interesting experiments take place in the laboratory. Naturally occurring phenomena also afford important research opportunities.

Additional Reading

The views of McCloskey et al. (1988; Cohen, McCloskey, & Wible 1990) have been challenged by Pillemer (1990).

Although the study of flashbulb memories has often focused on events experienced by an entire population, such as the assassination of President Kennedy or the *Challenger* disaster, Brown and Kulik (1977) noted that flashbulbs might be generated by "personal shocks." Personal shocks are events that are of primary importance to you and that take you by surprise. It might be useful to think through what kind of experiment you might do that would focus on such personal shocks. Examine the references in Pillemer (1990) for additional ideas.

Exploring the Characteristics of Naturally Occurring Processes

In Chapter 4 we considered the topic of quasi-experimental designs. Such experiments use naturally occurring variables rather than explicit laboratory manipulations. Recall Coren and Halpern's work (1991) on left- and right-handers, also discussed earlier. In this section we will examine quasi-experimental work that bears on the process of science itself.

The Process of Peer Review

How is it decided that a scientific paper is worthy of publication in a respected journal? Since you may someday wish to submit a paper to a journal for publication, this is more than just an "academic question," as it were. As we have already seen, there can be considerable debate concerning whether or not a particular piece of research has met the appropriate standards. Someone must make the decision to publish or not to publish the paper. Who should it be? Should the decision be left to the journal editor? Probably not, because that is too much responsibility to be placed in any one person's hands, no matter how competent he or she may be. Moreover, no one is an expert in all the subfields that make up a discipline. A better procedure, and one that has been very widely adopted, is to have papers in particular areas reviewed by acknowledged experts in that area. The judgment of these referees constitutes a system of *peer review*. Cicchetti (1991, pp. 119-120) has defined peer review as "a system of decision making by referees . . . [and] editors . . . in evaluating the quality of scientific research" and noted that reviewers are expected to assess manuscripts using such criteria as the following:

- Demonstrates knowledge of the relevant literature
- Is original and imaginative
- Uses viable research methodology
- Analyzes data appropriately
- Produces useful results
- Is well organized and well written

You can see that these criteria might not be easy to implement in all cases. In addition, since psychology journals typically use more than one reviewer for each manuscript, judgments about such attributes as *originality*, *imaginativeness*, *usefulness*, and *organization* might not be very reliable. Moreover, reviewers might use criteria other than the stated ones when they make a judgment about the manuscript. These possibilities give rise to at least two interesting research questions about reviewers' behavior:

1. Do reviewers agree in their assessment of a manuscript?
2. Do reviewers use criteria other than the stated ones to evaluate a manuscript?

Are Reviewers Biased?

Peters and Ceci (1982) did a study that called attention to the possibility that manuscript reviewers were biased in favor of some kinds of manuscripts rather than others. In their survey of previous studies of manuscript reviewer behavior, they note that the reliability of reviewers is far from perfect. There appears to be quite a bit of disagreement, even among reviewers of highly respected journals. Moreover, there is evidence that reviewers from prestigious universities evaluate a manuscript more favorably if it has been written by someone from another prestigious university than if it has been written by someone from a mediocre university. This suggests the possibility that reviewers are *biased* in favor of authors from prestigious universities. Peters and Ceci set out to test this hypothesis.

Peters and Ceci (1982) selected 12 highly respected psychology journals. A good measure of a journal's prestige is its *citation rate*, or the frequency with which articles published in the journal are cited by other authors. Another measure of a journal's prestige is its *rejection rate*, or the percentage of articles submitted that are rejected for publication. The 12 journals selected had high citation rates as well as high rejection rates (about 80%).

Having identified their target journals, Peters and Ceci then selected one recently published article from each journal. These articles were authored by faculty from prestigious psychology departments. A prestigious psychology department was one that had been named by previous surveys as particularly influential, according to such criteria as the frequency with which the work of members of the department was cited by other researchers.

Peters and Ceci then made superficial alterations in the 12 articles. They changed the names and affiliations of the authors to fictitious names and institutions (e.g., "Dr. Wade M. Johnston . . . at the Tri-Valley Center for Human Potential" and also altered the papers' titles, lists of key words, and abstracts (Peters & Ceci, 1982, p. 189). The altered papers were then submitted to the journals in which the originals had been published. None of the journals in the study employed the practice of *blind reviewing*, whereby the identity of the author is concealed from reviewers.

Intriguingly, it turned out that 9 in 12 of the altered articles "were not detected (by editors or reviewers) as having been previously submitted" (Peters & Ceci, 1982, p. 189). Moreover, of the 9 articles, 8 were rejected *by the same journal that had accepted them previously*. Most of the reviewers' criticisms of the altered articles centered on methodological flaws—which would, of course, have been in the original articles. Of 38 reviewers and editors who had seen one of the original articles, 35 failed to pick up the fact that the altered article was a minor variant of an article that had already been published in their journal.

Peters and Ceci (1982, p. 192) noted that their study might illustrate a phenomenon similar to experimenter bias (Rosenthal, 1967), which we considered in Chapter 4. Reviewers expect that good articles will be written by authors at prestigious institutions. This might also mean that if you are not at a prestigious institutions, then you will not be expected to write good articles, and reviewers will be biased against your work.

STOP

Do Peters and Ceci's findings (1982) unequivocally show that reviewers tend to judge an article in terms of where it comes from, rather than on the basis of its scientific merit? What do you think about the ethics of this study? Was it right to deceive editors and reviewers in this way?

It is interesting to note the reaction to the Peters and Ceci article on the part of editors of journals representing older and more established sciences. For example, Lazarus (1982), who is editor in chief for the society that publishes prominent physics journals, notes that even reviewers in physics often disagree about the merits of scientific papers. He also argues it is not surprising that an author's institutional affiliation should influence the way his or her paper is received. Lazarus (1982) asks, "Aren't a person's institution and reputation legitimate measures of the value of his work?" (p. 219). What do *you* think?

Rosenthal (1982) denied that the Peters and Ceci's findings (1982) could be taken as an experimental test of bias. He argued that any experiment, quasi- or otherwise, "requires assessing the effects on a dependent variable of a manipulated independent variable," and that the "authors *have not employed any independent variable*" (p. 235). In this case, a proper test of Peter and Ceci's hypothesis would have employed an experimental design similar to that in Table 7-4. This design has two independent variables: *author's prestige* (high versus low) and *type of manuscript* (previously accepted versus previously rejected). Notice that the manuscripts submitted would be presented as being written not only by low-prestige but also by high-prestige authors. This would enable the investigator to determine more precisely if the prestige of an author influenced rejection rates. Presumably high-prestige pseudo-authors would have lower rejection rates. The other manipulation involves submitting not only papers that had previously been accepted but also papers that had previously been rejected. Does the status of the author influence rejection rates independently of the kind of paper being submitted?

Additional Reading

Cicchetti (1991) provides a thorough review of current research on this topic. Cicchetti's article was published in *Behavioral and Brain Sciences*, a journal that employs "open peer commentary," a system whereby several peers of the writer(s) of a target article openly express their opinions of it, and the author then has a chance to reply.

TABLE 7-4 A Possible Experiment on Reviewer Bias

		Author	
		High-Prestige	Low-Prestige
Paper	Previously accepted		
	Previously rejected		

Is There a Home-Field Dis-*advantage?*

Earlier we considered Coren's work (e.g., Coren & Halpern, 1991) on left- and right-handers in baseball and noted that sports archives are a useful data source for testing hypotheses. Perhaps no one has been more ingenious in the use of such archives to test hypotheses than Baumeister (1984; Baumeister & Steinhilber, 1984).

Baumeister and Steinhilber (1984) studied the effects of supportive audiences on sports championships. They argued that typically a supportive audience improves a player's performance. That is why it is *usually* better for a team to play at home than on the road. Some performances are more important than others, however. In a particularly important game, the audience may make the performer more self-conscious than he or she usually is (Schlenker & Leary, 1982). Heightened self-awareness may not be a good thing when you are trying to execute an overlearned skill. Try to tie your shoelaces while being aware of every movement you make! I think that you will find it very difficult to execute a motor skill self-consciously if that skill normally runs itself off more or less automatically. The skills of professional athletes are extremely well practiced, and so one might expect self-awareness to interfere with their execution.

Baumeister and Steinhilber (1984) observed that there are two ways in which self-awareness can hinder performance:

1. The athlete is *distracted* from his real job. "The shortstop who is busy imagining himself celebrated as a World Series hero in a victory parade may misjudge a ball bouncing toward him and make a fielding error" (p. 86).
2. Paying attention to a skill that is normally performed automatically changes the way it is performed. "The shortstop who monitors the arm and hand muscle movements by which he throws a baseball to first base, after years of doing it automatically, may alter the skillful execution and make an error" (p. 86).

Whatever the relative contributions of each of these causes, it can be predicted that during particularly important contests (e.g., a decisive championship game), a home-team audience wants a victory even more than in routine home games. The crowd puts even more pressure on the home team to win than they usually do. This pressure is what makes home-team players more self-aware. They may wonder if they are really up to the championship role. This self-awareness causes their performance to suffer—they *choke under pressure* (Baumeister, 1984). This pressure is not experienced as intensely by visiting teams, and so their performance will be less affected.

STOP

How *exactly* would you test the Baumeister and Steinhilber (1984) hypothesis? What data do you need?

Baumeister and Steinhilber (1984) tested their hypothesis by comparing performance in World Series games for decisive and nondecisive contests. These data are presented in Table 7-5. Using the table, we can compare the outcomes of the first two games in the World Series with the outcomes of the the last game. The last game was the decisive game, and it could have been any of games 5, 6, and 7. (Baumeister and Steinhilber excluded series in which there was a four-game sweep, on grounds that such series were "mismatches" that were unlikely to show the influence of any home-field advantage or disadvantage.) Notice the reversal in fortune for the home team, which wins most of the first two games but loses the majority of the decisive games. This effect is still pronounced if one only compares games 1 and 2 with game 7. The home team tends to "choke" in decisive games.

Baumeister and Steinhilber (1984) conducted a series of ingenious analyses to investigate additional aspects of this phenomenon. One of these analyses is shown in Table 7-6. It addresses the question of whether the home team "chokes" because they are afraid of losing or because they are uncertain about claiming the winner's role. Data from game 6 is relevant to this question, because at the start of game 6, one team has already won three games, while the other team has lost two games. Thus the former team can be champions if they win, while the latter team will lose the series if they lose the game. Notice that when the home team must win just to stay in the series, then it tends to do so, but when the home team can win the championship, then it

TABLE 7-5 World Series Game Results, 1924–1982

	Winners		
Games	Home	Visitor	Home %
1 and 2	59	39	.602
Last game	20	29	.408
7	10	16	.385

Source: "Paradoxical Effects of Supportive Audiences on Performance under Pressure: The Home Field Disadvantage in Sports Championships" by R. F. Baumeister and A. Steinhilber, 1984, *Journal of Personality and Social Psychology, 47,* 87. Copyright 1984 by the American Psychological Association. Reprinted by permission.

TABLE 7-6   Outcome of Game 6 in World Series

Pressure	Winners		Home %
	Home	Visitor	
Home team must win	16	6	.727
Home team can clinch championship	6	10	.375

Source: "Paradoxical Effects of Supportive Audiences on Performance under Pressure: The Home Field Disadvantage in Sports Championships" by R. F. Baumeister and A. Steinhilber, 1984, *Journal of Personality and Social Psychology, 47*, 89. Copyright 1984 by the American Psychological Association. Reprinted by permission.

tends not to do so. This suggests that it is the possibility of *winning*, not the possibility of *losing*, that causes "choking."

Additional Reading
In their article, Baumeister and Steinhilber (1984) also analyze data from basketball championships. The topic of the home-field advantage has been extensively researched, not only in psychology but also in sociology (e.g., Schwartz & Barsky, 1977). If you are interested in this and similar issues, take a look at *Psychology of Sport* and *The Sociology of Sport Journal*. Archival sporting data have also been used to investigate other important social questions (e.g., Lavoie, Grenier, & Coulombe, 1987).

Finding the Explanation of a Known Effect

Harré (1983, p. 126) observed that scientific inquiry proceeds at different levels. Investigations may begin with a known relationship that has unknown causes. The known relationship is assumed to have a "deeper" cause than is apparent on the "surface." In this section we will review two studies that explore the causes of well-known psychological phenomena.

How Many Animals Did Moses Take on the Ark?

Reder and Kusbit (1991) have tried to uncover the reasons for the *Moses illusion*. This charmingly named cognitive illusion can be illustrated by the answer that people typically give to questions such as "How many animals of each kind did Moses take on the Ark?" The typical answer is "Two." This answer is often given quickly and without any apparent uncertainty. The problem with the answer is that *Moses* did not take any animals on the ark; *Noah* did.

The Moses illusion is named after the preceding example and is a very robust phenomenon, as the following examples, all taken from Reder and Kusbit (1991), show:

- *Question:* What country was Margaret Thatcher president of? *Answer:* United Kingdom
- *Question:* Who found the glass slipper left at the ball by Snow White? *Answer:* The prince
- *Question:* What superhero does Clark Kent become when he changes in a tollbooth? *Answer:* Superman

Did you notice the mistake in each question? Margaret Thatcher was prime minister, not president; it was Cinderella, not Snow White, who lost her slipper; and Clark Kent changes in a phone booth, not a tollbooth. Most people do not comment on the question but answer it anyway. Why do people apparently not notice the error in the question and respond instead to another version of the question?

STOP

Why do you think the Moses illusion occurs? What kind of experiment would you do to try to uncover its cause?

Reder and Kusbit considered several possible explanations, including the following:

- We know the question is incorrect, but we cooperate with the interrogator in order not to hurt his or her feelings by pointing out the mistake.
- Our memory is usually so bad that we cannot detect the mistake in the question.
- We do not have very high standards for what constitutes a proper match between question and answer, and so we are satisfied with just a partial match between question and answer.

In one experiment, subjects were given two types of questions and responded with two types of answers. The experimental design is illustrated in Table 7-7. One set of questions were ill formed, like those given above. They were designed to elicit the Moses illusion. Another set of questions were well

TABLE 7-7 An Experiment on the Moses Illusion, Contrasting Two Types of Question and Two Types of Answer

		Question	
		Well-formed	Ill-formed
Answer	Gist		
	Literal		

formed (i.e., did not contain mistakes). All subjects received both types of question. One group of subjects answered by just trying to get the *gist* of the question, while another group treated the questions *literally* and responded with "Can't say" if the question made no sense to them.

The result was that subjects took longer to answer questions when they took them literally. Thus it is "easier to ignore distortions than to have to detect them" (Reder & Kusbit, 1991, p. 390). This result suggests that people do not pick up the error in the question and then decide to cooperate with what they think the questioner wants.

In another experiment, subjects studied the correct answers to some of the questions prior to being given the questions. For example, they would be told that "Clark Kent becomes Superman when he changes in a phone booth." This prior knowledge did not reduce the Moses illusion. This result suggests that the Moses illusion cannot be the result of having inaccurate or incomplete information in memory. Rather, it appears that people are quite tolerant of mismatches between questions and answers. People do not try to recall specific items such as individual names. Rather, they perform a vague general match between what the question is requesting and what information they have in memory. The person probably does not even notice the distortion. The Moses illusion would be an example of our general tendency to be *flexible* in our demands on our memory. Such flexibility is adaptive, because it will often be the case that the information we are asked for will not exactly match what we have in memory. So, instead of retrieving the exact answer, we come up with what seems like a reasonable possibility. You can get a feel for this process by recalling how you go about trying to answer an examination question for which you have only partial information.

Additional Reading
The original study of the Moses illusion was done by Erickson and Mattson (1981).

Why Do Babies Smile?

Many of you will have had the opportunity to smile at a baby. It is always pleasant if the baby smiles back. Why does a baby smile? Jones, Collins, and Hong (1991) tried to answer this question. They pointed out that there are two possible explanations, one *emotional* and the other *social*. Perhaps infants smile when they are happy. On the other hand, perhaps they smile in response to someone else.

STOP

What kind of experiment is needed to determine which of these two explanations of infant smiling is correct?

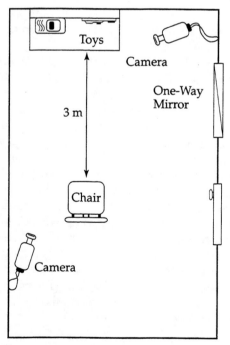

FIGURE 7-15 Experimental Setting

Source: "An Audience Effect on Smile Production in 10-Month-Old Infants" by S. S. Jones, K. Collins, and H. Hong, 1991, *Psychological Science*, 2, 46. Copyright 1991 by Cambridge University Press. Reprinted by permission.

Jones et al. cite a study by Kraut and Johnson (1979), who showed that bowlers do not smile immediately upon getting a strike. Rather, they smile when they turn to face their friends. This finding, and others like it, suggests that smiling in adults has a largely social function and is not merely the expression of an emotion. The question is, Do infants smile for purely emotional reasons, or are they also social smilers?

In their experiment, Jones et al. (1991) videotaped the behavior of 10-month-old infants (10 female and 10 male) in the setting shown in Figure 7-15. The child played with toys while the mother was seated behind. This allowed the child to turn and look at the mother. The mother was either *attentive* (responded as usual when the infant turned to her) or *inattentive* (ignored the infant). The videotapes were scored for the presence of smiles. This is not as difficult as you might imagine, since there is a standard scoring scheme for facial expressions (Ekman & Friesen, 1978).

The data summarized in Figure 7-16. Jones et al. (1991) found that "when mothers were attentive, infants directed a large majority of their smiles

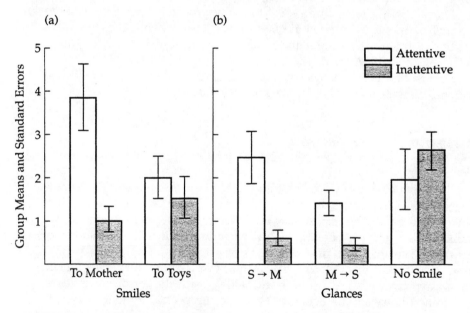

FIGURE 7-16 Means and Standard Errors of Smile and Glance Frequencies Produced by 10-Month-Old Infants During Toy Play with Mother Attentive versus Inattentive

Source: "An Audience Effect on Smile Production in 10-Month-Old Infants" by S. S. Jones, K. Collins, and H. Hong, 1991, *Psychological Science, 2,* 47. Copyright 1991 by Cambridge University Press. Reprinted by permission. (*a*) Smiles directed to infant's mother versus to the toys; (*b*) nonsmiling glances at mother, glances at mother followed by smiles (M → S), and existing smiles then turned toward mother (S → M).

towards their mothers, even though the babies were . . . engaged in a non-social activity," but "when mothers were inattentive, smiles directed back at the mother fell off dramatically" (p. 47). Moreover, the smiles that babies directed toward the mother did not appear always to be initiated by her. Rather, babies began to smile as they turned toward the mother, but before she came into view. This suggests that while a baby's smiling is influenced by the mother's attentiveness, it is also the result of the baby's ability to remember that mother had been attentive when the baby previously looked at her. Babies appear able to smile intentionally at mother; their smiles are not merely elicited by mother. Thus the smiling behavior of 10-month-old children reveals a social sensitivity and an ability to communicate that is more sophisticated than one might have imagined.

Additional Reading
Bavelas, Black, Lemery, and Mullett (1986) used a clever technique to uncover some aspects of the way in which adults communicate the fact that they empathically experience the pain that another person is experiencing.

Harré (1983) cited Gibson's ecological approach to perception as an example of finding the hidden mechanism of a known effect. Gibson's work has been extraordinarily influential, and an introduction to it may be found in Gibson (1966, 1969, 1979).

Superstition is a very widespread phenomenon that has been studied with revealing results by Rozin, Markwith, and Ross (1990).

Attempting to Demonstrate the Existence of a Psychological Entity

Psychologists often use words that appear to refer to unobservable psychological entities. Examples of such words are *habits, motives,* and *the self.* It is obviously a mistake to *reify* such words. Reification happens whenever we think a word refers to something real when in fact it is just a manner of speaking. Thus to speak of a person having a self may only be a way of describing the fact that the person does things with a particular style. It need not mean that there is a real thing, a *self,* hidden inside the person somewhere. Sometimes, however, the evidence points to the possibility that a concept refers to something that is really there, in some important sense. Such a concept is the *unconscious.*

Does the Unconscious Exist?

When we discussed Herbart and Kimble, we saw that there are good reasons for believing that psychological events can occur below threshold. Such

X path
X bridge
X ball
X soldier
X race
He really put his X in his mouth.

FIGURE 7-17 What Is X?

Source: "Revisioning the Unconscious" by K. S. Bowers, 1987, *Canadian Psychology, 28,* 93. Copyright 1987. Canadian Psychological Association. Reprinted with permission.

events are sometimes said to be unconscious. The concept of the unconscious has a very long history (Ellenberger, 1970). Many psychologists, however, have refused to accept the necessity of positing the existence of an unconscious. In this section we will examine some recent experimental evidence suggesting (if not proving) that the unconscious exists.

Consider Figure 7-17, which is taken from Bowers (1987). Most people have little or no difficulty guessing that X is *foot*. It seems obvious that *foot* is the right answer, even though it is difficult to say precisely why. Some ideas are just "intuitively obvious"; they just come to us without our actively seeking them. It is tempting to say, on the basis of demonstrations like this, that such ideas emerge as a result of unconscious psychological processes.

According to Bowers (1987), the unconscious is an idea that is *suggested* by a large number of facts, without there being any one piece of evidence that *proves* its existence. What sort of experimental evidence inclines at least some psychologists toward believing in the reality of the unconscious?

A good example of such an experiment is a recent study by Kihlstrom, Schacter, Cork, Hurt, and Behr (1990). They were interested in whether or not people undergoing surgery are able to remember events that took place while they were anesthetized (and therefore unconscious). Obviously, common sense tells you that patients are usually unable to remember consciously the events that took place while they were unconscious as a result of being anesthetized. Nevertheless, there is some anecdotal information suggesting that events that take place during surgery can have an effect on a patient's subsequent behavior even though the patient cannot consciously recall the events. As examples, Kihlstrom et al. (1990) mention that "patients occasionally show adverse postoperative responses—perhaps an inexplicable dislike for their surgeons, or a bad dream—that upon investigation, seem to be related to some untoward event that occurred during the operation" (p. 303). Thus while patients may have an amnesia for events during surgery, they may nevertheless indirectly show the effects of those events.

STOP

How would you go about demonstrating this phenomenon experimentally? You need to be able to measure a *dissociation* between two types of memory (Schacter, 1987, p. 501). The subjects must lack *explicit* memory (the kind that is consciously recalled) but nevertheless show *implicit* memory (an effect of previous experience of which the person is unaware). How could you test these two kinds of memory?

The first thing Kihlstrom et al. (1990) did was to create a set of "events" that people could be exposed to while under anesthesia. There were two sets of events, each recorded on a separate audiotape. Each tape contained 15 paired-associate items. Each of the items consisted of a stimulus word and a response word, and the two lists were matched in terms of the ease with which the stimulus word elicited the response word. Such matching is possible because of the existence of word association norms (e.g., Palermo & Jenkins, 1964). A *free associate* is the response that first comes to mind upon presentation of a stimulus. Thus most adults, when asked to name the first word they think of when they hear "chair" will say "table"; when they hear "body" adults most often say "mind," although they can think of other things as well (Deese, 1965). In the Kihlstrom et al. (1990) experiment, the stimulus word elicited the response word as a free associate approximately 50% of the time. That means that half the time people will give the word as an associate, and half the time they will give some other word as an associate.

Kihlstrom et al. report data for 25 patients who had been told that they would be given a tape-recorded message while under anesthesia, and later were tested to see if they could remember what had been played to them. The experimenters randomly selected one of the two tapes and played it to the subject while he or she was anesthetized. On average, subjects were under anesthesia for 82 minutes, during which time the tape played over and over again. Subjects typically had recovered to the extent that their memory could be tested approximately 87 minutes after surgery.

Subjects were given four different memory tests. The tests involved both the tape that had been played to them while under anesthesia (the critical tape) and the tape to which they had not been exposed (the neutral tape). The experimenter was not aware of which tape had been used during surgery. (If you recall our earlier discussion of experimenter bias and demand characteristics, you will know why the experimenter had to be "blind" to which tape was which.) One of the tests involved *free recall* of anything the subjects remembered from the time they were anesthetized. This test did not show any superiority for the critical, as opposed to the neutral, tape. The other memory tests were *cued recall, recognition,* and *free association.* In cued recall subjects are given a stimulus word and then try to recall the word that was paired with it. In recognition subjects are given the stimulus-response pairs and asked if they recognize any as having been read to them during anesthesia. Neither of these tests showed any superiority for the critical, as opposed to the neutral, tape. Thus the critical tape did not show any effect of cued recall or recognition when compared with the neutral tape. These are tests of explicit memory, and these results indicate that there is no evidence of explicit memory as a result of exposure to information under anesthesia. The fourth test, free association, did show such an effect. When subjects were given a stimulus word and asked for the first word that came to mind, they responded with more correct associates for the critical tape than for the neutral tape. This is a test of implicit memory, because subjects are not explicitly trying to remember anything. They are just saying whatever they think of first. The results of the fourth test show that implicit memory can occur in the absence of explicit memory.

For Kihlstrom (1987), experimental results such as these are persuasive evidence of unconscious mental events. It appears as if learning can take place unconsciously, and the effects of such learning can manifest themselves without the person's awareness.

Additional Reading
In a follow-up study, Wood, Bootzin, Kihlstrom, and Schacter (1992) have shown that implicit learning appears *not* to take place during sleep.

Another line of investigation leading to conclusions similar to Kihlstrom's was undertaken by Reber (e.g., 1989; Reber, Allen, & Regan, 1985). A critique of the concept of the unconscious can be found in Dulany, Carlson, & Dewey (1984, 1985).

Analyzing a Phenomenon

The Perception of Color

As Harré (1983, p. 167) observes, the study of color owes much to Isaac Newton's discovery that by passing sunlight thorough a prism it could be broken down into a set of different colors. This suggested that white light was made up of those colors and was thus a *complex* phenomenon that could be analyzed into simpler *elements.* The mixing of these elements would result in white. The research strategy of attempting to find simple elements that make up complex phenomena is very common. Developments in the study of color since Newton illustrate this research strategy.

Let us begin with some basic facts about the eye, with which you may already be familiar. The retina contains two main types of receptors, *rods* and *cones*. The rods are sensitive to light and dark; they are involved in *achromatic* perception. *Achromatic* means "without color," and achromatic perception is our perception that something is bright or dim, black or white. As a result of the rods' action, we can perceive light versus dark, black versus white. One early theory of color perception, advanced by Young (1802) and Helmholtz (1860) before the structure of the eye was well understood, held that there are three color receptors in the retina, corresponding to red, green, and blue. This is the Young-Helmholtz theory, and it can be interpreted as meaning that there are three types of cones, one for each of red, green, and blue. This theory holds that these three are the *primary colors*, which when mixed in different proportions give rise to all the other colors. By mixing primary colors, we can derive all the colors we are used to seeing.

STOP

Can you think of any examples of color mixture that could be used as evidence for a theory such as that of Young and Helmholtz?

Pictures on a color-television screen are typically made up of red, green, and blue dots. A venerable demonstration of color mixing is the so-called color wheel, illustrated in Figure 7-18. By varying the proportions of the colors on the wheel, and rotating the wheel at a high speed, one can see a variety of single colors. This is called *additive color mixture*, because individual colors are "mixed in the eye," as it were (Bremner & Prescott, 1984). There are many other ways of deriving colors, but they need not concern us here. All you need to understand is that the hypothesis that some colors can be broken down into more elementary colors can apparently be demonstrated using a simple apparatus such as the color wheel.

Of course, there is always an alternative interpretation of any phenomenon. The alternative to the Young-Helmholtz theory goes back to such eminent personages as Leonardo da Vinci and the great German poet Goethe (1810/1970). Goethe made the point that our *experience* of white cannot be decomposed into a set of more elementary colors. When I look at a white wall, for example, I see a *white* wall, not a wall made up of a mixture of any other colors. Goethe is appealing to our raw visual experience. If you examine your visual experience, don't you discover *four* basic colors? These colors are red, yellow, green, and blue. If you add our experience of the achromatic colors, then you get black, white, red, yellow, green, and blue as basic colors. Accord-

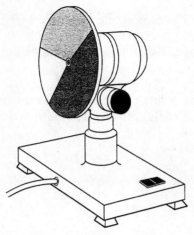

FIGURE 7-18   A Color Wheel

Source: Elements of Psychology by D. Krech and R. S. Crutchfield, 1969, New York: Knopf, p. 59. Copyright © 1958 by David Krech and Richard S. Crutchfield. Copyright © 1969 by Alfred A. Knopf, Inc. Reprinted by permission of the publisher.

ing to the alternative to the Young-Helmholtz theory, these are arranged in antagonistic pairs: black versus white, red versus green, and yellow versus blue (Hering, 1905–1911/1964). This approach is commonly called an *opponent-process* color theory (Hurvich & Jameson, 1957).

STOP

Can you think of any common experiences that lend themselves to an interpretation in terms of an opponent-process color theory?

Perhaps you have experienced *afterimages*. Afterimages occur as a result of the prolonged inspection of one color—blue, for example. Then if you close your eyes, you experience the opposite color, in this case yellow. Phenomena like this have been taken as supporting an opponent-process theory. Following the stimulation of one member of an opponent-process pair (such as blue versus yellow), there is a tendency for its opposite to be experienced when the first color is removed. Thus stimulation by blue gives rise to a yellow aftereffect, red gives rise to green, and white to black.

Once again you can see that the analysis of a phenomenon can often be accomplished by means of fairly simple demonstrations, such as afterimages. Keen observers are always on the lookout for naturally occurring phenomena that can be used to explore the underlying structure of psychological processes.

We should mention that both the Young-Helmholtz and the opponent-process theories have been integrated into a theory of color vision that captures the best features of each. The Young-Helmholtz approach seems to work best at the level of the retina, while opponent-process theory works well as color information is processed at higher levels of the visual system (Hilgard, 1987, p. 126).

Additional Reading

For a good overview of color theories, see Ratliff (1976) and Livingstone (1988).

Using the Right Experimental Technique

Is There a Difference between Seeing and Saying?

In an earlier chapter we considered the Greenwald, Spangenberg, Pratkanis, and Eskanazi study (1991) that attempted to determine whether or not so-called subliminal self-help audiotapes have any effect. We noted then that it is not easy to design experiments properly to evaluate the existence of so-called subliminal perception, or *subception*. There is a long history of experimental investigations of subception. You have probably heard about subliminal perception, or subception (e.g., Dixon, 1971; Lazarus & McCleary, 1951; Postman, Bruner, & McGinnis, 1948). These investigations have attempted to determine if a stimulus can have an effect on behavior even though it has been exposed too rapidly or at too low an intensity for the person to be able to identify it. Very often these experiments have presented subjects with words. The words are shown for very brief durations or at a very low intensity. That is, the words are below the subject's threshold. Nevertheless, there is some evidence that such weak stimuli can have strong effects on behavior (e.g., Erickson, Azuma, & Hicks, 1959; Wickens, 1970).

The problem with subception experiments is to determine whether or not the words are actually seen, even if the subjects do not say that they see them. If subjects actually see the words, even though they are very briefly exposed, then so-called subception effects would not be at all surprising. For example, suppose I show words to subjects for very brief durations. Is it possible that they *see* the words but, for whatever reasons, do not *say* them? How do we tell the difference between what a person *sees* and what a person *says* that he or she sees. At first it might seem impossible to be able to tease these two things apart. In order to explore such subtle distinctions, the experimenter must use ingenious experimental manipulations.

TABLE 7-8 Homophones Used in Neisser's Experiment

no	know
rain	reign
paste	paced
whirled	world
colonel	kernel
threw	through

Source: "An Experimental Distinction between Perceptual Process and Verbal Response" by U. Neisser, 1954, *Journal of Experimental Psychology, 47,* 400. Copyright 1954 by the American Psychological Association. Reprinted by permission.

Neisser (1954) took advantage of a useful feature of language to explore more precisely the difference between *seeing* a word and *saying* it. The feature of language he exploited involves *homophones*. Homophones are words that are pronounced the same but spelled differently. Table 7-8 contains some of the homophones that Neisser used in his experiment.

In the first phase of the experiment, subjects were shown a card with a list of words and told to try to keep this list in mind because it would help them to "see or guess" the words that they would be shown in the second phase of the experiment. Reading the list was supposed to establish an expectancy in the subject for the words shown. The experiment was designed to distinguish between the following two possibilities:

1. Reading the words makes it easier for you to *see* those words if they are shown to you again.
2. Reading the words makes it easier for you to *say* those words if they are shown to you again.

After reading the first list of words, subjects were shown a series of 15 words, one at a time, tachistoscopically. The 15 words included 5 words that they had read previously, 5 homophones of words that they had read previously, and 5 new, or control, words. The 15 words were exposed at longer and longer durations until they were recognized by the subject. The dependent variable was the length of exposure necessary for recognition to occur.

STOP

What predictions would you make if the first possibility is correct? What predictions would you make if the second possibility is correct?

Neisser reasoned that if reading the words makes it easier for you to *see* them on the next exposure, then thresholds should be lower for the words the subjects had seen before than for the homophones or new words. If reading the words makes it easier for you to *say* them on the next exposure, however, then thresholds should be lower for *both* the words the subjects had seen before *and* the homophones than for the new words, because both the words on the card and the homophones are *said* the same way. It turned out, however, that the words that had been seen before were recognized more quickly than either the homophones or the new words. This result supports the first possibility given above but does not support the second possibility.

A good experimental technique can be used in a variety of situations. Eich (1984) also used homophones to study a subtle distinction. Eich investigated implicit memory. Suppose people are presented with events to which they do not attend. They typically are not aware of remembering such events. However, they may show an effect of the previous exposure. This phenomenon is similar to the one we discussed earlier in our consideration of the reality of the unconscious and Kihlstrom et al.'s (1990) experiment.

In Eich's experiment (1984), subjects were given a *shadowing task*. Shadowing makes use of a very useful and widespread experimental technique called *dichotic listening*. Dichotic listening was employed in some of the most influential psychological experiments of all time (e.g., Broadbent, 1952/1992; Cherry, 1953). Dichotic listening involves "listening to one of two synchronous messages" (Broadbent, 1952/1992, p. 127). *Synchronous* means "at the same time." In a shadowing task, the subject wears headphones and is given one message in one ear, and another message in the other ear. The subject "shadows" one of the two messages by repeating it as it is heard.

In Eich's task (1984), the two messages were an 850-word excerpt from a humorous essay, and pairs of words. The second member of each word pair was a homophone, the interpretation of which could be influenced by the first member of the pair. For example, one of the pairs was *deep-sea*. In that case subjects would interpret the second word as *sea* and not *see*, because *sea* goes with *deep*.

Eich (1984) told subjects that "the primary purpose of the experiment was to investigate the influence of this extraneous information on an individual's ability to shadow, comprehend, and retain narrative material" (p. 107). Thus subjects were not instructed to try to recall the word pairs. After the dichotic listening task, subjects were asked to recall the gist of the essay. They were also given a recognition test, in which Eich spoke a word. Some of the words were homophones to which the subject had been exposed. The subject had to judge how confident he or she was that the word had been played in the unattended channel. Subjects were not very good at this recognition task. However, the interesting results occurred when the subjects were given a spelling test. When the author spoke a homophone, then subjects would tend to spell it in a way that was consistent with the interpretation that had been created by the earlier pair of words. Thus, for example, the subject would spell *sea* and not *see*. This suggests that the word pairs had an effect, even though subjects were not aware of having been exposed to them previously.

Notice how the use of homophones makes it possible to investigate a phenomenon we referred to earlier as *implicit memory*, or *memory without awareness* (Schacter, 1987, p. 501). This phenomenon is quite subtle and would elude investigators unless they employed sensitive experimental techniques. Sometimes experiments fail to demonstrate the existence of a phenomenon. Before concluding that the phenomenon does not exist, we would do well to consider whether or not the experimenter took enough care to utilize experimental techniques that were sensitive enough to give the phenomenon a chance to demonstrate itself.

Additional Reading
An important review of several experimental techniques in this area is provided by Tulving and Schacter (1990).

Finding the Right Test or Apparatus

As we saw in the previous section, the proper experimental technique can reveal psychological phenomena that we otherwise might not be able to investigate. It is also true that the right test, or experimental apparatus, can allow us to explore psychological processes that might otherwise remain unknown to us. A good example is the *Stroop task* (Stroop, 1935/1992), one of the most useful research tools ever invented (MacLeod, 1992).

What Happens When "Red" Is Blue?

The Stroop task (1935/1992) is named after the psychologist who first introduced it. An example of a Stroop task is presented in Figure 7-19. Of course, it is very easy to read the table of color names presented there. However, this task can become quite difficult if the color names are printed in different colors. Figure 7-20 gives you a list of colors for the words in Figure 7-19. The first word is red, and it is printed in *blue;* the second word is green, and it is printed in red; the third word is *blue*, and it is printed in *green;* and so on. It turns out to be very difficult to name the colors in which the words are printed.

It would be instructive for you to create your own Stroop task by coloring the words in Figure 7-19 in the colors given in Figure 7-20. First try reading the color names. Then try naming the colors of the words. You will find that the latter task is by far the more difficult of the two. One measure

red green blue green red yellow blue yellow blue green

yellow red blue yellow green red blue red blue yellow

blue yellow yellow blue red blue yellow green green red

red green green red green green green yellow red green

green blue blue yellow yellow yellow red red yellow green

yellow red green yellow blue green red green green blue

blue green red red green red green blue yellow yellow

red yellow yellow red blue yellow blue yellow green green

yellow blue red blue green green yellow blue blue red

green red yellow blue yellow blue red green red blue

blue red blue green red yellow blue blue yellow red

FIGURE 7-19 A Stroop Task

Source: A Factorial Study of Perception by L. L. Thurstone, 1944, Chicago: University of Chicago Press, p. 76. Copyright 1944 by The University of Chicago. All rights reserved. Reprinted by permission.

of the relative difficulty of the two tasks is how long it takes you to finish each one. Naming the colors of the words takes longer than reading the color words themselves. As an experience, naming the colors seems to require you to inhibit the tendency to read the names.

STOP

Why is it easier to read the color names than to name the colors in which they are printed?

The Stroop phenomenon is usually interpreted as reflecting the difference between *automatic* and voluntary, *or controlled*, processes (MacLeod,

blue red yellow blue green red yellow green red yellow

blue green red blue yellow green yellow blue yellow red

green blue green red green yellow blue red blue yellow

blue red blue green red yellow red blue green yellow

red yellow red blue green blue green yellow blue yellow

red blue yellow red green blue yellow red blue yellow

green red yellow blue yellow green red yellow green blue

green blue red yellow green red green blue red yellow

blue yellow green yellow blue red blue green red blue

red blue green red blue green yellow red green yellow

green yellow green yellow blue red yellow green red blue

FIGURE 7-20 Colors for the Words in Figure 7-19

Source: A Factorial Study of Perception by L. L. Thurstone, 1944, Chicago: University of Chicago Press, p. 78. Copyright 1944 by The University of Chicago. All rights reserved. Reprinted by permission.

1992). A skill that has been overlearned may tend to run itself off, whether we want it to or not. Once reading has become overlearned, then you read without thinking about it, as it were. In the Stroop situation, it is difficult not to read the words. Reading is an example of an automatic process. Such a process "takes care of itself." We do not need to pay attention to it in order for it to be done properly. By contrast, controlled processes require our attention if they are to be done properly (Shiffrin & Schneider, 1977). Naming the colors in which the words are printed is a controlled process (Shiffrin & Schneider, 1977).

Virtually anything can become an automatic process, in the sense that it can be executed without thinking. Such automaticity can lead to some very consequential errors. For example, a recent newspaper account told of a professor who owned and habitually drove a silver car but who had borrowed his wife's red car for the day. He parked the red car in the university parking lot, but when he left to go home he automatically went looking for the silver car he habitually drove. Not being able to find it, he reported it stolen. He apparently felt quite foolish when the police arrested his wife, who happened to be driving his silver car.

The distinction between automatic and controlled processes has been extensively investigated. The Stroop task is an invaluable device for such investigations. As MacLeod (1992) observes, the impact of the Stroop task can be measured by the fact that over 700 studies have employed it since it was introduced in 1935.

Additional Reading
MacLeod (1991) provides an extensive review of the literature devoted to the Stroop phenomenon.

Why Are We So Well Organized?

The Gestalt psychologists, who worked in Germany in the early part of this century, were among the most influential experimental psychologists of our time. In fact, they bequeathed the word *Gestalt* to our language. According to the *Oxford English Dictionary*, *gestalt* means "a shape, configuration, or structure which as an object of perception forms a specific whole or unity incapable of expression simply in terms of its parts (e.g., a melody in distinction from the notes that make it up)." The Gestalt psychologists believed that when we perceive things we tend to do so holistically. We organize our experience so as to make it as simple and coherent as possible (Koffka, 1935). The leader of the Gestalt psychologists was Max Wertheimer, who used *demonstrations* to illustrate his approach. A demonstration is a simple, easily observed phenomenon, usually requiring only a simple apparatus and having the same effect for almost everyone. Figure 7-21 illustrates a famous Gestalt demonstration called *phi phenomenon*, or apparent motion. The two lights can be alternately turned on by means of the switch. Each light casts a different shadow on the screen. However, at the right rate of alternation, a subject does not see *two* shadows but *one* shadow moving back and forth. The Gestalt psychologists took demonstrations like this as evidence that our perception need not be a copy of the stimulus conditions giving rise to it. Rather, our experience tended to be as simple as possible. Thus when conditions allow, we perceive one thing moving, rather than two things flashing on and off.

Phi phenomenon demonstrated to the Gestalt psychologists that experience could be simpler and more unified than the stimulus conditions giving rise to the experience. Instead of seeing two separate events, you see only one moving event.

Now examine the configurations in Figure 7-22. They are intended to illustrate the *Gestalt laws of organization*. These laws were supposed to describe

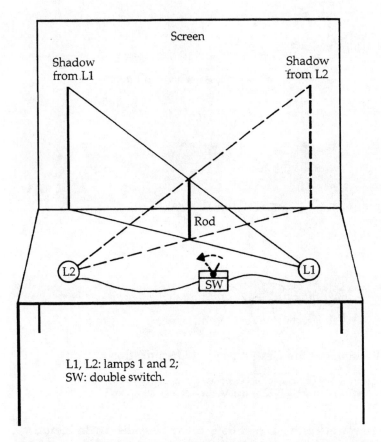

FIGURE 7-21 Apparatus to Demonstrate Apparent Motion

Source: The Task of Gestalt Psychology by W. Kohler, 1969, Princeton: Princeton University Press, p. 36. Copyright © 1969 by Princeton University Press. Reprinted by permission of Princeton University Press.

some of the basic ways in which we organize our experience as simply and coherently as possible. "When we are presented with a number of stimuli, we do not as a rule experience 'a number' of individual things. . . . Instead larger wholes . . . are given in experience; their arrangement and division are concrete and definite" (Wertheimer, 1923/1967, p. 72). For example, compare lines *A* and *B* in Figure 7-22. Notice that in line *B* there is a tendency to group the dots in pairs, but that there is no such tendency in *A*. This example illustrates the Gestalt principle of proximity: we tend to group things together that are close together in space. In Figure 7-22C, however, even though the

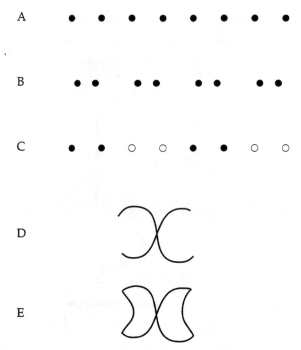

FIGURE 7-22 Examples of the Gestalt Laws of Organization

Source: "Common Region: A New Principle of Perceptual Grouping" by S. E. Palmer, 1992, *Cognitive Psychology, 24*, 437. Copyright © 1992 by the Academic Press. Reprinted by permission.

dots are equidistant, we see them in pairs because of *similarity*. In Figure 7-22D, we see two lines crossing. We do not see "two angles meeting at a point" (Palmer, 1992, p. 438). The principle operating here is called *good continuation*. In Figure 7-22E, however, we *do* see two forms meeting at a point. This is because of the principle of *closure*. We tend to make our experience as complete as possible. To summarize, the Gestalt psychologists believed that proximity, good continuation, and closure reflect a natural tendency toward "good forms" in our experience (Coren & Girgus, 1980).

Notice that the Gestalt psychologists used very simple methods to demonstrate the laws of organization. Such simple procedures can still lead to new discoveries. Palmer (1992; Rock & Palmer, 1990; Sekuler & Palmer, 1992) has recently demonstrated a new principle of organization, called *common region*. It is illustrated in Figure 7-23. "The proposed principle of common region states that, all else being equal, elements will be perceived as grouped together if they are located within a common region of space, i.e., if they lie within a connected, homogeneously colored or textured region or within an enclosing contour" (Palmer, 1992, p. 438).

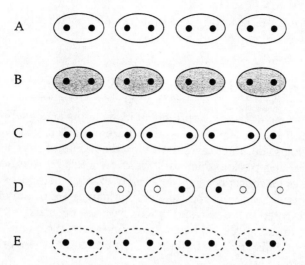

FIGURE 7-23 Palmer's New Gestalt Principle: Common Region

Source: "Common Region: A New Principle of Perceptual Grouping" by S. E. Palmer, 1992, *Cognitive Psychology, 24*, 439. Copyright © 1992 by the Academic Press. Reprinted by permission.

Observe that in Figure 7-23A and B, we see the dots in pairs even though they are equidistant from each other. This is because we see the pairs as sharing a common region. Common region can overcome the effects of other grouping principles. In Figure 7-23C, even though the first and second dots are closer together than the second and third dots, we tend to group the second and third, fourth and fifth, sixth and seventh, dots together because they share a common region. This shows common region overriding the effects of proximity. Common region can also override the effect of similarity, as shown in Figure 7-23D. Without the oval enclosures, we would see the filled dots as a pair, followed by the empty dots as a pair, and so on. Common region, however, makes us see a series of groups consisting of one filled and one empty dot. It is not that we cannot see the dots as grouped in some other way, but that common region inclines us to see them in a particular way, as opposed to some other way.

Palmer's research illustrates an important point. It is not necessary to have an elaborate apparatus to make interesting and important discoveries. His simple demonstrations, like Wertheimer's before him, allow us to see simple but important regularities that we might otherwise overlook.

Additional Reading
If you are interested in reviewing particularly well-known experiments in psychology, see Hock (1992). A new journal, *Current Directions in*

Psychological Science, contains up-to-the-minute reviews of current research in central areas in psychology.

Names and Concepts to Understand and Remember

The following are some of the most influential ideas in the area we have just reviewed. Some concepts are quite general and are not associated with any particular psychologist. In other cases, however, the names of psychologists are paired with the concepts for which they are known. Read through the list. If any of the names or concepts seem unfamiliar to you, then go back and reread the appropriate section of the chapter. The names are in the order in which they are presented in the text, and the concepts are italicized in the text, so they are easy to find. You should be able to define each concept and briefly discuss it. You should also be able to write a brief account of the work done by each person on the list.

mental rotation
mental chronometry
autobiographical memory
Galton's number
psychophysics
just noticeable difference (jnd)
Weber's law
rival hypotheses
arousal
Wundt-Berlyne curve
nonsense shapes
yoked-subjects design
computer simulation
imitation game
Turing's test
artificial intelligence
thinking aloud
concurrent and retrospective verbalization
catastrophe theory
catastrophe machine
control variable
state variable
hysteresis
cusp catastrophe
control plane
Newton's second law of motion

limen
blind variation and selective retention
flashbulb memories
Now Print mechanism
peer review
citation rate
rejection rate
blind reviewing
choke under pressure
Moses illusion
dissociation
explicit versus implicit memory
free recall
cued recall
rods and cones
achromatic
primary colors
additive color mixture
opponent process
afterimages
subception
homophones
shadowing task
dichotic listening
memory without awareness
Stroop task
automatic versus controlled processes
demonstration
phi phenomenon
Gestalt laws of organization

References

Alexander, R. A., Herbert, G. R., DeShon, R. P., & Hanges, P. J. (1992). An examination of least-squares regression modeling of catastrophe theory. *Psychological Bulletin, 111,* 366–374.

American Psychological Association. (1985). Guidelines for ethical conduct in the care and use of animals. Washington, DC: Author.

American Psychological Association (1989). *Directory of the American Psychological Association.* Washington, DC: Author.

American Psychological Association. (1992). *Ethical principles of psychologists and code of conduct.* Washington, DC: Author.

Amundson, R. (1985). Psychology and epistemology: The place versus response controversy. *Cognition, 20,* 127–153.

Anastasi, A. (1965). *Individual differences.* New York: Wiley.

Anderson, M. G. (1989). Lateral preferences and longevity. *Nature, 341,* 112.

Anzai, Y., & Simon, H. A. (1979). The theory of learning by doing. *Psychological Review, 86,* 124–140.

Arkes, H. R., & Hammond, K. R. (1986). *Judgement and decision making: An interdisciplinary reader.* New York: Cambridge University Press.

Arnheim, R. (1974). *Art and visual perception.* Berkeley, CA: University of California Press.

Bahrick, H. P., & Hall, L. K. (1991). Lifetime maintenance of high school mathematics content. *Journal of Experimental Psychology: General, 120,* 20–33.

Bakan, D. (1967). *On method.* San Francisco: Jossey Bass.

Baumeister, R. F. (1984). Choking under pressure: Self-consciousness and paradoxical effects of incentives on skillful performance. *Journal of Personality and Social Psychology, 46,* 610–620.

Baumeister, R. F., & Steinhilber, A. (1984). Paradoxical effects of supportive audiences on performance under pressure: The home field disadvantage in sports championships. *Journal of Personality and Social Psychology, 47,* 85–93.

Bavelas, J. B., Black, A., Lemery, C. R., & Mullet, J. (1986). "I *show* how you feel": Motor mimicry as a communicative act. *Journal of Personality and Social Psychology, 50,* 322–329.

Benjafield, J., Frommhold, K., Keenan, T., Muckenheim, R., & Mueller, D. (1993). Imagery, concreteness, goodness, and familiarity ratings for 500 proverbs sampled from the *Oxford Dictionary of English Proverbs. Behavior Research Methods. Instruments and Computers 25,* 27–40.

Benjafield, J., & Muckenheim, R. (1989). Dates-of-entry and measures of imagery, concreteness, goodness, and familiarity for 1,046 words sampled from the *Oxford English Dictionary. Behavior Research Methods, Instruments and Computers, 21,* 31–52.

Berlyne, D. E. (1965). *Structure and direction in thinking.* New York: Wiley.

Berlyne, D. E. (1971). *Aesthetics and psychobiology.* New York: Appleton-Century-Crofts.

Beveridge, W. I. B. (1957). *The art of scientific investigation.* New York: Vintage Books.

Birnbaum, M. H., & Mellers, B. A. (1979). Stimulus recognition may mediate exposure effects. *Journal of Personality and Social Psychology, 37,* 391–394.

Blumenthal, A. L. (1975). A reappraisal of Wilhelm Wundt. *American Psychologist, 30,* 1081–1088.

Bohannon, J. N. (1988). Flashbulb memories for the Space Shuttle disaster: A tale of two theories. *Cognition, 29,* 179–196.

Boneau, C. A. (1990). Psychological literacy: A first approximation. *American Psychologist, 45,* 891–900.

Boring, E. G. (1923). Intelligence as the tests test it. *New Republic, 35,* 35–37.

Boring, E. G. (1942). *Sensation and perception in the history of experimental psychology.* New York: Appleton-Century-Crofts.

Boring, E. G. (1945). The use of operational definitions in science. In R. I. Watson & D. T. Campbell (Eds.), *History, psychology, and science* (pp. 200–209). New York: Wiley.

Boring, E. G. (1950). *A history of experimental psychology* (2nd ed.). New York: Appleton-Century-Crofts.

Bower, G. (1992). Reviewing the basics. *APS Observer, 5*(2), 2.

Bowers, K. S. (1987). Revisioning the unconscious. *Canadian Psychology, 28,* 93–104.

Bowers, K. S., Regehr, G., Balthazard, C., & Parker, K. (1990). Intuition in the context of discovery. *Cognitive Psychology, 22,* 72–110.

Braver, M. C., & Braver, S. L. (1988). Statistical treatment of the Solomon four-group design: A meta-analytic approach. *Psychological Bulletin, 104,* 150–154.

Bremner, D., & Prescott, A. (1984). Painting with light. *New Scientist, 102,* 38–42.

Bridgman, P. W. (1927). *The logic of modern physics.* New York: Macmillan.

Broadbent, D. E. (1992). Listening to one of two synchronous messages. *Journal of Experimental Psychology, General, 121,* 51–55. (Original work published 1952)

Brooks, J. O., & Watkins, M. J. (1989). Recognition memory and the mere exposure effect. *Journal of Experimental Psychology: Learning, Memory and Cognition, 15,* 968–976.

Brown, R., & Kulik, J. (1977). Flashbulb memories. *Cognition, 5,* 73–99.

Bruce, D. (1985). The how and why of ecological memory. *Journal of Experimental Psychology: General, 114,* 78–90.

Bruner, J. S., Goodnow, J. J., & Austin, G. A. (1956). *A study of thinking.* New York: Wiley.

Brunswik, E. (1952). *The conceptual framework of psychology.* Chicago: University of Chicago Press.

Campbell, D. T. (1960). Blind variation and selective retention in creative thought as in other knowledge processes. *Psychological Bulletin, 67,* 380–400.

Campbell, D. T., & Stanley, J. C. (1963). *Experimental and quasi-experimental designs for research.* Boston: Houghton Mifflin.

Carnap, R. (1959). Psychology in physical language. In A. J. Ayer (Ed.), *Logical positivism* (pp. 165–198). Glencoe, IL: Free Press. (Original work published 1935)

Carroll, J. B. (1967). On sampling from a lognormal model of word-frequency distribution. In H. Kucera & W. N. Francis (Eds.), *Computational analysis of present-day American English* (pp. 406–413). Providence: Brown University Press.

Carroll, J. B. (1971). Statistical analysis of the corpus. In J. B. Carroll, P. Davies, & B. Richman (Eds.), *The American Heritage word frequency book* (pp. xxi–xl) Boston: Houghton Mifflin.

Carroll, J. B., Davies, P., & Richman, B. (1971). *Word frequency book.* Boston: Houghton Mifflin.

Catania, A. C., & Harnad, S. (1984). The canonical papers of B. F. Skinner. *Behavioral and Brain Sciences, 7,* 473–724.

Cherry, E. C. (1953). Some experiments on the recognition of speech with one and with two ears. *Journal of the Acoustical Society of America, 25,* 975–979.

Cicchetti, D. V. (1991). The reliability of peer review for manuscript and grant submissions: A cross-disciplinary investigation. *Behavioral and Brain Sciences, 14,* 119–186.

Cohen, J. (1962). The statistical power of abnormal-social psychological research: A review. *Journal of Abnormal and Social Psychology, 65,* 145–153.

Cohen, J. (1968). Multiple regression as a general data-analytic system. *Psychological Bulletin, 70,* 426–443.

Cohen, J. (1988). *Statistical power analysis for the behavioral sciences.* Hillsdale, NJ: Erlbaum.

Cohen, J. (1990). Things I have learned so far. *American Psychologist, 45,* 1304–1312.

Cohen, J. (1992). A power primer. *Psychological Bulletin, 112,* 155–159.

Cohen, J., & Cohen, P. (1983). *Applied multiple regression/correlation analysis for the behavioral sciences* (2nd ed.). Hillsdale, NJ: Erlbaum.

Cohen, M. R., & Nagel, E. (1934). *An introduction to logic and scientific method.* New York: Harcourt, Brace & World.

Cohen, N. J., McCloskey, M., & Wible, C. G. (1990). Flashbulb memories and underlying cognitive mechanisms: Reply to Pillemer. *Journal of Experimental Psychology: General, 119,* 97–100.

Colby, K. M. (1981). Modeling a paranoid mind. *The Behavioral and Brain Sciences, 4,* 515–560.

Colby, K. M., Watt, J. B., & Gilbert, J. P. (1966). A computer method of psychotherapy: Preliminary communication. *Journal of Nervous and Mental Disease, 142,* 148–152.

Coope, C., Geach, P., Potts, T., & White, R. (1970). *A Wittgenstein workbook.* Berkeley, CA: University of California Press.

Coren, S., & Girgus, J. S. (1980). Principles of perceptual organization and spatial distortion: The Gestalt illusions. *Journal of Experimental Psychology: Human Perception and Performance, 6,* 404–412.

Coren, S., & Halpern, D. F. (1991). Left-handedness: A marker for decreased survival fitness. *Psychological Bulletin, 109,* 90–106.

Coren, S., & Porac, C. (1977). Fifty centuries of right-handedness: The historical record. *Science, 198*, 631–632.

Coren, S., & Ward, L. M. (1989). *Sensation and perception.* New York: Harcourt Brace Jovanovich.

Cosmides, L. (1989). The logic of social exchange: Has natural selection shaped how humans reason? Studies with the Wason selection task. *Cognition, 31*, 187–276.

Cowles, M. (1989). *Statistics in psychology: An historical perspective.* Hillsdale, NJ: Erlbaum.

Cronbach, L. J. (1957). The two disciplines of scientific psychology. *American Psychologist, 12*, 671–684.

Crouse, J., & Trusheim, D. (1988). *The case against the SAT.* Chicago: University of Chicago Press.

Crovitz, H. F. (1970). *Galton's Walk.* New York: Harper & Row.

Crovitz, H. F., & Schiffman, H. (1974). Frequency of episodic memories as a function of their age. *Bulletin of the Psychonomic Society, 4*, 517–518.

Crovitz, H. F., Schiffman, H., & Apter, A. (1991). Galton's number. *Bulletin of the Psychonomic Society, 29*, 331–332.

Danziger, K. (1983). Origins and basic principles of Wundt's *Volkerpsychologie. British Journal of Social Psychology, 22*, 303–314.

Danziger, K. (1990). *Constructing the subject: Historical origins of psychological research.* New York: Cambridge University Press.

Davison, M. L., & Sharma, A. R. (1990). Parametric statistics and levels of measurement: Factorial designs and multiple regression. *Psychological Bulletin, 107*, 394–400.

Deese, J. (1965). *The structure of associations in language and thought.* Baltimore: Johns Hopkins University Press.

Devenport, L. D., & Devenport, J. A. (1990). The laboratory animal dilemma: A solution in our backyards. *Psychological Science, 1*, 215–216.

Dixon, N. F. (1971). *Subliminal perception: The nature of a controversy.* London: McGraw-Hill.

Donlon, T. F. (1984). *The College Board Technical Handbook for the Scholastic Aptitude Tests.* New York: College Entrance Examination Board.

Dulany, D., Carlson, R., & Dewey, G. (1984). A case of syntactical learning and judgement. *Journal of Experimental Psychology: General, 113*, 541–555.

Dulany, D., Carlson, R., & Dewey, G. (1985). On consciousness in syntactic learning and judgment: A reply to Reber, Allen, and Regan. *Journal of Experimental Psychology: General, 114*, 25–32.

Eich, E. (1984). Memory for unattended events: Remembering with and without awareness. *Memory and Cognition, 12*, 105–111.

Ekman, P., & Friesen, W. V. (1978). *The facial action coding system.* Palo Alto, CA: Consulting Psychologists Press.

Ellenberger, H. F. (1970). *The discovery of the unconscious.* New York: Basic Books.

Epstein, R. (1991). Skinner, creativity, and the problem of spontaneous behavior. *Psychological Science, 2*, 362–370.

Erickson, T. A., & Mattson, M. E. (1981). From words to meaning: A semantic illusion. *Journal of Verbal Learning and Verbal Behavior, 20*, 540–552.

Ericsson, K. A., & Simon, H. A. (1980). Verbal reports as data. *Psychological Review, 87*, 215–251.

Ericsson, K. A., & Simon, H. A. (1984). *Protocol analysis*. Cambridge, MA: MIT Press.

Eriksen, C. W., Azuma, H., & Hicks, R. (1959). Verbal discrimination of pleasant and unpleasant stimulus prior to specific identification. *Journal of Abnormal and Social Psychology, 59,* 114–119.

Estes, W. K. (1960). Learning theory and the new mental chemistry. *Psychological Review, 67,* 207–223.

Estes, W. K. (1990). Introduction: Principles of psychology. *Psychological Science, 1,* 149–150.

Estes, W. K. (1991). The animal rights debate. *Psychological Science, 2,* 202.

Ethical principles of psychologists. (1989). *American Psychologist, 45,* 390–395.

Fancher, R. E. (1979). *Pioneers of psychology*. New York: Norton.

Fancher, R. E. (1989). Galton on examinations: An unpublished step in his invention of correlation. *Isis, 80,* 446–455.

Fisher, R. A. (1991). *Statistical methods, experimental design, and scientific inference.* Oxford: Oxford University Press. (Original work published 1925)

Franklin, N., & Tversky, B. (1990). Searching imagined environments. *Journal of Experimental Psychology: General, 119,* 63–76.

Freeman, G. R. (1990). Kinetics of nonhomogeneous processes in human society: Unethical behavior and societal chaos. *Canadian Journal of Physics, 68,* 794–798.

Fryer, D. M., & Marshall, J. C. (1979). The motives of Jacques de Vaucanson. *Technology & Culture, 20,* 257–269.

Gaito, J. (1980). Measurement scales and statistics: Resurgence of an old misconception. *Psychological Bulletin, 87,* 564–567.

Galton, F. (1869). *Hereditary genius: An inquiry into its laws and consequences.* New York: Macmillan.

Galton, F. (1879a). Psychometric experiments. *Brain, 2,* 148–160.

Galton, F. (1879b). Psychometric facts. *The Nineteenth Century,* 425–433.

Galton, F. (1886). Regression toward mediocrity in hereditary stature. *Journal of the Anthropological Institute, 15,* 246–263.

Galton, F. (1889). *Natural inheritance.* New York: Macmillan.

Gardner, H. (1985). *The mind's new science.* New York: Basic Books.

Gardner, M. (1968). *Logic machines, diagrams, and Boolean algebra.* New York: Dover.

Gibson, J. J. (1962). Observations on active touch. *Psychological Review, 69,* 477–491.

Gibson, J. J. (1966). *The senses considered as perceptual systems.* Boston: Houghton Mifflin.

Gibson, J. J. (1969). *Outline of a theory of direct visual perception.* Paper presented at the Conference on the Psychology of Knowing, Edmonton.

Gibson, J. J. (1979). *The ecological approach to visual perception.* Boston: Houghton Mifflin.

Gigerenzer, G. (1981). External validity of laboratory experiments: The frequency-validity relationship. *American Journal of Psychology, 2,* 185–195.

Gigerenzer, G. (1991). From tools to theories: A heuristic of discovery in cognitive psychology. *Psychological Review, 98,* 254–267.

Gigerenzer, G., & Murray, D. J. (1987). *Cognition as intuitive statistics.* Hillsdale, NJ: Erlbaum.

Gilovich, T., Vallone, R., & Tversky, A. (1985). The hot hand in basketball: On the misperception of random sequences. *Cognitive Psychology, 17,* 295–314.

Gleick, J. (1987). *Chaos: Making a new science.* New York: Viking Penguin.

Goethe, J. W. von. (1970). *Theory of colors*. (C. L. Eastlake, Trans.). Cambridge, MA: MIT Press. (Original work published 1810)

Goldman, W. P., Wolters, N. W., & Winograd, E. (1992). A demonstration of incubation in anagram problem solving. *Bulletin of the Psychonomic Society, 30,* 36–38.

Gordon, P. C., & Holyoak, K. J. (1983). Implicit learning and the "mere exposure" effect. *Journal of Personality and Social Psychology, 45,* 492–500.

Gorman, M. (1986). How the possibility of error affects falsification on a task that models scientific problem solving. *British Journal of Psychology, 77,* 85–96.

Gorman, M. E. (1989). Error, falsification, and scientific evidence. *Quarterly Journal of Experimental Psychology, 41A,* 385–412.

Gould, S. J. (1991). The median isn't the message. In S. J. Gould (Ed.), *Bully for Brontosaurus* (pp. 473–478). New York: Norton.

Greenwald, A. G., Spangenberg, E. R., Pratkanis, A. R., & Eskanazi, J. (1991). Double-blind tests of subliminal self-help audiotapes. *Psychological Science, 2,* 119–122.

Griggs, R. A., & Cox, J. R. (1982). The elusive thematic materials effect in Wason's selection task. *British Journal of Psychology, 73,* 407–420.

Griggs, R. A., & Newstead, S. E. (1983). The source of intuitive errors in Wason's THOG problem. *British Journal of Psychology, 74,* 451–459.

Guastello, S. J. (1992). Clash of the paradigms: A critique of an examination of the polynomial regression technique of evaluating catastrophe theory hypotheses. *Psychological Bulletin, 111,* 375–379.

Guilford, J. P. (1942). *Fundamental statistics in psychology and education*. New York: McGraw-Hill.

Gunderson, K. (1964). The imitation game. In A. R. Anderson (Ed.), *Minds and machines* (pp. 60–71). Englewood Cliffs, NJ: Prentice Hall.

Halpern, A. R. (1988). Mental scanning in auditory imagery for songs. *Journal of Experimental Psychology: Learning, Memory and Cognition, 14,* 433–443.

Halpern, D. F., & Coren, S. (1988). Do right-handers live longer? *Nature, 333,* 213.

Hanson, N. R. (1969). *Patterns of discovery*. Cambridge, UK: Cambridge University Press.

Harré, R. (1983). *Great scientific experiments*. Oxford: Oxford University Press.

Heidbreder, E. (1933). *Seven psychologies*. New York: Appleton-Century-Crofts.

Heinrichs, R. W. (1984). Verbal responses to human figure paintings: A test of the uncertainty hypothesis. *Canadian Journal of Psychology, 38,* 512–518.

Helmholtz, H. F. von. (1924). *Treatise on physiological optics* (Vols. 1–3, 3rd ed.; J. P. Southall, Ed.). Rochester, NY: Optical Society of America. (Original work published 1856–1866; 3rd ed. augmented by A. Gullstrand, J. von Kries, & W. Nagel, 1909–1911)

Herbart, J. F. (1891). *A textbook in psychology: An attempt to found the science of psychology on experience, metaphysics, and mathematics* (2nd ed.; W. T. Harris, Ed., M. K. Smith, Trans.). New York: Appleton. (Original work published 1816)

Hering, E. (1964). *Outlines of a theory of the light sense* (L. M. Hurvich & D. Jameson, Trans.). Cambridge, MA: Harvard University Press. (Original work published 1905–1911)

Higbee, K. L., & Millard, R. J. (1983). Visual imagery and familiarity ratings for 203 sayings. *American Journal of Psychology, 96,* 211–222.

Hilgard, E. R. (1987). *Psychology in America: An historical survey.* New York: Harcourt Brace Jovanovich.

Hinde, R. A. (1970). *Animal behaviour* (2nd ed.). New York: McGraw-Hill.

Hirst, W., & Levine, E. (1985). Ecological memory reconsidered: A comment on Bruce's "The how and why of ecological memory." *Journal of Experimental Psychology: General, 114,* 269–271.

Hock, R. R. (1992). *Forty studies that changed psychology.* Englewood Cliffs, NJ: Prentice Hall.

Holland, C. A., & Rabbitt, P. M. A. (1991). Ageing memory: Use versus impairment. *British Journal of Psychology, 82,* 29–38.

Holmes, C. B., & Buchanan, J. A. (1984). Color preference as a function of the object described. *Bulletin of the Psychonomic Society, 22,* 423–425.

Huck, S. W., & Sandler, H. M. (1979). *Rival hypotheses.* New York: Harper & Row.

Hull, C. L. (1952). *A behavior system.* New Haven: Yale University Press.

Hulse, S. H., & Green, B. F. (1986). *One hundred years of psychological research in America.* Baltimore: Johns Hopkins University Press.

Hurvich, L. M., & Jameson, D. (1957). An opponent process theory of color vision. *Psychological Review, 64,* 384–404.

James, W. (1890). *Principles of psychology* (Vols. 1 and 2). New York: Holt.

Jankowicz, A. D. (1987). Whatever became of George Kelly? *American Psychologist, 42,* 481–487.

Jaynes, J. (1973). Animate motion in the 17th century. In M. Henle, J. Jaynes, & J. J. Sullivan (Eds.), *Historical conceptions of psychology* (pp. 166–179). New York: Springer.

Johnson, D. (1990a). Public perception, public good, and the modal scientist. *Psychological Science, 1,* 79–80.

Johnson, D. (1990b). Animal rights and human lives: Time for scientists to right the balance. *Psychological Science, 1,* 213–214.

Johnson, R. C., MacClearn, G. E., Yuen, S., Nagoshi, C. T., Ahern, F. M., & Cole, R. E. (1985). Galton's data a century later. *American Psychologist, 40,* 875–892.

Johnson-Laird, P. N., & Wason, P. C. (1970). A theoretical analysis of insight into a reasoning task. *Cognitive Psychology, 1,* 134–148.

Jones, S. S., Collins, K., & Hong, H. (1991). An audience effect on smile production in 10-month-old infants. *Psychological Science, 2,* 45–49.

Judson, H. F. (1984). Century of the sciences. *Science 84,* 41–43.

Kahneman, D., & Tversky, A. (1972). Subjective probability: A judgement of representativeness. *Cognitive Psychology, 3,* 430–454.

Kant, I. (1929). *Critique of pure reason* (N. K. Smith, Trans.). New York: St. Martin's Press. (Original published in 1781)

Kaplan, E. (1983). Process and achievement revisited. In S. Wapner & B. Kaplan (Eds.). *Toward a holistic developmental psychology.* Hillsdale, NJ: Erlbaum.

Katz, A., Paivio, A., & Marschark, M. (1985). Poetic comparisons: Psychological dimensions of metaphoric processing. *Journal of Psycholinguistic Research, 14,* 365–383.

Katz, S., Lautenschlager, G. J., Blackburn, B., & Harris, F. H. (1990). Answering reading comprehension items without passages on the SAT. *Psychological Science, 1,* 122–127.

Kelly, G. A. (1955). *The psychology of personal constructs*. New York: Norton.

Kihlstrom, J. F. (1987). The cognitive unconscious. *Science, 237*, 1335–1352.

Kihlstrom, J. F., Schacter, D., Cork, R., Hurt, C., & Behr, S. (1990). Implicit and explicit memory following surgical anesthesia. *Psychological Science, 1*, 303–306.

Kimble, G. A. (1990). Mother Nature's bag of tricks is small. *Psychological Science, 1*, 36–41.

Koffka, K. (1935). *Principles of Gestalt psychology*. New York: Harcourt, Brace.

Kohler, W. (1969). *The task of Gestalt psychology*. Princeton, NJ: Princeton University Press.

Kosslyn, S. M., Ball, T. M., & Reiser, B. J. (1978). Visual images preserve metric spatial information: Evidence from studies of image scanning. *Journal of Experimental Psychology: Human Perception and Performance, 4*, 47–60.

Kraut, R. E., & Johnson, R. E. (1979). Social and emotional messages of smiling: An ethological approach. *Journal of Personality and Social Psychology, 37*, 1539–1553.

Krueger, L. E. (1989). Reconciling Gechner and Stevens: Toward a unified psychological law. *Behavioral and Brain Sciences, 12*, 251–320.

Kucera, H., & Francis, W. N. (1967). *Computational analysis of present-day American English*. Providence: Brown University Press.

Kuhn, D. (1989). Children and adults as intuitive scientists. *Psychological Review, 96*, 674–689.

Kuhn, T. (1970). *The structure of scientific revolutions* (2nd ed.). Chicago: University of Chicago Press.

Lakatos, I. (1970). Falsification and the methodology of scientific research programmes. In I. Lakatos & A. Musgrave (Eds.), *Criticism and the growth of knowledge*. Cambridge, UK: Cambridge University Press.

Langer, E. (1989). *Mindlessness/mindfulness*. Reading, MA: Addison-Wesley.

Lavoie, M., Grenier, G., & Coulombe, S. (1987). Discrimination and performance differentials in the National Hockey League. *Canadian Public Policy, 13*, 407–422.

Lazarus, D. (1982). Interreferee agreement and acceptance rates in physics. *Behavioral and Brain Sciences, 5*, 219.

Lazarus, R. S. (1984). On the primacy of cognition. *American Psychologist, 39*, 124–129.

Lazarus, R. S., & McCleary, R. (1951). Autonomic discrimination without awareness: A study of subception. *Psychological Review, 58*, 113–122.

Lederer, S. E. (1985). Hideo Noguchi's luetin experiment and the antivivisectionists. *Isis, 76*, 31–48.

Leeuwenberg, E., & Boselie, F. (1988). Against the likelihood principle in visual form perception. *Psychological Review, 95*, 485–491.

Lehman, D. R., Lempert, R. O., & Nisbett, R. E. (1988). The effects of graduate training on reasoning. *American Psychologist, 43*, 431–442.

Lerner, R. M. (1986). *Concepts and theories of human development*. New York: Random House.

Livingston, R. (1967). Reinforcement. In G. Quarton, T. Melenchuk, & F. Schmidt (Eds.), *The neurosciences: A study program*. New York: Rockefeller University Press.

Livingstone, M. S. (1988). Art, illusion, and the visual system. *Scientific American, 258*, 78–85.

Lockhart, R., Lamon, M., & Gick, M. L. (1987). Conceptual transfer in simple insight problems. *Memory and Cognition, 16*, 36–44.

Loehlin, J. C. (1987). *Latent variable models: An introduction to factor, path, and structural analysis.* Hillsdale, NJ: Erlbaum.

Loehlin, J. C. (1989). Partitioning environmental and genetic contributions to behavioral development. *American Psychologist, 44*, 1285–1292.

Loftus, E. F. (1991). The glitter of everyday memory . . . and the gold. *American Psychologist, 46*, 16–18.

Logan, F. A. (1959). The Hull-Spence approach. In S. Koch (Ed.), *Psychology: A study of a science (Vol. 2)* (pp. 293–358). New York: McGraw-Hill.

Lopes, L. L. (1982). Doing the impossible: A note on induction and the experience of randomness. *Journal of Experimental Psychology: Learning, Memory and Cognition, 8*, 626–636.

Lorenz, K. (1952). *King Solomon's Ring.* New York: Crowell.

Losee, J. P. (1985). [Review of "Great scientific experiments that changed the world"]. *Isis, 76*, 92–93.

Luchins, A. S., & Luchins, E. H. (1968). New experimental attempts at preventing mechanization in problem solving. In P. C. Wason & P. N. Johnson-Laird (Eds.), *Thinking and reasoning* (pp. 65–80). Baltimore: Penguin. (Original work published 1950).

Luscher, M., & Scott, I. (1969). *The Luscher color test.* New York: Random House.

Lycan, W. G. (Ed.). (1990). *Mind and cognition: A reader.* Oxford: Basil Blackwell.

MacLeod, C. M. (1991). Half a century of research on the Stroop effect: An integrative review. *Psychological Bulletin, 109*, 163–203.

MacLeod, C. M. (1992). The Stroop Task: The "Gold Standard" of attentional measures. *Journal of Experimental Psychology: General, 121*, 12–15.

Markus, H. (1990). On splitting the universe. *Psychological Science, 1*, 181–184.

Marschark, M., Richman, C. L., Yuille, J. C., & Hunt, R. R. (1987). The role of imagery in memory: On shared and distinctive information. *Psychological Bulletin, 102*, 28–41.

Maxwell, S. E., & Delaney, H. D. (1985). Measurement and statistics: An examination of construct validity. *Psychological Bulletin, 97*, 85–93.

McCloskey, M. (1983a). Intuitive physics. *Scientific American, 284*, 122–130.

McCloskey, M. (1983b). Naive theories of motion. In D. Gentner & A. L. Stevens (Eds.), *Mental models.* Hillsdale, NJ: Erlbaum.

McCloskey, M., & Kargon, R. (1988). The meaning and use of historical models in the study of intuitive physics. In S. Strauss (Ed.), *Ontogeny, phylogeny, and historical development.* Norwood, NJ: Ablex.

McCloskey, M., & Kohl, D. (1983). Naive physics: The curvilinear impetus principle and its role in interactions with moving objects. *Journal of Experimental Psychology: Learning, Memory and Cognition, 9*, 146–156.

McCloskey, M., Wible, C. G., & Cohen, N. J. (1988). Is there a special flashbulb-memory mechanism? *Journal of Experimental Psychology: General, 117*, 171–181.

McManus, I. C. (1981). The aesthetics of colour. *Perception, 10*, 651–666.

Mednick, S. A. (1967). *The remote associations test.* Boston: Houghton Mifflin.

Meehl, P. E. (1978). Theoretical risks and tabular asterisks: Sir Karl, Sir Ronald, and the slow progress of soft psychology. *Journal of Consulting and Clinical Psychology,* *46*, 806–834.

Metcalfe, J., & Wiebe, D. (1987). Intuition in insight and non-insight problem solving. *Memory and Cognition, 15*, 238–246.

Michotte, A. (1963). *The perception of causality.* New York: Basic Books.

Mill, J. S. (1973). A system of logic, ratiocinative and inductive. In J. M. Robson (Ed.), *Collected works of John Stuart Mill* (Vol. 7). Toronto: University of Toronto Press. (Original work published 1846)

Miller, G. A. (Ed.). (1964). *Mathematics and psychology.* New York: Wiley.

Mischel, T. (1967). Kant and the possibility of a science of psychology. *The Monist, 51*, 599–622.

Mischel, T. (1969). Scientific and philosophical psychology: An historical introduction. In T. Mischel (Ed.), *Human Action* (pp. 1–40). New York: Academic Press.

Morawski, J. G. (1988). *The rise of experimentation in American psychology.* New Haven: Yale University Press.

Moreland, R. L., & Zajonc, R. B. (1977). Is stimulus recognition a necessary condition for the occurrence of exposure effects? *Journal of Personality and Social Psychology, 35*, 191–199.

Moreland, R. L., & Zajonc, R. B. (1979). Exposure effects may not depend on stimulus recognition. *Journal of Personality and Social Psychology, 37*, 1085–1089.

Morgan, C. L. (1894). *Introduction to comparative psychology.* London: Walter Scott.

Mozart, W. A. (1970). A letter. In P. E. Vernon (Ed.), *Creativity* (pp. 55–56). Baltimore: Penguin. (Original written in 1789)

Mumford, M. D., & Gustavson, S. B. (1988). Creativity syndrome: Integration, application, and innovation. *Psychological Bulletin, 103*, 27–43.

The National Hockey League. (1991). *National Hockey League Official Guide & Record Book.* Montreal: Author.

Neisser, U. (1954). An experimental distinction between perceptual process and verbal response. *Journal of Experimental Psychology, 47*, 399–404.

Neisser, U. (1967). *Cognitive psychology.* New York: Appleton-Century-Crofts.

Neisser, U. (1976). *Cognition and reality.* New York: Freeman.

Neisser, U. (1978). Memory: What are the important questions? In P. M. Morris & R. N. Sykes (Eds.), *Practical aspects of memory.* London: Academic Press.

Neisser, U. (1982). *Memory Observed.* San Francisco: Freeman.

Neisser, U. (1985). The role of theory in the ecological study of memory: Comment on Bruce. *Journal of Experimental Psychology: General, 114*, 272–278.

Neisser, U., & Weene, P. (1962). Hierarchies in concept attainment. *Journal of Experimental Psychology, 64*, 640–645.

Newell, A. (1977). On the analysis of human problem solving protocols. In P. N. Johnson-Laird & P. Wason (Eds.), *Thinking: Readings in cognitive science.* Cambridge, UK: Cambridge University Press.

Newell, A., & Simon, H. (1962). The processes of creative thinking. In H. E. Gruber, G. Terrell, & M. Wertheimer (Eds.), *Contemporary approaches to creative thinking.* New York: Atherton.

Newman, J. R. (1956). *The world of mathematics.* New York: Simon & Schuster.

Neyman, J., & Pearson, E. S. (1928a). On the use and interpretation of certain test criteria for purposes of statistical inference. (P. 1). *Biometrika, 20A*, 175–240.

Neyman, J., & Pearson, E. S. (1928b). On the use and interpretation of certain test criteria for purposes of statistical inference (P. 2). *Biometrika, 20A,* 263–294.

Nisbett, R. E., Krantz, D. H., Jepson, C., & Kunda, Z. (1983). The use of statistical heuristics in everyday inductive reasoning. *Psychological Review, 90,* 339–363.

Oakhill, J. V., & Johnson-Laird, P. N. (1985). Rationality, memory, and the search for counterexamples. *Cognition, 20,* 79–94.

Ofir, C., Reddy, S. K., & Bechtel, G. G. (1987). Are semantic response scales equivalent? *Multivariate Behavioral Research, 22,* 21–38.

Orne, M. T. (1965). The nature of hypnosis: Artifact and essence. In R. E. Shor & M. T. Orne (Eds.), *The nature of hypnosis.* New York: Holt, Rinehart & Winston.

Paivio, A. (1965). Abstractness, imagery, and meaningfulness in paired-associate learning. *Journal of Verbal Learning and Verbal Behavior, 4,* 32–38.

Paivio, A. (1971). *Imagery and verbal processes.* New York: Holt, Rinehart & Winston.

Paivio, A. (1983). The empirical case for dual coding. In J. Yuille (Ed.), *Imagery, memory and cognition: Essays in honor of Allan Paivio* (pp. 307–332). Hillsdale, NJ: Erlbaum.

Paivio, A., Yuille, J., & Madigan, S. (1968). Concreteness, imagery, and meaningfulness values for 925 nouns. *Journal of Experimental Psychology Monograph Supplement, 76* (1, P. 2).

Palermo, D. S., & Jenkins, J. J. (1964). *Word association norms: Grade school through college.* Minneapolis: University of Minnesota Press.

Palmer, S. E. (1992). Common region: A new principle of perceptual grouping. *Cognitive Psychology, 24,* 436–447.

Parker, T. (1983). *Rules of thumb.* Boston: Houghton Mifflin.

Pedhazur, E. J. (1982). *Multiple regression in behavioral research.* New York: Holt, Rinehart & Winston.

Peters, D. P., & Ceci, S. J. (1982). Peer-review practices of psychological journals: The fate of published articles submitted again. *Behavioral and Brain Sciences, 5,* 187–255.

Pfungst, O. (1911). *Clever Hans (the horse of Mr. von Osten): A contribution to experimental animal and human psychology.* New York: Holt.

Piaget, J. (1957). *Logic and psychology.* New York: Basic Books.

Pierce, C. S. (1934). *Collected papers.* Cambridge, MA: Harvard University Press.

Pillemer, D. B. (1990). Clarifying the flashbulb memory concept: Comment on McCloskey, Wible & Cohen (1988). *Journal of Experimental Psychology: General, 119,* 92–96.

Pinker, S., & Finke, R. A. (1980). Emergent two-dimensional patterns in images rotated in depth. *Journal of Experimental Psychology: Human Perception and Performance, 6,* 244–264.

Plous, S. (1991). An attitude survey of animal rights activists. *Psychological Science, 2,* 194–196.

Poincaré, H. (1960). *Science and method.* New York: Dover. (Original published 1924)

Popper, K. R. (1965). *The logic of scientific discovery.* New York: Harper.

Porac, C., Coren, S., & Searleman, A. (1986). Environmental factors in hand preference formation: Evidence from attempts to switch the preferred hand. *Behavior Genetics, 16,* 251–261.

Posner, M. (1986). *Chronometric explorations of mind.* Oxford: Oxford University Press.

Postman, L. (1962). Repetition and paired-associate learning. *American Journal of Psychology, 75,* 372–389.

Postman, L., Bruner, J., & McGinnis, E. (1948). Personal values as selective factors in perception. *Journal of Abnormal and Social Psychology, 43,* 142–154.

Poston, T., & Stewart, I. (1978). *Catastrophe theory and its applications.* London: Pitman.

Poston, T., & Woodcock, E. R. (1973). Zeeman's catastrophe machine. *Proceedings of the Cambridge Philosophical Society, 74,* 217–226.

Pribram, K. (1981). The brain, the telephone, the thermostat, the computer, and the hologram. *Cognition and Brain Theory, 4,* 105–122.

Rao, C. R. (1992). R. A. Fisher: The founder of modern statistics. *Statistical Science, 7,* 34–48.

Ratliff, F. (1976). On the psychophysiological bases of universal color terms. *Proceedings of the American Philosophical Society, 120,* 311–330.

Reber, A. S. (1985). *The Penguin dictionary of psychology.* London: Penguin.

Reber, A. S. (1989). Implicit learning and tacit knowledge. *Journal of Experimental Psychology: General, 118,* 219–235.

Reber, A. S., Allen, R., & Regan, S. (1985). Syntactical learning and judgement, still unconscious and still abstract: Comment on Dulany, Carlson, and Dewey. *Journal of Experimental Psychology: General, 114,* 189–221.

Reder, L. M., & Kusbit, G. W. (1991). Locus of the Moses illusion: Imperfect encoding, retrieval or match? *Journal of Memory and Language, 30,* 385–406.

Reed, J. G., & Baxter, P. M. (1992). *Library use: A handbook for psychology* (2nd ed.). Washington, DC: American Psychological Association.

Reichenbach, H. (1938). *Experience and prediction.* Chicago: University of Chicago Press.

Reichler, J. L. (Ed.). (1979). *The baseball encyclopedia.* New York: MacMillan.

Robinson, A., & Katzman, J. (1986). *Cracking the system: The SAT.* New York: Villard.

Rock, I. (1957). The role of repetition in associative learning. *American Journal of Psychology, 70,* 186–193.

Rock, I., & Heimer, W. (1959). Further evidence of one-trial associative learning. *American Journal of Psychology, 72,* 1–16.

Rock, I., & Palmer, S. (1990). The legacy of Gestalt psychology. *Scientific American, 263,* 84–90.

Rock, I., Wheeler, D., & Tudor, L. (1989). Can we imagine how objects look from other viewpoints? *Cognitive Psychology, 21,* 185–210.

Rodgers, J. L. (1990). About APS: Structural models of the American Psychological Society at birth. *Psychological Science, 1,* 81–84.

Rogers, C. R. (1952). Client-centered psychotherapy. *Scientific American, 187,* 66–74.

Rogers, C. R. (1961). *On becoming a person.* Boston: Houghton Mifflin.

Rosch, E. (1988). What does the tiny vajra refute? Causality and event structure in Buddhist logic and folk psychology. *Cognitive Science Reports.* Berkeley, CA: Institute for Cognitive Studies.

Rosenfeld, H. M., & Baer, D. M. (1969). Unnoticed verbal conditioning of an aware experimenter by a more aware subject: The double agent effect. *Psychological Review, 76,* 425–432.

Rosenthal, R. (1966). *Experimenter effects in behavioral research.* New York: Appleton-Century-Crofts.

Rosenthal, R. (1967). Covert communication in the psychological experiment. *Psychological Bulletin, 67,* 356–367.

Rosenthal, R. (1982). Reliability and bias in peer-review practices. *Behavioral and Brain Sciences, 5,* 235–236.

Rosnow, R. L., & Rosenthal, R. (1989). Statistical procedures and the justification of knowledge in psychological science. *American Psychologist, 44,* 1276–1284.

Rozin, P., Markwith, M., & Ross, B. (1990). The sympathetic magical law of similarity, nominal realism, and neglect of negatives in response to negative labels. *Psychological Science, 1,* 383–384.

Rubin, D. C., & Friendly, M. (1986). Predicting which words get recalled: Measures of free recall, availability, goodness, emotionality, and pronounceability for 925 nouns. *Memory and Cognition, 14,* 79–94.

Rubin, D. C., Wetzler, S. E., & Nebes, R. D. (1986). Autobiographical memory across the lifespan. In D. C. Rubin (Ed.), *Autobiographical memory.* Cambridge, UK: Cambridge University Press.

Russell, B. (1959). *Wisdom of the West.* New York: Doubleday.

Saunders, P. T. (1980). *An introduction to catastrophe theory.* London: Cambridge University Press.

Schacter, D. L. (1987). Implicit memory: History and current status. *Journal of Experimental Psychology: Learning, Memory and Cognition, 12,* 432–444.

Schacter, D. L., & Graf, P. (1986). Effects of elaborative processing on implicit and explicit memory for new associations. *Journal of Experimental Psychology: Learning, Memory and Cognition, 12,* 432–444.

Schacter, S. S., Christenfeld, N., Ravina, B., & Bilous, F. (1991). Speech disfluency and the structure of knowledge. *Journal of Personality and Social Psychology, 60,* 362–367.

Schlenker, B. A., & Leary, M. R. (1982). Social anxiety and self-presentation: A conceptualization and model. *Psychological Bulletin, 92,* 641–669.

Schlick, M. (1962). Meaning and verification. In W. Barrett & H. D. Aiken (Eds.), *Philosophy in the twentieth century* (Vol. 3) (pp. 28–51). New York: Random House. (Original work published 1938)

Schuh, F. C. (1968). *The masterbook of mathematical recreations.* New York: Dover.

Schultz, D. P., & Schultz, S. E. (1992). *A history of modern psychology.* Fort Worth: Harcourt Brace Jovanovich.

Schwartz, B., & Barsky, S. (1977). The home advantage. *Social Forces, 55,* 641–661.

Scientific genius and creativity. (1987). New York: Freeman.

Sears, F. W., & Zemansky, M. W. (1970). *University physics.* Reading, MA: Addison–Wesley.

Sedlmeier, P., & Gigerenzer, G. (1989). Do studies of statistical power have an effect on the power of studies? *Psychological Bulletin, 105,* 309–316.

Sekuler, A. B., & Palmer, S. E. (1992). Perception of partly occluded objects: A microgenetic analysis. *Journal of Experimental Psychology: General, 121,* 95–111.

Senders, V. L. (1958). *Measurement and statistics.* New York: Oxford.

Shepard, R. N. (1978). The mental image. *American Psychologist,* 125–137.

Shepard, R. N. (1984). Ecological constraints on internal representation: Resonant kinematics of perceiving, imagining, thinking, and dreaming. *Psychological Review, 91, 91,* 417–447.

Shepard, R. N., & Cooper, L. A. (1982). *Mental images and their transformations.* Cambridge, MA: MIT Press.

Shepard, R. N., & Metzler, J. (1971). Mental rotation of three-dimensional objects. *Science, 171,* 701–703.

Shiffrin, R. M., & Schneider, W. (1977). Controlled and automatic human information processing: II, Perceptual learning, automatic attending, and a general theory. *Psychological Review, 84,* 155–171.

Simon, H. A. (1975). The functional equivalence of problem solving skills. *Cognitive Psychology, 7,* 268–288.

Simon, H. A. (1979). *Models of thought.* New Haven: Yale University Press.

Simonton, D. K. (1981). The library laboratory: Archival data in personality and social psychology. In L. Wheeler (Ed.), *Review of Personality and Social Psychology.* Beverly Hills, CA: Sage.

Simonton, D. K. (1984). *Genius, creativity, and leadership.* Cambridge, MA: Harvard University Press.

Simonton, D. K. (1988). *Scientific genius.* New York: Cambridge University Press.

Skinner, B. F. (1956). A case history in scientific method. *American Psychologist, 11,* 221–233.

Sluckin, W., Colman, A. M., & Hargreaves, D. J. (1980). Liking words as a function of the experienced frequency of their occurrence. *British Journal of Psychology, 71,* 163–169.

Smedslund, J. (1963). The concept of correlation in adults. *Scandinavian Journal of Psychology, 4,* 165–173.

Smith, L. D. (1986). *Behaviorism and logical positivism.* Stanford, CA: Stanford University Press.

Smyth, M. M., & Clark, S. E. (1986). My half-sister is a THOG: Strategic processes in a reasoning task. *British Journal of Psychology, 77,* 275–287.

Solomon, R. L. (1949). An extension of control group design. *Psychological Bulletin, 46,* 137–150.

Solomon, R. L., & Lessac, M. S. (1968). A control group design for studies of developmental processes. *Psychological Bulletin, 70,* 145–150.

Steering Committee of the Physicians' Health Study Research Group. (1988). Preliminary report: Findings from the aspirin component of the ongoing physicians' health study. *New England Journal of Medicine, 318,* 262–264.

Steinfeld, G. J., & Rock, I. (1968). Control for item selection and familiarization in the formation of associations. *American Journal of Psychology, 61,* 42–46.

Sternberg, R. J. (1982). Natural, unnatural, and supernatural concepts. *Cognitive Psychology, 14,* 451–488.

Stevens, P. S. (1974). *Patterns in nature.* Boston: Little, Brown.

Stevens, S. S. (1951). Mathematics, measurement, and psychophysics. In S. S. Stevens (Ed.), *Handbook of experimental psychology* (pp. 1–49). New York: Wiley.

Stevens, S. S. (1968). Measurement, statistics, and the schemapiric view. *Science, 161,* 849–856.

Stewart, I. (1983). Catastrophe theory modeling in psychology. *Psychological Bulletin, 94,* 336–362.

Stigler, S. M. (1986). *The history of statistics: The measurement of uncertainty before 1900.* Cambridge, MA: Harvard University Press.

Stroop, J. R. (1992). Studies of interference in serial verbal reactions. *Journal of Experimental Psychology: General, 121,* 15–23. (Original work published 1935)

Suls, J. M., & Rosnow, R. L. (1988). Concerns about artifacts in psychological experiments. In J. Morawski (Ed.), *The rise of experimentation in American psychology* (pp. 163–187). New Haven: Yale University Press.

Taylor, J. G. (1966). Perception generated by training echolocation. *Canadian Journal of Psychology, 20,* 64–81.

Tchaikovsky, P. I. (1970). Letters. In P. E. Vernon (Ed.), *Creativity* (pp. 57–60). Baltimore: Penguin. (Original written in 1878)

Thom, R. (1975). *Structural stability and morphogenesis.* New York: Benjamin-Addison-Wesley.

Thompson, D. W. (1929). Excess and defect: Or the little more and the little less. *Mind, 38,* 43–55.

Thorndike, E. L., & Lorge, I. (1944). *The teacher's word book of 30,000 words.* New York: Teacher's College, Columbia University.

Toglia, M., & Battig, W. (1978). *Handbook of semantic word norms.* Hillsdale, NJ: Erlbaum.

Tolman, E. C. (1959). Principles of purposive behavior. In S. Koch (Ed.), *Psychology: A study of a science* (Vol. 2) (pp. 92–157). New York: McGraw-Hill.

Tolman, E. C., & Honzik, C. H. (1930). Degrees of hunger, reward and non-reward, and maze learning in rats. *University of California Publications in Psychology, 4,* 241–256.

Tulving, E., & Schacter, D. (1990). Priming and human memory systems. *Science, 247,* 301–306.

Tuohy, A. P. (1987). Affective asymmetry in social perception. *British Journal of Psychology, 78,* 41–51.

Turing, A. (1950). Computing machinery and intelligence. *Mind, 59,* 433–450.

Tversky, A., & Kahneman, D. (1971). Belief in the law of small numbers. *Psychological Bulletin, 76,* 105–110.

Tversky, A., & Kahneman, D. (1974). Judgement under uncertainty: Heuristics and biases. *Science, 185,* 1124–1131.

Ulrich, R. E. (1991). Animal rights, animal wrongs, and the question of balance. *Psychological Science, 2,* 197–201.

Underwood, B. J., Rehula, R., & Keppel, G. (1962). Item-selection on paired associate learning. *American Journal of Psychology, 75,* 353–371.

van der Maas, H. L. J., & Molenaar, P. C. M. (1992). Stagewise cognitive development: An application of catastrophe theory. *Psychological Review, 99,* 395–417.

Vernon, P. E. (Ed.). (1970). *Creativity.* Baltimore: Penguin.

Vinacke, W. E. (1974). *The psychology of thinking.* New York: McGraw-Hill.

Wallas, G. (1926). *The art of thought.* London: Cape.

Wanner, K. (1990). *A comparative study of filled pauses in introductory and advanced university lectures.* Unpublished honors thesis, Columbia University, New York.

Wason, P. C. (1960). On the failure to eliminate hypotheses in a conceptual task. *Quarterly Journal of Experimental Psychology, 12,* 129–140.

Wason, P. C. (1966). Reasoning. In B. M. Foss (Ed.), *New horizons in psychology* (pp. 135–151). Harmondsworth, UK: Penguin.

Wason, P. C. (1977a). "On the failure to eliminate hypotheses . . . "—A second look. In P. N. Johnson-Laird & P. C. Wason (Eds.), *Thinking: Readings in cognitive science.* Cambridge, UK: Cambridge University Press.

Wason, P. C. (1977b). Self-contradictions. In P. N. Johnson-Laird & P. C. Wason (Eds.),

Thinking: Readings in cognitive science. Cambridge, UK: Cambridge University Press.

Wason, P. C. (1978). Hypothesis testing and reasoning. In *Cognitive Psychology* (Block 4, Unit 25). Milton Keynes, UK: Open University Press.

Wason, P. C., & Brooks, P. G. (1979). THOG: The anatomy of a problem. *Psychological Research, 41,* 79–90.

Wason, P. C., & Evans, J. St. B. T. (1975). Dual processes in reasoning? *Cognition, 3/2,* 141–154.

Wason, P. C., & Johnson-Laird, P. N. (1972). *Psychology of reasoning: Structure and content.* London: Batsford.

Webb, E. J., Campbell, D. T., Schwartz, R. D., & Sechrest, L. (1966). *Unobtrusive measures.* Chicago: Rand McNally.

Werner, H. (1937). Process and achievement: A basic problem of education and developmental psychology. *Harvard Educational Review, 7,* 353–368.

Wertheimer, M. (1967). Laws of organization in perceptual forms. In W. D. Ellis (Ed.), *A source book of Gestalt psychology.* New York: Humanities Press. (Original work published 1923)

White, P. A. (1990). Ideas about causation in philosophy and psychology. *Psychological Bulletin, 108,* 3–18.

Wickens, D. D. (1970). Encoding categories of words: An empirical approach to meaning. *Psychological Review, 77,* 1–15.

Winer, B. J. (1971). *Statistical principles in experimental design* (2nd ed.). New York: McGraw-Hill.

Wittgenstein, L. (1953). *Philosophical investigations.* Oxford: Basil Blackwell.

Wittgenstein, L. (1974). *Tractatus logico-philosophicus.* London: Routledge & Kegan Paul. (Original work published 1921)

Wood, E. K. (1988). Less sinister statistics from baseball records. *Nature, 335,* 212.

Wood, J. M., Bootzin, R. R., Kihlstrom, J. F., & Schacter, D. L. (1992). Implicit and explicit memory for verbal information presented during sleep. *Psychological Science, 3,* 236–239.

Woodworth, R. S., & Schlosberg, H. (1958). *Experimental Psychology.* New York: Henry Holt.

Wundt, W. (1973). *An introduction to psychology.* New York: Arno Press. (Original work published 1912)

Young, T. (1802). On the theory of light and colours. *Philosophical Transactions, 92,* 12–48.

Zajonc, R. B. (1980). Feeling and thinking: Preferences need no inferences. *American Psychologist, 35,* 151–175.

Zajonc, R. B. (1984). On the primacy of affect. *American Psychologist, 39,* 117–123.

Zeeman, R. (1977a). *Catastrophe theory: Selected papers 1972–1977.* Reading, MA: Addison-Wesley.

Zeeman, R. (1977b). A catastrophe machine. In R. Zeeman (Ed.), *Catastrophe theory: Selected papers 1972–1977* (pp. 409–415). Reading, MA: Addison-Wesley. (Original work published 1972)

Index